Socialist ownership
and political systems

By the same author

The market in a socialist economy (1972)
The economics and politics of socialism (1973)

Socialist ownership and political systems

Włodzimierz Brus

Translated by R. A. Clarke

Routledge & Kegan Paul
London and Boston

First published in 1975
by Routledge & Kegan Paul Ltd
Broadway House, 68–74 Carter Lane,
London EC4V 5EL and
9 Park Street,
Boston, Mass. 02108, USA
Set in Monotype Times New Roman
and printed in Great Britain by
Willmer Brothers Limited, Birkenhead
© Włodzimierz Brus 1975

ISBN 0 7100 8247 9

Contents

Contents

Introduction

> Just as our opinion of an individual is not based on what he thinks of himself, so can we not judge of such a period of transformation by its own consciousness. – Marx: Preface to *A Contribution to the Critique of Political Economy*.

The present work in a sense continues my book on the functioning of a socialist economy.[1] The subject of both works is socialist production relations and the laws of their evolution, which is the expression of the development of internal contradictions in the system. The previous book was limited to the analysis of the system of functioning of the economy – the degree of centralisation of economic decisions, the role of the market mechanism, the form of material incentives, etc. – without examining the totality of production relations, and, in particular, ownership of the means of production. This was, as some critics pointed out, too narrow an approach, in that it made it difficult to distinguish between effects which could be obtained by reform of the system of functioning of the economy (economic reform, according to the popular definition) and those requiring deeper changes, extending to the foundations of the system. Experience also proves that changes in the functioning of the economy proceed in close connection with other elements of the relations of production. Without considering them in totality, therefore, one cannot, for example, explain the sources, methods and degree of effectiveness of the obstruction of economic reform, be it the continuous retarding observed in the USSR, Poland and other countries or the forcible arresting of reform which we witnessed in Czechoslovakia in 1968. Nor can we explain what influence great political upheavals like the 1956 Hungarian uprising or the workers' demonstrations in Poland in 1970 have on the undertaking or acceleration of economic reforms.

This book is an attempt to broaden the subject of study. It is primarily concerned with examining the connection between social ownership and political system under socialism against the background of the conditions in which the development of productive forces takes place in the modern age. True, the problems of changes in the system of functioning of the economy appear again, but this time in the context of the whole, from the point of view of the role which they play in the process of socialisation and in the evolution of the political system.

Consideration of the political aspect as an integral element of the analysis of the economic system is justified today more than at any time, under every kind of political structure, owing to the important and continually growing economic role of the state. This applies all the more to a socialist system, where the role of the state becomes so great that one can speak of a qualitative change. I, for my part, have tried to draw certain conclusions from this in certain works published during the years 1965–9.[2]

The book is not historical, yet it stems from the aim of generalising real experiences which seem sufficiently long to afford the appropriate perspective. The author approaches this attempt at generalisation from a specific methodological position – Marxist historical materialism. In general terms, this position is expressed in the conviction that the evolution of society is subject to laws at the basis of which lie the processes of development of productive forces. Accepting this methodological plane, I treat it nevertheless exclusively as a working hypothesis, the usefulness of which for the study of socialism must be verified in the course of the analysis, in order to eliminate the drawing of conclusions from *a priori* assumptions. Hence also – at the risk of boring the reader – the attempts to make certain concepts more precise, particularly those which have become so current in Marxist literature that frequently we no longer think of their real meaning. This also applies to such central concepts for Socialism as 'social ownership of the means of production' or 'socialisation of the means of production'.

My personal experience and works hitherto have been limited basically to the problems of the form of socialism which has developed in the USSR and the East European people's democracies (it would be simplest to cover this whole group of countries with the term 'Soviet-type countries', but in view of the undesirable political implications it is better to reject it). It is this form of socialism which is primarily the subject of the present book. I thus pass over not only the question of the rise of socialism in the West, but also the problems of the Asian and Latin American countries, and, which requires stressing particularly, I abstract from the many specific problems of the development of Yugoslav socialism. True, the Yugoslav model is discussed in the book – indeed, it plays a significant part in it – but not as an independent subject of research; rather, I view it as a possible alternative solution, thus enabling myself to cast the problems of the book in stronger relief.

In the discussion the actual course of events is compared with the theoretical concepts of socialism. The book is not so much concerned, however, with the discussion of different individual conceptions, but primarily with the broadly accepted ideo-political doctrines which have been expressed in the general line of action of the parties in power, and thus exerted a direct influence on what happened. This creates specific difficulties since the normal method of quoting scientific literature becomes scarcely applicable here. In some cases one can make use of programme documents (e.g. the 1958 programme of the League of Communists of Yugoslavia, to some extent the 1919 programme of the RKP(b) and the 1961 CPSU programme); at times, however, they do not exist at all (e.g. in Poland) and in any case they often do not exhaust the matter. Hence the necessity of resorting to my own presentation, built up equally from such programme documents as exist and my own reconstruction of the doctrine on the basis of historical practice. This holds certain dangers, since it introduces a subjective factor not only into the results of the comparison with actual practice but into the presentation of the doctrine itself as well. It is my duty to warn the reader of this.

The fundamental question which the present work seeks to answer can be formulated as follows: do there exist *economic* laws postulating the real socialisation of the means of production and thus defining the plane of further evolution of socialism – in relation to the form which it has taken in the USSR and the people's democracies? This covers above all the question of economic conditioning of the evolution of the political system. It does not, on the other hand, cover the problem which many readers will consider the most pertinent: the evaluation of the chance, form and timing of changes which would fulfil the postulate of real socialisation of the means of production. The author considers this justified, among other things, by the limits of competence of an economist, even one who understands his discipline most literally as *political* economy. The verdict on whether this is in fact so and whether, within these specific and rather rigorously maintained limits, problems of sufficient importance are posed, belongs to the reader.

Notes

1   *Ogolne problemy funkcjonowania gospodarki socjalistycznej*, 1st Polish ed., 1961, 2nd ed. 1964; translated into Italian, Czech, Hungarian, French, Spanish, German, Japanese, English; English edition, *The Market in a Socialist Economy*, Routledge & Kegan Paul, London and Boston, 1972.
2   The majority were reprinted in the collection of essays *The Economics and Politics of Socialism*, published in Italy by Editori Riuniti, Rome (1972), in Germany by Suhrkamp Verlag (1972), and in Great Britain by Routledge & Kegan Paul (1973). An example of the interdependence of the economic and political factors in relation to the Polish events of 1970 is provided in the article 'Six Months after the Baltic Crisis', *Rinascita*, 25 June 1971.

1

Socialisation of the means of production in the Marxist model of development

According to the Marxist model of the development of society, accepted here as the most general methodological platform, the factors determining the rise and evolution of socialism must be sought in the relationships which Oskar Lange called respectively the first and second laws of sociology: the law of necessary conformity of the relations of production with the character of the productive forces and the law of necessary conformity of the superstructure with the relations of production (the economic base).[1] What does this mean in concrete terms, above all in relation to the rise of socialism as a product of the evolution of the capitalist system?

The classical formulation of Marx runs as follows:[2]

In the social production of their life men enter into definite relations that are indispensable and independent of their will – relations of production which correspond to a definite stage of development of their material productive forces. The sum total of these relations of production constitutes the economic structure of society, the real foundation on which rises a legal and political superstructure and to which correspond definite forms of social consciousness. ... At a certain stage of their development the material productive forces of society come in conflict with the existing relations of production, or – what is but a legal expression for the same thing – with the property relations within which they have been at work hitherto. From forms of development of the productive forces these relations turn into their fetters. Then begins an epoch of social revolution.

The productive forces of the *époque* of capitalism give the process of production a social character in the sense that the final product is the collective result of many interconnected activities. Understood in this way, the process of production is a complicated and multi-stage process of cooperation by people – gathered together in a particular factory and participating in an extended division of labour among enterprises, regions and branches of production. Kuznets considers[3] that 'the wide-spread application of science to problems of economic production' has been a feature of the industrialised countries of today since at least the beginning of the nineteenth century; which would lead to the conclusion that capitalist production cooperation – broadly understood – began to embrace scientific production too relatively early.

As the productive forces of the *époque* of capitalism develop, the social character of production is continuously being deepened. The scale of production and outlays, especially of investment, grows; the period for which resources are tied up lengthens; and the external connections of every undertaking become more complicated, including connections with the scientific infrastructure and with the creation of 'human capital'. It is clear that a process of this type must be accompanied by changes in the 'economic structure of society', and thus in the relations of production. As long as capitalism remains capitalism these changes take place on essentially the same general base, namely, the dominance by private ownership of the means of production with all its consequences: deprivation of ownership of the direct producers – the employed workers; the antagonistic class character of the distribution of income; the maximisation of profit on capital as the main criterion for allocation of resources; the conflict between 'the conditions of production and the conditions of sale'; and the resultant tendency to cyclical fluctuations in the level of use of productive capacity and of the labour force, etc., etc. Yet even the most orthodox interpretation of the Marxist model of development does not deny the importance of the continuous process of transformation of the relations of production within the limits of capitalism. No strand in Marxism has maintained, or does maintain, that at a certain moment the productive forces developing within the framework of capitalism encounter a rigid, immutable wall of capitalist production relations which is incapable of adaptation. On the contrary, all generations of Marxists, from Marx and Engels themselves onwards, have followed the process of evolution of the economic structure of capitalist society attentively, trying to predict precisely from this evolution the prospects and forms of the transition to socialism. The differences – some extremely deep – have concerned, and still concern, their conclusions about the limits of adaptation of the capitalist system; their evaluation of particular stages in this adaptation from the point of view of the continuity or discontinuity of the process of transition from capitalism to socialism; the changes in the social structure and in the political aspirations of particular classes which the adaptation causes; and finally, the strategy and tactics of socialist movements.

These rather elementary observations have a twofold significance for our subject. First, they remind us that the dialectics of conflict between productive forces and relations of production embrace not only the 'jump' solution – the transition from one systemic 'quality' to another – but also the continuous process of transformation of the economic structure of society within the framework of a particular formation, which preserves its features of continuity and progressiveness the more it displays 'elasticity of adaptation'. Second, they teach us to view the problem of socialism as a product of historical development not only in a negative way (does socialism, and if so to what extent, meet the requirements of the development of productive forces by virtue of the fact that it is the opposite of capitalism?) but also as a form of continuity (is socialism, and to what extent, a result of and a further link in those tendencies which already characterise the evolution of the relations of production within the limits of capitalism?).

The evolution of the relations of production within the framework of capitalism is expressed above all in transformations in the ownership of the means of production. The following seems to be the most concise way of presenting the course of these changes.

The early, from a certain point of view 'classical', phase of capitalism is characterised by close dependence of actual disposition over the means of production on private ownership in the simplest form, the juridical and economic aspects of which are not separated and are most frequently personified in the shape of the *individual*

capitalist-entrepreneur. The process of concentration and centralisation of capital, brought about by technological and economic conditions, proceeds for some time within this form (but already causing changes of degree in the nature of competition through the
growth of elements of 'imperfection'). As this process continues the
individual form of private ownership becomes too restricted for the
growing scale of production and the need to raise larger and larger
sums of capital; it is replaced – at least as the dominant factor – by
the corporate form, by the joint-stock company.

The rise of joint-stock companies sets in motion structural
changes which appear particularly sharply in *the modern large capitalist corporation.*[4] Without going into a detailed description of the
functioning of the modern corporation, we must note two features
distinguishing it from the individual capitalist enterprise which are
essential for our problem.

First, the division of the single form of private ownership into
individual ownership of capital (in the form of shares) and corporate ownership of the real assets forming the means of production;
corporate ownership is private ownership as opposed to public
ownership, but at the same time it is ownership through association
as opposed to individual private ownership.[5]

Second, the separation of effective disposition over the means of
production from their legal ownership, in the sense that the direct
and virtually automatic dependence of the leading role in the management structure on capital ownership disappears. This still does
not mean the severing of the dependence of disposition over the
means of production on individual private ownership, especially
when the latter is concentrated. The extent of this dependence is the
subject of numerous controversies in economic literature, but the
fact itself can scarcely be denied. It is nevertheless a dependence
which is significantly more indirect and takes forms which cause the
modern capitalist corporation to retain at least relative autonomy
vis-à-vis its shareholders and to use criteria and methods of operation different from those typical of enterprises directed by individual capitalists. In particular this applies to the time horizon,
attitude to the market and competition, and the distribution of
profit. On the other hand the corporate form of enterprise by itself
changes nothing in the relationship between capital and labour.

The next link in this schematic chain of evolution is *the public
sector.* It is next, not necessarily because a definite succession in

time could always be observed, but in view of the fact that the growth of the role of the public sector in the capitalist economy may be explained, in my opinion, by the fact that the development of productive forces also encounters obstructions and obstacles from private ownership when this appears in corporate form. In certain cases the state as entrepreneur is in a position not only to mobilise resources on a larger scale than private investors could (and would want to), but is also able to take into account external effects and costs ('externalities') over a considerably wider area, adopt a broader time horizon and insure more adequately against risk. And precisely these factors, reflected among other things in the various forms of planning or programming, are today playing a more and more essential role from the point of view of the development of productive forces.

In the public sector the formal dependence of disposition over the means of production on private ownership is completely broken. Factual dependence exists in so far as the state is an apparatus for the rule of the class of private owners over the means of production. Let us note, however, that here the lines of dependence become even more complicated and general: first, the dominant members of the private sector are the big corporations, in which the relations between ownership and real disposition over the means of production have themselves undergone far-reaching modifications; second, influencing the policy of the state in the interests of particular groups requires the use of political mechanisms, and these in turn, must to some extent – particularly under a democratic system – be subject to pressure from mass social movements.

The public sector *sensu stricto* – most frequently in the form of commercialised state enterprises – is today only one element of state interference in economic life, although it is in general a very important element, which to a significant extent determines the effectiveness of other forms of interference, especially when it is a question of giving them the coordinated form of a plan. These forms, which along with the public sector comprise the system of state intervention, can be divided into three groups.

(1) Regulation of the activity of private and particularly corporate capital. This covers restrictions of the anti-trust legislation type, licensing of certain kinds of activity, control over the location of investment projects and their influence on the general conditions of

life, as well as interference in wage disputes, the control of prices, etc.

(2) Influencing the economic conditions of allocation of resources by an active policy on market magnitudes (prices, interest rates), redistribution of incomes (taxes, subsidies), government purchases and public works, control over foreign transactions and influence on their structure, etc.

(3) Active and growing participation in the development of 'scientific infrastructure' and the reproduction of 'human capital', particularly in the field of training. The modern 'welfare state' is on the one hand the result of social pressure, and on the other an essential form of safeguarding of the general development conditions in a purely economic sense.

The growth of the economic role of the state in modern capitalism is undoubtedly connected with the evolution of capitalist private ownership, in particular with the growth of the specific weight of big corporations. On the one hand, and which can be found already in Marx[6], the increase in the area of state interference is a necessary condition of the maintenance of the overall equilibrium of the system, an equilibrium which would be threatened by the uncontrolled power of corporate giants. On the other hand, the creation of conditions favouring the activity of the 'mature corporation', directed at long-term aims, requires an increase in state interference at many points in the functioning of the economic system (relative stabilisation of markets, safeguarding against the risks of investment, etc.).[7]

Despite its close connection with the development of big corporation capitalism, state interventionism should not be treated only as a factor supplementing the previous transformations within the framework of private ownership. It is at the same time the expression of a new, higher stage in the evolution of production relations within the limits of capitalism. It is not only that the state performs the allocation of resources on the basis of macro-criteria and that, through the role it plays in the economy, it can at least partially impose these criteria on private entrepreneurship;[8] it also has consequences of a socio-economic nature which are extremely relevant from the point of view of the Marxist development schema. Extended state interventionism becomes a source of 'politicisation of the economy', and begins to alter the relations between the economic base and the political superstructure. If ownership in an economic sense is understood as actual and relatively permanent disposition over means of production, the direction of dependence begins to be modified here, since in some areas power no longer stems from ownership but rather ownership stems from power. We must add, too, that this circumstance gives a political overtone to the economic demands of workers, which in turn leads to a sort of politicisation of trade unions. Of course, if we continue to look upon the modern capitalist state as simply and exclusively 'a committee managing the common interests of the whole bourgeoisie',[9] then the changes we have mentioned must be classified as formal. But even if one adopts such an extreme and undoubtedly oversimplified view – which both obliterates the conflicts within the different groups of capital and also ignores the effects of many decades of struggle by the workers' movement – the problem of the direction of dependence remains, since the socio-economic essence of public ownership of means of production can only be defined in conjunction with a definition of the class character of the state.

The above remarks should not, obviously, be treated as an attempt at a characterisation of the complicated and many sided – economic, social and political – process of changes occurring in capitalism. It is a question of extracting, so to say – of distilling from the whole the single most general trend in the evolution of ownership relations and of showing – again in extremely schematic form – the link between this trend and what in Marxist terminology are called the requirements of the development of productive forces.

If we now look at *socialism* from this point of view, it seems justifiable – at least as one possible interpretation – to treat it as a systemic formation placed further along the trend line, and thus as a system which does not appear by chance, but rather as a result of definite development processes.

It is precisely in this way that Schumpeter formulates socialism and its relationship to modern capitalism.[10] By socialism he understands, as is well known, 'an institutional pattern in which the control over means of production and over production itself is vested with a central authority – or as we may say, in which, as a matter of principle the economic affairs of society belong to the public and not to the private sphere.'[11] The rise of this type of institutional structure is prepared by the development of capitalism itself, in which the gradual depersonalisation of ownership and management accompanies to some extent the transformation of private owner-

B

ship of the means of production into public. This is not, according to Schumpeter, a threat to the effectiveness of the system; on the contrary, its reliance on public ownership increases the possibility of rational management of the economy, since:

(a) it permits the allocation of resources according to the criterion of overall interest, by which the conditions of equilibrium become determined (as distinct from oligopolistic competition, where they are virtually undetermined);

(b) it creates the conditions for selection and subsequent implementation of a particular rate of growth, and for the elimination of cyclical fluctuations – the latter due to the possibility of adjusting aggregate demand to aggregate supply, among other things as a result of an appropriate income distribution policy.

Because of these factors, the possibility arises of planned coordination of activities on the scale of the whole economy, which eliminates (or at any rate significantly diminishes) uncertainty about the actions of competitors and about the market situation.

Schumpeter presents arguments in favour of socialism as an economic system answering modern requirements in a way which is in many respects close to the Marxist concept of the dialectics of development of productive forces and relations of production, although he uses a different language. The most important element in these arguments is the statement that the replacement of private ownership by public ownership is the next link in the evolutionary process, which brings out all the more sharply the necessity of calculation of effects and outlays on a macro-economic scale (and thus the internalisation of externalities), and the separation of incomes from ownership, which is a condition of pursuit of an incomes policy compatible with general economic criteria.

Referring to our previous remarks, we have thus a strong emphasis on *the aspect of continuity* in the relationship between capitalism and socialism. It would be hard to reconcile oneself with the undoubted one-sidedness of this concept on examining the social and political impulses of the process of transition from capitalism to socialism in the real world; on the other hand, from the point of view of abstract analysis of the historical laws determining the general tendencies of development, it has a number of merits.

Putting the emphasis on the aspect of continuity permits us, among other things, to take up a position in relation to the view once expressed by Joan Robinson, that 'socialism is not a stage beyond capitalism but a substitute for it – a means by which the nations which did not share in the Industrial Revolution can imitate its technical achievements, a means of achieving rapid accumulation under a different set of rules of the game'.[12] Obviously the importance of socialism for the countries which are only just facing industrialisation cannot be denied. Imitation of the capitalist road of development – apart from very exceptional circumstances – would be impossible for them today; making up for their lateness requires essentially state forms of accumulation and planned allocation of resources according to macro-economic criteria. However, if the line of reasoning cited above is correct, it must be accepted that socialism can prove economically rational in less-developed countries *not because of but in spite of* their immaturity, and the 'jumping of stages' involves a number of negative consequences.[13] It is precisely from the changes taking place in the world of mature capitalism that one can derive, amid zigzags and conflicts, with varying strength in different countries, the continuing tendency towards socialism as the stage logically following capitalism.

The position presented here also determines the author's attitude to the so-called theory of convergence of socialism and capitalism.

The question of whether capitalism and socialism are evolving in convergent directions was posed particularly clearly in the well-known article by Jan Tinbergen in 1961.[14] Tinbergen catalogues the factual changes which have taken place in both systems, taking as his starting-point for socialism very early and short-lived forms which arose under the influence of the needs of the moment or of the ideological naïveties which always accompany great turning points. Thus in his catalogue of 'converging' changes in socialism we have not only the reforms in the system of functioning of the economy which are mentioned everywhere today (the growth in importance of monetary as distinct from physical instruments and plan indicators, the area of decentralisation associated with this, the new elements in the system of economic incentives, etc.) but also matters long since regarded as obvious in the socialist countries: the abandonment of rationing in favour of the principle of free choice in the sphere of consumption, of drastic egalitarianism in favour of the principle of differentiation of incomes, and of extreme forms of 'popular' management of enterprises in favour of a principle of organisation under which specialised managerial personnel play the appropriate role. As far as capitalism is concerned, a number of the points listed – regulation of market processes, planning in different forms, the creation of infrastructure. etc., amount to a character-isation of the basic tendency, which is the growth of the public sector and other forms of state influence on the economy. Tinbergen puts special emphasis on the development of public education, including higher education. Among the many additions to Tinbergen's list, the observation of 'convergence' in the evolution of consumer requirements, particularly for durable goods, deserves attention.[15]

In the copious and persistent discussion the existence of a number of factual signs of convergence has not in general been questioned, if we exclude, on both sides, contributions which are *par excellence* ideological, depicting every attempt at objective analysis of the phenomenon as subversion. The answer to the question thus boils down to interpretation of the facts.

In the light of the position set out above, any evaluation of the signs observed must, in our opinion, be differentiated for socialism on the one hand and for capitalism on the other. In respect of socialism we interpret them as signs of adaptation of the mechan-isms of functioning of the economy to economic conditions within the compass of the existing system of production relations, based on public ownership; this adaptation in certain cases means abandon-ment of too far-reaching institutional solutions (among other things in relation to the 'jumping of stages' mentioned above), in others it is simply an expression of the fact that the foundations of a system of socialism permit, within a certain area, a diversity of forms. On the other hand, in respect of capitalism, we interpret them as funda-mental structural changes, manifestations of the objective laws of development towards socialism. This view does not involve either an assertion that the developed countries of the West have already entered socialism, nor that they will attain this stage in the course of automatic evolution. It means only that a need is appearing for even greater inclusion of socialist elements in the existing economic structure, and thus that the system, which is characteristic of a number of capitalist countries today, of coexistence between public and private elements, with the latter having the dominant role, cannot be a state of permanent equilibrium but must change in favour of the public element. A particular complex of social and political reasons can prevent these needs being met, and thus, to use

Isaac Deutscher's pertinent description,[16] cause a state of 'over-maturity', with the threat of particularly severe conflicts.

Our discussion hitherto has served, in the main, the purpose of providing evidence for the thesis that the evolution of the economic structure of the developed capitalist countries can be interpreted according to the Marxist model of development, which treats the rise of socialism as an expression of historical laws. But even in our understanding this is not synonymous with acceptance of all the detailed elements of the model, particularly in relation to the later stages of development of capitalism. What is more, we have tried to draw attention to the point that, precisely as a result of a process taking place according to the initial assumptions of the model, some relationships are modified so far that their original interpretation loses – completely or partially – its justification. This applies in particular to the relationship between economic structure and political institutions, which is so essential for the theory of historical materialism: at a certain stage of development the treatment of the relationship between them in the categories of 'base' and 'superstructure' ceases to be adequate, or at any rate requires verification anew.

The author is fully aware of the highly controversial nature of his position – both as regards his general conception of the dialectics of productive forces and relations of production, and his assertion of the succession of socialism after capitalism. In modern economic and sociological literature we find not only criticism of the assumptions of the Marxist model and of the thesis that the process of changes leads towards socialism, but also a series of attempts at constructing alternative models.[17] However, these introductory considerations do not include a comparison of the different conceptions of the development process and its direction. For the purpose of this work it is quite sufficient to state that there exist grounds for recognising the model presented here as one of the possible methodological planes.

Does the interpretation of the operation of the 'law of necessary conformity of the relations of production with the character of productive forces' accepted here define exhaustively and unambiguously the features of socialism as an economic system? The answer to this question is of fundamental importance for the correct posing of the problem of social ownership and the general laws of the evolution of socialism.

So far we have cited only one – Schumpeter's – definition of socialism as an economic system. This is a characteristic and typical definition in as far as it uses categories which are simple and also directly comprehensible in a formal legal conception. In practice in the existing nation-states, the central authority to which – according to the definition – 'control over the means of production and over production itself' belongs, is the state authority. If we treat 'control' as ownership in the economic sense, then we can say that this definition of socialism turns on the assertion of dominance of state ownership of the means of production, without the necessity of closer definition of the character of the state as the *subject* of ownership. State ownership understood in this way we shall call *public ownership*.

The thesis that socialism meets the requirements of the law of necessary conformity of the relations of production with the character of productive forces would mean – if we accept Schumpeter's or an analogous definition – that the requirements of the development of modern productive forces are satisfied by the fact of creation of the institutional preconditions for allocation of resources on the scale and from the point of view of the system *as a whole,* i.e. according to macro-economic criteria. The point is that the state should secure the capacity for effective allocation of resources on a national economic scale, without limitation by the hurdles of private ownership, which are the source of particular interests and accordingly of allocation decisions based on private criteria of economic rationality. Effective disposition on a macro scale does not of itself predetermine *forms* of organisation, nor allocation mechanisms (the scope of delegation of decisions to lower levels, the proportions between direct orders and market steering instruments, etc.) as long as the precedence of general economic criteria is safeguarded.

The state as the subject of *public ownership* can be connected with society in very varied ways and can be pursuing widely-differing aims and interests. This is precisely the basis for Schumpeter's position that recognition of a system as socialist does not prejudge its other features, in particular the features by which one evaluates it. Socialism in this conception can be either democratic or autocratic, peaceful or aggressive, rich or poor. Obviously, from a humanistic point of view, these alternatives are not immaterial. But the definition of socialism on the basis of the category of public ownership does not lead to any consequential definition of the probability of particular alternatives, nor of a direction of development, e.g. from less to more desirable.

Whilst in its understanding of socialism as a product of historical development Schumpeter's conception displays a number of points of resemblance to the Marxist position as most generally understood, in its actual definition of socialism and the problems connected with it there is a clear difference to be seen. The difference lies not so much in the rejection of elements of the Schumpeter definition and of his arguments for the thesis that there are economic laws determining the evolution from private to public ownership of the means of production – as in the treatment of them as incomplete, insufficient. With reference to the concepts introduced above, it could be said that the resemblance concerns the aspect of continuity (of socialism in relation to capitalism) whereas the differences relate to the *aspect of negation*; in Schumpeter this aspect barely exists, whereas in the Marxist conception it is at least of equal importance.

Marxists are not satisfied with the socially anonymous characterisation of socialist ownership as public ownership, just as they are not satisfied with the anonymous characterisation of public, corporate or individual ownership under capitalism. Ownership is a social relationship realised through the relationship of people to things, in particular to the material factors in the process of reproduction of the material conditions of life. On account of this, every form of ownership requires a characterisation of its essence, exposing the social relationship which is formed on the basis of it. Private ownership means monopolisation of the means of production in the hands of a particular sector of society, and thus deprives another sector of society of the means of production; the result is relations of dominance and subordination which, under conditions where there is personal freedom of the direct producer, take the form of *hired labour*. To put it paradoxically, in this – essential – sense *every form* of ownership can be private ownership, including public ownership, if it means the accumulation of *de facto* disposition over the means of production in the hands of an established group holding state power, which in turn means deprivation of the majority of society of this right of disposition.[18] What is more, in certain situations the relations of dominance and subordination based on public ownership can be far more relentless than those which are based on private ownership in the generally accepted sense, since (1) the state, gathering in one centre disposition over all – or almost all – the places and conditions of work, has in its hands an instrument of *economic coercion* the scale of which cannot be equalled by individual capitalists and corporations; (2) the state can directly link economic coercion with *political coercion,* in particular in a totalitarian system which actually liquidates political rights, the right of assembly and freedom of speech.

Marx's critique of private ownership relates not to its specific forms, but to its essence, which is based on the opposition of labour to ownership and the subordination of the former to the latter. In every form of such subordination are to be found the sources of *alienation of labour,* its alienation in relation to the means and aims of its activity. Alienation cannot be overcome by replacing one system of subjection in work by another system, e.g. by replacing hired labour for an individual owner by hired labour for the state (however, this does not mean that forms are completely immaterial!) – but by means of liquidation of all subordination of labour to ownership and the creation of 'a union of free people working with the aid of social means of production and consciously expending their personal individual labour power as a *single* social labour power'.[19]

These premises are the basis of the Marxist understanding of socialism as a system which in the contemporary *époque* fulfils the requirements of 'the law of necessary conformity of the relations of production with the character of the productive forces'. Socialism is claimed to meet these requirements not only because it eliminates the obstacles to allocation of resources on the scale and by the criteria of the national economy as a whole; if it were a matter of this otherwise essential aspect alone, the solution would be *public ownership* without further qualifications. The conformity of socialist production relations with the character of the productive forces is held to depend on the point that under socialism public ownership acquires certain specific features which make it *social ownership.*

What arguments are there to justify this crucial thesis for the Marxist conception? We face here an extremely subtle problem which is rarely taken up in Marxist literature. The brunt of the economic argument for socialism has always been directed against a system based on private ownership in the narrow sense which is thus unable to make full use of potential productive capacity or to overcome the anarchy of the market and the associated cyclical fluctuations, etc. Clearly, arguments of this type are not applicable to the problem of social ownership versus *public* ownership. Similarly, one cannot refer to the economic results of the socialist countries, unless there is evidence that these results stem from *socialisation* of the means of production, and not only from making them publicly owned (*nationalisation*).[20]

The relationship between public ownership and social ownership is in fact a central problem of this book. Therefore we shall only be able to attempt our own answer to the question of the justification of the Marxist conception outlined above after the end of our discussion – on the basis of more concrete analysis of the evolution of the existing forms of socialism. At this point, however, we must at least note the general direction of the arguments which, if not directly formulated in the literature, may nevertheless be deduced indirectly. I think they can be divided into three interconnected groups.

1 The question of the possibility of full or at any rate sufficiently broad nationalisation from the point of view of the requirements of economic rationality without simultaneous radical change in socio-political relations. Some prominent Marxists have also not excluded the possibility of full nationalisation of the means of production under a capitalist state aiming at total subordination of society to itself on the pattern of the literary vision of the 'iron foot' of Jack London. Rudolf Hilferding, for example, considered this type of solution possible[21] in the form of a 'general cartel' with the basic means of production under its disposition and planning the whole economy centrally. The experience of the highly developed capitalist countries – if we abstract from the period of the war economy, in particular in the Hitlerian form, seems not to support this theoretical hypothesis. The extent of nationalisation has grown, but by no means to such a degree that private capital has become marginal. Against this background a relentless and complicated struggle proceeds. Despite the fact that the state, in Marxist terminology, retains a bourgeois character and that nationalisation of certain sectors, particularly those connected with infrastructure, is favourable to private capital, the latter opposes extension of the area of public ownership of the means of production. This opposition is not only on principle, but also in order to maintain the socio-economic positions which all nationalisation, including bourgeois, must to some degree disturb. In this connection

it is sometimes observed that the Schumpeter definition (effective disposition over the means of production and over production itself by a central authority) could only really be fulfilled given radical socio-political transformations, and a change in the class content of the state authority which already shifts the problem to a different plane. One could say – formulating it most carefully, so as not to run ahead – that this argument leads to the conclusion that consistent nationalisation requires something more than simple passing of the means of production into public ownership; it requires also a socio-political revolution.

2 Nationalisation of the means of production does not fully solve the problem of internalisation of external costs and benefits ('externalities'), which problem, as we have seen, plays a crucial role in determining the principles of the direction of changes in production relations. Under conditions where separate individual *households* exist, nationalisation does not and cannot mean the formation of a single economic macro-unit directly embracing all portions of the process of reproduction: production, distribution, exchange and consumption. Even in the case of extreme centralisation, integrating the *national economy* in a kind of monolithic grand corporation, we also have to deal with other units, namely with the worker-consumer *households*. The division between the national economy and households corresponds to the division into two types of income – where the *income* of households becomes a *cost* to the national economy and vice versa (when the state is not only the sole producer and employer, but also the sole distributor-seller of consumer goods). In these conditions internalisation of costs and benefits within the national economy does not extend directly to the household economy. Cost and benefit from the point of view of the national economy and the household economy are not identical, so there is a problem of balancing the financial and material flows between the one and the other, etc.[22] The advantages of the national economy are not identical with the advantages of households, but can also be directly opposed to them, and the one may only be attainable at the expense of the others.

3 The position of man as producer in the process of production and distribution and the associated question of his subjective posture towards work and the means of production. The following line of argument is the best known and appears most often in Marxist literature: the productive forces will continue to develop without

hindrance on condition that labour is not only organised by planning on a national economic scale, but also becomes 'labour for itself', free labour, creative and not alienated.[23] Public ownership *per se,* without further qualification, is not – from the points of view discussed above – a sufficient condition for the postulated change in the objective position and the subjective posture of man in the process of production. This requirement is fulfilled when public ownership is given certain specific features which make it social ownership.

The last argument reflects the fundamental position of the Marxist philosophy of history, which treats the acts of human society as a progressive process: the development of productive forces is accompanied – and must be accompanied, if we view it over a sufficiently large time scale – by the gradual improvement of the position of man as creator of material and spiritual goods. The passage from a lower to a higher socio-economic formation, at least in the mainstream of civilisation, required first that people would be kept alive (the transition from the primitive community to slavery) and then successive extensions of the area of freedom and of the interest of the producer in the results of his labour. In this conception communism is supposed to be the logical and historical continuation of the trend, in that it transforms the means of production into the social property of all working people and thus makes them free in a social sense and totally interested in the multiplication of their material wealth and spiritual community.

The whole conception of the unequivocally progressive character of the development of human society is criticised today from various quarters as an over-optimistic legacy of nineteenth-century evolutionism; the vision of communism is often treated as the next social utopia, and also typical of the great reforming ideologies of the past which appealed to the imagination of the masses. Without going into an evaluation of the justification of these criticisms, let us, however, turn our attention to a certain aspect which gives a wholly pragmatic merit to the postulate of development in society of the posture of collective ownership of the means of production. This is the question of the possibility and the conditions for creating the motivation, which would permit the proper use of potential capacity, inherent in 'the principle that the economic affairs of society belong to the public, and hardly at all to the private sphere' (Schumpeter). It is well known that in his polemic with Lange, F. A.

Hayek[24] advanced the argument that the manager of a state enterprise, not of course being in a position to bear personal material responsibility for the consequences of wrong decisions, finds himself permanently between the Scylla of excessive risk and the Charybdis of bureaucratic playing for safety, so that it is impossible to make him effectively interested in striving towards a long-term goal, etc. These arguments have been refuted – more or less convincingly – several times, but experience proves that they should not be disregarded. The correct organisation of the functioning of the economy and economic incentives can make a substantial improvement in the situation and counteract bureaucratic distortions, but it cannot – here again we anticipate a conclusion, the basis for which will be fully worked out considerably later – finally solve the problem. Such a solution requires the inclusion of a social motivation stemming from a feeling of common ownership. It would be an exaggeration to say that the Marxist conception of socialism assumes a dominant role for this type of motivation right from the moment the new order arises; the view seems correct, however, that it must assume *progress* in this field with the passage of time. If the opposite is the case the proportions of light and shade associated with the passage of the economic affairs of society into the public sphere will change unfavourably.

So much for the main lines of the arguments in favour of the Marxist proposition that the development of productive forces requires the basing of production relations on social ownership, and not just on public ownership. It may be that these arguments – at least in the form presented here – carry more conviction in a negative sense (public ownership is still not a satisfactory solution) than in a positive sense (social ownership is such a solution). This results among other things from the imprecision of the concept of social ownership itself – of which more below. What has been said up till now seems, however, to provide sufficient justification at least for the intention of verifying the thesis of objective necessity of socialisation of the means of production. The introductory stage of this must be an attempt at a definition of social ownership, and the next an attempt to present and contrast with practice those conceptions of socialisation which have been manifested in the socialist countries of Eastern Europe.

One further preliminary remark. In this book we aim primarily to verify the hypothesis that the direction of evolution of the system of

ownership of the means of production under socialism is conditioned by the laws of development of productive forces. But what
are we to understand by the concept 'development of productive
forces'? Can we, for example, – as is frequently done, explicitly or
implicitly – identify the development of productive forces with
economic growth, i.e., with increase in the national product over
time? Can we measure the efficiency of an economic system, and
thus also indirectly the degree to which production relations are
suited to the requirements of the development of productive forces,
simply by the long-term rate of growth? This seems to be too simplified, an example of the characteristic fanaticism of growth ('growth-
manship'). It is hard to deny that growing productive potential and
the ability to make the fullest possible use of it are an expression of
progress and that up to the time a certain level of development is
attained this can in essence be treated as the basic criterion of the
economic efficiency of a system of production relations. For many
countries of the world – for the majority, rather – this is still the
basic criterion today: despite the appearance of inescapable
negative consequences of growth, in these countries – taking the
matter in the most general terms – the decisive factor for the
improvement of human life is capacity for accelerated economic
growth, increase in labour productivity, industrialisation and urban-
isation. At the same time, however, we are more conscious today
that there may come, or may even have arrived, the moment (which
will certainly be different for different countries) when the positive
effects of economic growth cease to outweigh the negative ones. This
means that the broadly accepted conditions of life may not be
subject to improvement but, on the contrary, to deterioration, if the
increasingly growing productive potential of society is directed
exclusively or mainly to the growth of production and consumption
of material goods and services of the conventional type. Could one
say of a society which gave up a part or even the whole of the
attainable increase in output and consumption in the conventional
sense in favour of reduced working time and a lower degree of
tension than is characteristic of life today, or in favour of the protection and regeneration of the natural environment, etc., could one
say of such a society that it was arresting the development of its
productive forces? The author thinks not – as long as we stop considering that the development of productive forces is always in line
with economic growth and can in every case be measured by indi-

cators of growth. In our understanding, development of productive forces is increasing the capacity to satisfy broadly understood social needs. In certain circumstances it may turn out that for the development of productive forces understood in this way the unrestrained growth of production is less essential than the formation of a more appropriate structure of needs, such as would ensure harmony between the different sides of the human personality and would further the maintenance of equilibrium between man and his environment.

These few general remarks obviously do not claim to be a solution to the problem of the relation between the concepts of economic growth and development of productive forces (among other things simplifications of the opposite type are possible – e.g. the primitive postulate of total cessation of growth as an antidote to its negative ecological consequences). It remains only to emphasise that when we use the concept of development of productive forces in our further discussion we shall understand it as increasing the capacity to satisfy the needs of people broadly understood, and not as the simple growth of productive potential in the conventional sense.

Notes

1 *Ekonomia polityczna* (*Political Economy*), 3rd ed., Warsaw, 1963, Vol. 1, p. 31.
2 Preface to *A Contribution to the Critique of Political Economy*, Marx and Engels, *Selected Works*, Moscow, 1950 (English text), vol. 1, pp. 328–9.
3 Simon Kuznets, *Modern Economic Growth*, Connecticut, 1966, p. 9.
4 John K. Galbraith (*The New Industrial State*, London, 1967) distinguishes the modern 'mature corporation' from the 'entrepreneurial corporation', which was characteristic of the initial period of corporate capitalism, in which an individual entrepreneur was still largely dominant.
5 Marx formulated this even more sharply:
   Formation of stock companies. Thereby: ... (2) The capital, which in itself rests on a social mode of production and presupposes a social concentration of means of production and labour-power, is here directly endowed with the form of social capital (capital of directly associated individuals) as distinct from private capital, and its undertakings assume the form of social undertakings as distinct from private undertakings. It is the abolition of capital as private property within the framework of

capitalist production itself (*Capital*, Moscow, 1962 (English text), vol. 3, part V, ch. 27, p. 427).

6 [The development of share companies] establishes a monopoly in certain spheres and thereby requires state interference, *Capital*, vol. 3, p. 429.

7 Hence, among other things, the tendencies to cooperation between top management of corporations and the state apparatus. Galbraith (*The New Industrial State*) seems to me to overstate these tendencies in his definition of 'the technostructure', and not to pay enough attention to the conflicts – but the phenomenon can undoubtedly be observed, and is particularly clear in the mechanism of so-called indicative planning (as in France).

8 An excellent picture of this type of transformation in the economic system of the developed capitalist countries is given by Andrew Shonfield, *Modern Capitalism: The Changing Balance of Public and Private Power*, Oxford, 1965.

9 *The Communist Manifesto*. This assertion is by no means considered only of historical importance. Its full relevance today is defended, for example, by Paul A. Baran and Paul M. Sweezy in *Monopoly Capital: An essay on the American Economic and Social Order*, Harmondsworth, 1966.

10 Joseph Schumpeter, *Capitalism, Socialism and Democracy*, 7th ed., London, 1957.

11 Ibid., p. 167.

12 Joan Robinson, *Marx, Marshall and Keynes*, Collected Economic Papers, vol. 2, Oxford, 1960, p. 15.

13 It would be difficult to discuss these consequences here, but we may point, for example, to the connection between transition to socialism 'in conditions of immaturity' and drastic forms of industrialisation policy, to the negative effects of the lack of experience of the functioning of large corporations and commercialised state enterprises, etc. We shall return to some of these problems.

14 'Do communist and free economies show a converging pattern?', *Soviet Studies*, vol. 16, No. 4.

15 H. Myint emphasised this factor in his contribution to the symposium 'Convergence and divergence of economic systems in the process of socio-economic development', organised by the Association for Comparative Economics (Bellagio, September 1967). A report was published in duplicated form.

16 *The Unfinished Revolution, Russia, 1917–1967*, ch. 6, Oxford, 1967.

17 Two works of this type, in our opinion the most characteristic, are: Walt W. Rostow, *The Stages of Economic Growth, An Anti-Communist Manifesto*, Cambridge, 1960, and Ralf Dahrendorf, *Class and Class Conflict in Industrial Society*, Routledge & Kegan Paul, 1959.

18 The seemingly Marxist conception which identifies state ownership in the socialist countries with social ownership is sharply opposed by, among others, J. Kuroń and K. Modzelewski: 'State ownership can conceal different class contents depending on the class character of

the state' (*List Otwarty do Partii* (*An Open Letter to the Party*), ed. Instytut Literacki, Paris, 1966, p. 127).

19 Marx, *Capital*, vol. 1.

20 The fundamental distinction between public ownership and social ownership makes a terminological distinction necessary here, too: we shall call the passing of the means of production into public ownership *nationalisation*, and reserve *socialisation* for fulfilment of the postulates which Marxists apply to socialisation of the means of production. Although the proposed terminology may be contrary to deep-rooted custom and contains a certain impreciseness as regards the term 'nationalisation' (public ownership need not necessarily be state ownership but, for example, local authority ownership) it seems to the author to be the best solution.

21 *Das Finanzkapital*, Frankfurt am Main, 1968, ch. 25.

22 The problem of the limitations of internalisation of externalities in a socialist economy is discussed by Alec Nove in 'Internal economies', *Economic Journal*, vol. 79, no. 316, December 1969, though mainly from the point of view of the influence of organisational structures, which we pass over here.

23 See Edward Lipiński, *Teoria ekonomii i aktualne zagadnienia gospodarcze* (*Economic Theory and Current Economic Problems*), Warsaw, 1961 (chapter on 'Alienation'), and *Karol Marks i zagadnienia współcznesności* (*Karl Marx and the Problems of Today*), Warsaw, 1969 (chapter on the 'Marxist Theory of Alienation of Labour').

24 'Sozialistische Wirtschaftsrechnung, III – Wiedereinführung des Wettbewerbs' (Socialist economic calculus III – the re-introduction of competition), in the collection *Individualismus und Wirtschaftliche Ordnung* (*Individualism and Economic Order*), Erlenbach, Zürich, 1952.

2

Socialisation in the conception and practice of East European socialism

1 The basic criterion of socialisation

The distinction between public and social ownership of the means of production requires an extremely careful definition of social ownership, which must be public ownership endowed with certain specific features. Despite what one might expect, in view of the widespread and frequent use of the term 'social ownership of the means of production', it is hard to find a definition in the literature of the socialist countries which is neither ambiguous nor a truism. The relatively few attempts at more rigorous definitions have started from the most general premise that ownership in an economic sense is tantamount to effective disposition over the object owned by its owner in his interests, broadly understood. Thus, by analogy with this, social ownership of the means of production would have to meet two criteria: (1) the means of production must be employed in the interests of society, and (2) society must have effective disposition over the means of production it owns. This is how socialisation of the means of production was understood by Oskar Lange,[1] and it is also the way I have formulated the problem.[2]

This formulation seems to me to contain the most essential components characterising social ownership. But from the point of view of our further discussions, and in particular for constructing a criterion to evaluate the actual practice in the socialist countries, one

c

further step is necessary, namely to consider the interrelationship between the two components of the definition: the social interest and effective disposition by society over the public means of production.

The concept of ownership is closely connected in the human mind with the interests of the owner, and it is difficult to imagine a definition of social ownership without the element of 'social interest'. In justification of the need for socialisation of the means of production socialist ideology always refers to the social interest – to material interest (in this most general sense socialism always allows for material incentives), freedom, the development of culture and personality, national liberation, etc. By examining the ways the existing forms of socialism have developed, their objective results and their reflection in social consciousness, we can verify again to what degree and by what methods social interests are satisfied. It might even seem that this component, 'the social interest', is the more measurable, at least as far as material interest is concerned, and thus that it is better fitted for the role of criterion to evaluate the reality of socialisation of the means of production, or of progress in this direction, if we treat socialisation as a process rather than as a once-for-all act.

And yet, if we try to apply this criterion the clarity and palpability of the social interest turn out to be illusory. We shall pass over the problems of the general theory of interests, their objective and subjective aspects, as well as the whole of the highly important and rich field of extra-economic interests,[3] and concentrate exclusively on economic interests, taking their narrowest possible expression, in the form of the level and growth of real household incomes; even with this, the most simplified formulation possible, we cannot make the social interest an *independent* criterion for evaluation of a system of ownership of the means of production. This is not only because of the difficulties, well known to welfare economics, in measuring the magnitudes and rates of change of aggregates, but something more: the problem concerns the connection between people's material situation and their position in relation to the means of production. At first glance this seems none too clear, so we must develop this idea a little.

Every Marxist accepts that the character of the means of production in capitalist countries cannot be judged on the basis of the level of wages. *Mutatis mutandis,* observation of the level and rate of growth of incomes in socialist countries does not by itself afford conclusive evidence on whether the means of production are socially owned or not. We know well that from time to time there are periods of sacrifice which are accepted by society and therefore are not treated as contradictory to the socialisation of the means of production; there also occur, on the other hand, favourable changes in incomes which can in no way be interpreted as gathering the fruits of common ownership, but can only be a manifestation of a better bargaining position attained by a particular social group in conflict with whoever has actual disposition over the means of production. The history of the socialist countries contains plenty of examples of changes in economic policy in favour of the population made under direct pressure of social action. This applies probably to all stages, with the exception – as far as one can be certain – of the period of full Stalinism, which testifies not so much to the absence of causes for pressure as to the effectiveness, at least temporarily, of mass and indiscriminate terror.

Let us assume, however (employing the terminology used in chapter I) that there is no subjective conflict of interest between the national economy and the household economy, that the intentions of the economic leadership are the best possible. There remains the problem of interpretation and in fact of reaching a consensus-definition of the social interest. Let us take, for example, the classical problem in the theory and practice of planning, the problem of the time horizon. It is well known that the problem of optimal allocation of resources from the point of view of maximisation of consumption cannot be solved without specifying the length of the period over which it is to be done; even a theoretically perfect solution (the so-called 'golden rule of accumulation') can prove sub-optimal if we take into account the relation between benefits and costs in the so-called transition periods.[4] At the same time there is no 'objectively determined' time horizon which could be accepted as corresponding to the social interest; this appears different for the household, the factory workforce and the nation, although each of the larger groups mentioned includes the smaller. How can we give a simple answer to the question of whether later improvement of living standards is in the social interest and is sufficient justification for the sacrifices of the period of forced industrialisation, and if so, how much later and with what level of costs and benefits, etc.? Clearly, there is and can be no single answer to this.

The same applies to the problem of income distribution, where egalitarian tendencies continually clash, as they are bound to, with the maintenance of differential rewards in the name of productivity growth, where both the egalitarian requirements (equal pay? equal income per head? equal opportunity?) and those of differentiation (the limits and criteria of differentiation) demand continual reformulation and adaptation to concrete situations, taking account of indirect effects, etc.

All this does not mean rejection of the category 'the social interest' or 'social preferences', nor abandoning comparison of practice with possibilities of realisation of the social interest. It does mean, though, that a definition of what is and is not in the social interest is impossible – except in particularly simple cases, when the choice is obvious – without putting into operation some mechanism for revealing contradictions and reaching solutions which in the nature of things will contain an element of compromise; it is thus impossible without ensuring for society an active role in the process of taking economic decisions (we are confining ourselves to this plane), of setting the aims of plans and the basic methods for their implementation. Use of the concept 'the social interest' in a situation when society does not play such a role is in general unfounded, and frequently becomes simply misuse to favour the interests of the rulers.

It would follow from this that the two components of the definition of social ownership of the means of production are not of equal importance. The second component is decisive: does society have effective disposition over the means of production as their owner? And if so, investigation of whether public ownership in the socialist countries is or is becoming social ownership must cover primarily the problem of democratism in the management of the economy in the broadest sense. With the predominance of public ownership this problem is inextricably linked with political democratism, although it is worth observing that the links between them follow different lines in different models of socialism.

The basic criterion of socialisation of the means of production therefore, in our understanding, is the criterion of democratism.[5] It is difficult to imagine this formulation disturbing any spokesman of official socialist doctrine, which after all has always based its claims regarding the social character of ownership on the argument that the means of production are in the hands of the toiling masses.

Controversy only begins when we try to elucidate the essence of this formulation and to make a more adequate evaluation of actual relations. We attempt such an evaluation below, from the point of view of the criterion we have put forward – treating separately the two types of solution which are found both in theoretical conceptions and in practice. The first type, with which we shall deal in more detail, is the Soviet solution, transferred in its basic features to the peoples' democracies; we shall call it the *etatist model*. The second type, which, as we said in the Introduction, we shall use primarily for the purpose of contrast, is the Yugoslav solution, which we call the *self-management model*. Of course, both terms are used here as conventional abbreviations.[6]

But before we go on to analyse these two models of socialism from the point of view of the criterion of socialisation of the means of production, we must, albeit briefly, deal with a problem which is essential to clearing the ground for further discussion, namely, the relation between political democratism and social democratism.

Deeply rooted in the Marxist tradition is the critique of political democracy with no basis in the form of social democratism; it is no accident that the political movement which grew from this tradition generally used the name social-democratic for so long. The accumulation of the means of production in the hands of the bourgeoisie and the resultant property, cultural and professional inequalities, the possibility of privileged influence on the mass media, etc., all mean that even the most refined system of political democracy and civil rights and freedoms does not in the least ensure real democracy (although obviously it creates more favourable conditions than autocracy for a campaign for the realisation of the political and socio-economic demands of the masses). As Carl Landauer correctly observes,[7] freedom depends not only on the absence of coercion but also on a sufficiently broad real range of choice, which is determined primarily by socio-economic situation.

Against this background it must be clearly stated that our thesis about the link between the social character of ownership of the means of production and political democratism relates to a different situation from the one being discussed above. By abolishing capitalist ownership of the means of production, radically altering the sources and pattern of distribution of incomes, and opening up opportunities for receiving education and access to public positions to hitherto underprivileged social classes, etc., the October Revolution and the analogous changes in the other East European countries after the Second World War created a favourable starting point for the extension of the real range of choice. This starting point, the 'big push' in socio-economic relations, exerted over the whole of the following period, and today exerts, a great influence on life in the socialist countries, and partially determines their essential features, development trends and ideology. But, if this is so, the slighting criticism and accusations of formalism directed at democratic political institutions, particularly by the communist wing of Marxism, lose their basis. The situation is, in a sense, reversed: it is no longer the absence of a social basis that destroys the chance of political democratism, but the lack of political democratism that threatens the future of the social achievements, and thus *a fortiori* the possibilities of satisfying the need to enrich them further.

We shall return to these problems, which have merely been indicated here, when discussing the two models of socialism we have distinguished – the etatist and the self-management.

2   The etatist model

Our initial reservation about the possibility of using the authentic doctrine of socialisation of the means of production, word for word as formulated in the programmes and authoritative pronouncements by party leaders, applies particularly to the etatist model. For this there are, I think, two completely different reasons. First, the creation of the socialist system in the USSR was begun with no previous experience, which meant, among other things, that many problems were simply ignored, among them the need for precise distinction between nationalisation and socialisation of the means of production; second, the etatist model was already fully formed in the Stalin period, when programme documents, party leaders' speeches and also work in the field of the social sciences blurred over all real problems and, from the point of view of what we are interested in, fulfilled a purely apologetic function. For these reasons our presentation of the *conception* of socialisation in the etatist model will be to a relatively greater extent a reconstruction based on what has been done historically in practice.

A certain problem arises here, which requires a brief discussion. The evolution of the general outlines of the etatist model of socialism in the Soviet Union was completed in the middle of the 1930s.

The features of the period, later known as Stalinist, were bound to leave their imprint on the concrete form taken by the etatist model. This applied all the more to the following phase, from the Great Purge to the death of Stalin, when the system ruling in the USSR, and imposed on the peoples' democracies, took the extreme form of totalitarian dictatorship, in the Byzantine garb of the cult of personality. This form of the etatist model may be accepted as its logical conclusion and thus used as a basis for generalisation. But one can also in a certain sense abstract from this extreme form by, as it were, stopping at an earlier stage and examining the question whether the etatist model fulfils the criterion of socialisation under – let us use the word – more normal conditions. Our choice falls on the second course, primarily because it allows us to get closer to the sources of the model and to guard against superficial judgment on the basis of obvious signs of degeneration; it will also be easier to evaluate the changes in the post-Stalin period, with which we shall deal in chapter 3.

The solution adopted has nevertheless many negative, or at least inconvenient, aspects. In certain problems there is simply no way of keeping within the defined historical framework; this applies for example to any reference to the experience of the peoples' democracies, which plunged directly into the Stalinist form of the etatist model.

Finally, we must point out that we do not cover the otherwise essential question of the nature of the link between the general features of the etatist model and its extreme forms in the second phase of the Stalin period. To attempt this would push us still more towards historical analysis and deflect us from the main task of this work.

In the etatist model socialisation *boils down* to transfer of the means of production to the ownership of the socialist *state*. In the programme of the Russian Communist Party (bolsheviks) we read (emphasis mine):[8]

> It is essential to continue and finally complete the expropriation
> of the bourgeoisie, which has been begun and in principle
> already concluded, the transfer of the means of production and
> working capital to the ownership of the Soviet Republic,
> *that is,* to the common ownership of all working people.

It is true that in some of Lenin's pronouncements reservations can be found against the identification of socialisation with confiscation of capitalist property and its transfer to the socialist state,[9] but these ideas were never developed, and a mass of other formulations, identical in content with the passage cited from the programme, supports our thesis.

Thus, if we abstract from the time needed for solving the organisational questions concerning the internal affairs of enterprises and their links with the national economy as a whole, the change in the character of the relations of production takes place immediately, by means of a once-for-all act. In this sense we can speak of a *static* conception of socialisation.

This description does not contradict the theory of the transition period from capitalism to socialism. This theory contains a dynamic element in so far as it concerns the process of development of socialism, but – at least in the conception presented in the USSR and the peoples' democracies – the dynamic aspect relates to the *quantitative* extent of socialist production relations in the whole economy. The means of production in state enterprises *are* socialised, production relations *are* socialist and do not have to go through some process to become so – on the other hand, the economy is transitional as long as these socialist relations are not exclusive or at least predominant. The fulfilment of this condition – in the USSR more or less in the mid 1930s – means the end of the transition period and the building of socialism.

The theory of two stages of communism does on the other hand contain certain dynamic elements, involving the evolution of social ownership. The transition from the lower stage of communism (socialism) to the higher (full communism) depends not on quantitative extension of the area of socialist production relations, but on deepening them, which leads to full integration of social and individual interests, the transformation of work into an 'elementary necessity of life', the replacement of the principle of distribution according to work by the principle of distribution according to need, the withering away of the state, among other things due to the disappearance of the function of control over 'norms of work and norms of consumption', etc., etc. This otherwise methodologically interesting conception of the rise of communism as a process has, however, no direct significance for our problem, since (1) it remains in the sphere of eschatology, with no possibility of verification by experience, and (2) it does not alter the fundamental thesis that at the lower stage of communism 'the means of production belong to the whole of society,'[10] as a result of nationalisation by the socialist state.

The theoretical identification of this type of nationalisation with socialisation has undoubtedly exerted an influence on the practice of socialism in the USSR and the peoples' democracies. In particular this influence can be discerned in the following essential components of the etatist model: (1) the very broad area of nationalisation of the means of production; (2) the extreme centralisation of the system of functioning of the state economy; and (3) the etatisation of non-state collective forms of economy, above all of the cooperatives. We shall discuss these briefly.

The tempo and extent of nationalisation were in fact analogous in the USSR and the peoples' democracies, despite all the differences in conditions. In both cases expropriation of private owners was carried out quickly – by historical standards – at most within a few years of gaining power. In both cases, too, nationalisation was not confined to the basic means of production, but was extremely extensive, bringing the (legal) private sector right to the margin; the exceptions were East Germany in respect of non-agricultural sectors and Poland in respect of agriculture. As a result the state became virtually a monopolist in production and trade and in employment.

The system of functioning (planning and management) of the economy, formed in the USSR at the beginning of the 1930s and subsequently transferred in basically unchanged form to the peoples' democracies, has been so widely and comprehensively presented in the literature of economics that any more detailed description of it is superfluous here. Using our own terminology,[11] we can say that an adequate generalisation of this system of functioning is provided by the 'centralistic model', characterised by concentration of all basic economic decisions (apart from individual choices in the sphere of employment and consumption) at central level, a hierarchical structure of plans, transmission of decisions from above to below in the form of commands, and a passive role of money. From the point of view of the object of our analysis it is essential to emphasise that extreme centralisation of planning and management was bound to mean the removal of the basis for any real forms of self-management or participation by workers in the management of enterprises, and thus for direct economic democracy. Clearly, then, the lack of any field of decision at enterprise level deprives such forms of their content. This aspect of the system of functioning has great importance in so far as the socialist revolution was always connected in the minds of its adherents with a radical change in the relations between people directly at their place of work, in the organisation of the production process, in the methods of taking decisions about the use of factors of production and about the use of the products. The elimination of hired labour – labour for someone – was to mean the elimination of the division into managers and managed in the daily operation of the economy, the elimination of the situation in which decisions in the factory are taken by a narrow group of managers and the function of the mass of workers is purely to carry out these decisions.

In contrast to the two previous points, *the etatisation of cooperatives* requires somewhat broader discussion. It is well known that official doctrine in the USSR and the peoples' democracies distinguishes two forms of socialist ownership: the higher – state or 'all-national' – and the lower – group ownership, of which the most important form is cooperative (apart from cooperatives, other organisations can also be group owners of means of production in a certain sphere, but we shall not concern ourselves with this in view of its minor importance). Formally, the cooperative is a voluntary, self-managing association, and cooperative unions analogous associations of associations. Precisely in these features Lenin[12] saw the chance of using cooperatives as a bridge between the individual economy and the nationally organised economy; at the same time, however, he stressed that cooperatives could only fulfil this mission in conditions where the state form of socialist ownership and planning predominates. The question of the relationship between this second part of Lenin's view of cooperatives and later practice can be the subject of different interpretations, but there can be no doubt that in practice the real economic differences between state and cooperative forms of ownership were quickly reduced to a minimum. Even if certain differences were preserved these were too small to be taken into account on the level of generalisation on which we are operating in our characterisation of the etatist model.

Cooperatives other than in agriculture (trade, small-scale industry and services, housing cooperatives) retain the character of ownership by an association of members to a certain extent as long as they are small, economically marginal units. Growth in their number or field of operation is accompanied by obligatory inclusion in the system of centralised organisations, functioning – apart from minor concessions to tradition and the cooperative form – in a way analogous to the corresponding state systems, both in respect of subordination to the plan and of discretion over personnel policy, distribution of incomes, etc., etc. It is no accident that in the Soviet Union whole sectors of the economy in towns passed at one stroke of a pen from the sphere of 'cooperative ownership' to the hands of the state (trade, housing), unnoticed even by the vast majority of the members of the cooperatives. Polish experience also illustrates that, in general, cooperativisation has proved to be a particular form of nationalisation, and the main occasion when it was not so was when it served as a screen for the illegal activity of private capital. . . .

The most significant problem, however, is the agricultural production cooperative, which (1) concerns one of the fundamental sectors of the economy, and (2) concerns the peasantry, that is to say a whole social class of enormous importance in the USSR and the peoples' democracies. The Soviet kolkhozes, even from the formal legal aspect, have had significantly fewer elements of co-operative ownership of the means of production than it might have seemed from their presentation in the economic literature as the main representative of 'the lower form of socialist ownership': they have operated on nationalised land with machinery and equipment – apart from hand tools and live draught power – owned by state machinery stations which were not simple hirers of equipment but fulfilled statutorily the function of management organisations for agriculture. Control of production – the determination of its structure, the way it was used, etc. – was only formally in the hands of the kolkhozes; in fact it was in the hands of the state, through the strict directives of the plan, the system of payments in kind for the services of the MTS, compulsory deliveries and direct subordination on the party-administrative plane. In addition, neither the internal organisation nor, still less, the composition of the kolkhoz authorities could be freely decided by the members. Besides this, as was pointed out many times after Stalin's death, in particular in Khrushchev's speeches, the *de facto* deprivation of the kolkhozes of control over the means of production or their production itself was used as an instrument for the distribution of income in a way which was drastically unfavourable for the peasants (high norms for payments in kind to the MTS and for deliveries, low – at one period purely symbolic – prices). Thus the actual owner with economic disposition was surely the state, at least to the same extent as with state enterprises. The cooperative form was not without significance, but of a very peculiar nature; it proved a suitable camouflage for the real character of production relations. In no state enterprise (excepting of course the forced labour camps), even at the worst moments of the Stalin period, could the level of wages be reduced as low as it was in the kolkhozes, where in many regions for years at a time the sole source of maintenance for the family was the individual allotment; the same applies to social insurance and even to minimum civil rights such as the freedom to change one's place of employment and residence.

In the peoples' democracies the situation never became so drastic, and since for other reasons the creation of higher-level amalgamations (centres) for agricultural cooperatives was avoided, elements of real cooperative relations were able to appear at times more strongly than outside agriculture. In sum, however, the differences were only quantitative in character, and did not change the basic fact that it was essentially the state which had control over the means of production which had really passed into the hands of cooperatives (in some cases means of production formally transferred to cooperatives were in fact under the control of their former private owners).

The components of the etatist model which we have discussed – the very broad area of nationalisation, the extreme centralisation of the system of functioning, the etatisation of cooperatives – may partly derive from the objective conditions in which Russia and some of the peoples' democracies found themselves, at the starting point of their socialist development. I have in mind their relative economic backwardness, which meant that these countries entered socialism in, using Schumpeter's description again, 'a state of immaturity'. This immaturity was typified, among other things, by the lack of sufficiently broad and long-lasting experience of state intervention in the sphere of operation of private capital, and in steering the economy through instruments of indirect influence rather than exclusively by administrative means. In this situation attempts to bring the whole economy within effective control, and all the more so, attempts at active planning, were bound to produce relations between the state and private owners which tended to push towards accelerated nationalisation over the broadest possible area.

Neither side could succeed in coexisting with the other since both the state and the private owners saw only one form of effective control: transfer of ownership. Hence, in the activity of the state, the tendency to extend the area of nationalisation, as well as to 'etatise' the cooperatives, and, in the activity of private entre-preneurs, the principle of *carpe diem* – predatory exploitation in order to extract the maximum profit in the shortest possible time, before expropriation. It is interesting that both at the time of the October Revolution and in the first stage of the existence of the peoples' democracies party programme documents proclaimed nationalisation only of the basic means of production ('the key economic positions', 'the commanding heights', to use Lenin's description); yet in both cases this limit was quickly and radically exceeded. The extreme centralisation of the system of functioning of the nationalised economy is also at least partly connected with the backward economic structure and the absence of broad experience of the operation of state enterprises on principles of full commercial autonomy.

This objective factor should not, however, overshadow the role of ideological positions, which are closely involved in the etatist con-ception of socialisation. Czesław Bobrowski correctly described the clear tendency in the USSR in the 1920s to identify socialist plan-ning with maximum centralisation:[13]

> The problem of the limits of useful planning is regarded as
> non-existent. On the contrary, detail is regarded as a basic
> positive feature of the plan, hence the tendency for breaking the
> indicators down to the smallest possible time periods and to the
> lowest level (if possible right down to the place of work)
> and leaving nothing to the improvisation and initiative of the
> executants. . . . Only categorical directives, supported by checks
> and sanctions, are regarded as effective instruments. . . . The
> concept of effective planning is identified with the principle of
> commands and compulsion.

It appeared similarly with the area of nationalisation: each success-ive act was regarded as a step forward on the road to socialism, even if small shops and craftsmen's workshops were nationalised. The preponderance of ideological positions over objective factors is evi-dent, among other things, in the copying of the USSR's practice by the peoples' democracies, although the twenty-five year time lag and the different economic level had changed the conditions to an important degree. Obviously an essential element of the tendency to a very broad area of nationalisation, to extreme centralisation of the system of functioning and to the etatisation of cooperatives was political requirements, but we shall pass over this question in the meantime as going beyond the present stage of our discussion.

On the other hand, we must now – without drawing final conclusions, which involve the problems of the political system – examine *the direct consequences of the etatist model for the character of production relations.*

It may look at first like a truism, a tautology, but the most important consequence from this point of view is the fact that the function of owner of the means of production is fulfilled directly by the *state as such.* The impression of truism should, however, vanish if we remind ourselves that not every nationalisation has such consequences; for example nationalising an enterprise while preserving its commercial autonomy is not at all the same as replacing the former capitalist-worker relationship by a state-worker relationship, but can mean the rise of a more anonymous state enterprise-worker relationship.[14] One can have long disputes on the differences or analogies between the character of production relations in the (private) Citroën car factory and the (state) Renault factory, but it would be difficult to maintain that the French state behaves directly as the employer of the Renault workers. In conditions corresponding to the etatist model of socialism, on the other hand, precisely such a situation arises. The state, being the political organisation of society, appears at the same time directly in the role of an economic agent, and in fact an agent regulating not only relations within the enterprise, but also the whole of the external factors which determine the positions of enterprises and households. Formally the work contract is between the enterprise and the worker, but the conditions of this contract, in particular the level and principles of remuneration, are determined by the state as the *de facto* employer. It is in addition not one of many employers, but the dominant employer, and for many categories of employees the only one. Practically the whole of the economic surplus is concentrated in its hands ('the socialist surplus product') and thus it decides the future directions of development of production and employment, in other words the structure of the supply of jobs, and also the extent and directions of training of personnel, and the structure of demand for work. The state has disposition over the overwhelming mass of the goods and services produced, and at the same time is the body determining the conditions (in the first place – prices) on which these goods are made available to customers; it thus controls not only the level of nominal incomes, but their real value too, and it collects the basic part of the surplus through the difference between prices and costs, using direct taxes only as a supplementary instrument.

There is no need to continue this description – the universal economic power of the state in the etatist model is evident. What we described in chapter 1[15] as the problem of the relation between households and the national economy takes the concrete form, basically, of the relation between households and the state. Because the centralistic organisation of the economy necessarily requires its own vast bureaucratic apparatus, these problems move to a significant extent on to the plane of the relation between the population and *the state apparatus in the broad sense*.

In our analysis of the etatist model so far we have not been able to discover *in the economy itself* elements which would justify calling the ownership of the means of production social as distinct from public. On the contrary, virtually universal nationalisation, etatisation of cooperatives and centralisation of the system of functioning, taken together, create unfavourable premises for real disposition over the means of production by society, for the display of creative initiative and other phenomena, which may reflect the attitude of co-owners. Thus the whole weight of the problem of socialisation is shifted to the *political plane*. In singling out democratism in the disposition over the means of production as the paramount criterion of socialisation we have underlined the connection between economic and political democratism whenever public ownership is the predominant form, but at the same time we have drawn attention to the different character of this connection in various models of socialism. This connection is strongest in the etatist model, since here society is deprived of the prerequisites for disposition over the means of production directly in the economic sphere and retains only the possibility of control or influence by means of political instruments. *The test of socialisation for the etatist model, then, turns on whether the political system ensures subordination of the state to the will of society – both as regards setting out the directions of policy and as regards control over their implementation.*

This presentation of the problem is, as we have already indicated, in general conformity with the official doctrine, which justifies identification of nationalisation with socialisation primarily by the democratic character of the socialist state, true democracy as distinct from the formal pseudo-democracy of the capitalist state. According to Marxist theory, every state is an instrument of class rule, and thus in this sense a dictatorship of a particular social class or classes. The overthrow of the political and economic rule of the bourgeoisie by the socialist revolution opens the way to the liquidation of the class structure of society and thus to the abolition of class rule and the withering away of the state. Because this cannot be achieved by means of a single act, the state is preserved after the revolutionary change as the instrument of the new ruling class, the proletariat, united with the working peasantry and other working strata. Having thus become the instrument for the rule of the great majority of society, the dictatorship of the proletariat, the socialist state, has the task of finally breaking the resistance of the former exploiting classes and defending itself against the external class enemy (in conditions of so-called capitalist encirclement), and also of ensuring the observance of certain essential norms in socio-economic relations, particularly in connection with implementation of the principle of distribution according to work. The *differentia specifica* of the dictatorship of the proletariat – according to Lenin – is that it prepares the premises for the abolition of all dictatorship, all *political* rule, since the socialist state, while being the apparatus for the suppression of 'the minority, that is, the exploiters', at the same time introduces the broadest democratism for the working people, and thus the suppression 'is compatible with the diffusion of democracy among such an overwhelming majority of the population that the need for a *special machine* of suppression will begin to disappear'.[16]

Whence this conviction, this unwavering certainty rather, that the state which arises from the revolution guarantees this postulated, virtually absolute, democratism in political relations? What conditions have to be fulfilled for democracy which is 'false, for the rich' to be transformed into true democracy, assuring the people real power and abolishing the division into managing and managed in society at work? The justification, explicitly or implicitly, is based on three elements: (1) genetic (2) socio-economic and (3) political systemic. Let us discuss them in turn – though in point (3) we shall have to take account to a considerably greater extent than hitherto of the actual political evolution of the USSR; our concern, however, remains generalisation rather than the history of the political system.

1 *The genetic factor* The establishment of the dictatorship of the proletariat in the USSR was the work of a revolutionary movement whose social support came from oppressed strata, primarily the industrial workers and the agricultural proletariat or semi-proletariat. At the head of the victorious movement stands the party, which bases its claim to legitimacy on years of self-sacrificing campaign for the interests of the working masses, proclaims the ideology of the proletarian revolution, and forms part of the international workers' revolutionary movement. Such a party's accession to power is supposed in itself to be the fundamental guarantee of the democratism of the new state.

Legitimation by revolutionary origin also fulfils an analogous function in supporting the claim to democratism of the socialist states which came into being after the Second World War, and not only in the countries where the communist parties played an independent or semi-independent role in gaining power (China, Yugoslavia), but also in those where external force – of the Soviet Union – was decisive, and was supported in very varying degrees by internal force (the most in Czechoslovakia). The genetic factor, therefore, does not necessarily apply to the way in which the political revolution was carried out (although the official historiography of each country is at pains to create the impression that the revolution enjoyed the support of the majority of society), but primarily to the revolutionary past of the communist party and of the people placed by it in the leading state positions.

2 *The socio-economic factor* This part of the justification of the socialist state's claim to democratism is connected with the interdependence between social and political democratism touched on in the introduction to this chapter. Apart from considerations of a general nature – like the elimination of incomes from capital and the radical reduction of property and income differentials, the opening up of possibilities for social and professional advancement through economic expansion, in particular industrialisation, the adaptation of the education system to provide equality of oppor-

D

tunity, etc. – the foremost proof of democratism is usually given by pointing out the revolution in the personal composition of the organs of power. This process took place in different forms and at different *tempi* – most precipitately where power was gained in a revolutionary outbreak – but it took place everywhere: people from the former possessing classes or associated with them were replaced in state positions at all levels by revolutionary activists, workers and peasants. This also applies to economic positions, which in any case in the etatist model have a clear political significance; the mass promotion of workers to managerial positions – initially alongside the old personnel to exercise political control over them, later, with the development of a training system – becomes the normal means of forming the 'officer corps' of the socialist economy.

There can be no doubt that both what we have called the genetic factor and the socio-economic factor have an essential significance and must be taken into account in evaluating the political democratism of the socialist countries. However, first, the weight of these factors diminishes with the passage of time, and, second, they never, even in the immediate post-revolution period, solve the problem. The transformation of the revolutionaries and proletarians of yesterday into members of the party leadership, ministers and directors, is no guarantee against the transformation of the new state into a power standing above society and employing an alienated bureaucratic apparatus. The division into managing and managed is not only, and not so much, connected with opposition between persons as with opposition between social roles and with constitutional conditions which perpetuate and deepen this opposition by making the 'top' independent of the 'bottom'. One could say, then, that the political significance of the genetic and the socio-economic factors can only become fundamental and long-lasting when the problem of the political system is appropriately solved. Lenin, who categorically defended the principle of one-man management in matters of economic organisation, regarded self-management in factories with reluctance, saw the main element of the new social relations in the appointment of workers to leading positions in industry and, where the political system was concerned, considered that the crucial question was the creation of forms of state which would permit real involvement of the masses in management and thus make the alienation of the apparatus of power from society impossible ('so that everybody became a "bureaucrat" for a certain time, and as a result nobody could remain a "bureaucrat" ').

3 *The political-systemic factor* In this, the decisive point, the official doctrine bases its claim to democratism of political relations (1) on the break-up of the old apparatus of state power, and (2) on the use of constitutional forms which ensure the subordination of the state to society in all essential aspects: election of authorities at each level, the setting out of policy, control. Obviously there are no perfect solutions and at the conclusion of a certain stage some shortcomings or other in democracy come to light – yet the doctrine maintains unwaveringly that, in general, the worker-peasant, popular, national character of power is never violated; on the contrary, it is continually strengthened, which is synonymous with strengthening the social character of ownership of the means of production.

The self-satisfaction of the authorities and the substitution of apology for analysis reach a peak precisely at this point, and therefore it requires the most meticulous possible analysis.

The form of state on which the October Revolution pinned its hopes of implementing socialist democracy was to be based on *soviets*. In contrast to the classical form of parliamentary democracy, the distinctive features of the 'soviets of workers', peasants' and soldiers' delegates' were:

(a) combination of the legislative and executive functions of power, which was regarded as essential to ensure democracy not only occasionally, at the time of an election, but from day to day;

(b) direct election of the members of the lowest level of soviets at the place of work (factory, village, etc.) and of higher soviets indirectly by the lower level soviets, which was regarded as essential in view of the involvement of the state authorities with production, with the problems of the basic cells of the social organism.

The overt emphasis on the class character of the soviets was expressed, among other things, in the deprivation of persons originating from the former privileged classes of political rights (the so-called *lishentsy*) and in the differentiation of the proportions of representatives in elections to the soviets, with the aim of ensuring a majority of representatives for the proletariat, *vis-à-vis* the much more numerous peasantry.

Neither the theme of this work nor the competence and interests of the author permit dwelling on the question of how realistic and satisfactory this conception of the soviet form of state was, either in general or for Russian conditions at the time. It is, however, worth recalling how much attention and effort Lenin and his colleagues devoted to working out the structure of this 'semi-state', which the socialist republic was to become. Symptomatic of this, among other things, is the precise codification of the limitations and inequalities in the enjoyment of political rights, which is treated with the greatest seriousness as a means of preventing the influence of the former possessing classes and of 'the petit-bourgeois element' on the fate of the state, which, after all, was completely ruled by the holders of active and passive elective rights to the soviets, in particular the workers, who enjoyed the highest norms of representation. . . .

Yet in the actual process of evolution of the political system this long and hotly debated soviet form of state played a minimal role. The question of socialist democratism proved to be completely independent of whether, and in what way, the system of soviets differed from a system based on the Montesquieu division of authority and of how effectively it ensured the numerical preponderance of workers in the soviets. In practice the decisive factor, as Rosa Luxemburg wrote,[17] was the political, organisational, ideological and information monopoly of a single party, which in addition, itself very quickly lost all real internal democracy and was transformed into the instrument of power of 'a handful of politicians', reinforced by a powerful and continually strengthening apparatus.

Defending the soviets against charges of lack of democracy Lenin,[18] in his polemic with Kautsky in 1918, still used the customary set of arguments about the growth of the influence of the bolsheviks in the soviets in comparison with the influence of other groups, and cited data on the electoral successes of communist candidates. But arguments of this type very quickly lost all sense: no other group apart from the communist party any longer had the legal possibility of competing for influence in the soviets in an organised way, of presenting its political platform, of critical evaluation of government policy, of giving independent information to the public, etc. Thus the problem of gaining influence in the soviets simply ceased to exist, and what in practice began to become more and more essential was the requirement to use the soviets as an instrument for mobilising the population to implement policy already set out, and their executive organs as a normal administrative apparatus. This, in turn, was bound to lead to guaranteeing to the higher links of the system effective influence over the personal composition of the lower links of the soviets themselves and particularly of their executive organs, and to the absolute predominance of the latter (and their clerical apparatus) over the elective bodies, which were finally transformed into a purely decorative element.

This process took place at different *tempi* in different periods and in different areas; it appears, for example, that in view of the nature of a number of local problems in the countryside, particularly in the period preceding mass collectivisation, the rural soviets at the lowest level succeeded for longest in preserving certain elements of independence in their activity and influence on policy, at least from the aspect of means of implementing it. It was similar later, for example in Poland, where relatively the greatest area of autonomy was found in elections to the lowest level local councils. But these are matters of no great significance for an evaluation of the general direction of development. The system as a whole gradually became the opposite of the hopes and prognostications – both as concerns the 'vector of dependency' (dependence of the bottom on the top instead of dependence of the top on the bottom) and the relation between the legislature and the executive, and also the slogan 'all power to the soviets'. Politically emasculated, not elected but selected from above, subordinated to the executive link at higher levels – the soviets not only did not hold 'all state power' in their hands, but became deprived of any power, remaining in this respect far behind a bourgeois-democratic parliament and, in the case of local soviets, behind some other forms of local self-government. Taking into account as well the need, inseparably linked with the development of the 'economic organisational' function of the socialist state, to construct an apparatus for planning and management, the soviet system could in no way fulfil the role of a factor counteracting the separation of the state 'special machine' from society. This was a result of the fundamental features of the way the soviets functioned in practice, which totally removed them from real choice between political, economic and social alternatives and also precluded the soviets from control over the executive authorities. This made it impossible for the soviets to place any limits on the executive authorities. The authorities did not feel themselves obliged to make any real effort to seek public approval for their actions or for particular representatives.

Lenin fairly soon perceived this gap between the practice and the theoretical assumptions. In the last period of his life he feverishly sought a remedy for the increasing 'bureaucratic distortion' of the worker-peasant state. His articles, notes and letters from this period testify forcibly to his sense of the threat to the future of the system which its evolution at that time already presented. Where therapy is concerned, on the other hand, it did not go beyond the plane of changes or improvements in the *forms* of activity (particularly in the field of social control over the functioning of the apparatus), not touching the crux of the problems of the political system at all. This was presumably connected with the conviction that bureaucratism is to a considerable extent a product of economic backwardness and its social consequences, the numerical weakness of the working class and the low cultural level of the masses. This may explain, on the one hand, his sharply growing anxiety in the years 1922–3 (the entry of capitalism into a period of 'relative stability' and thus the shattering of the hopes that the soviet system would be put into effect in the developed countries, particularly Germany) and, on the other, the rather modest set of remedial measures which were supposed to suffice for the time being, since, in the longer run, rapid industrial development would simply remove the grounds of 'bureaucratic excrescences'.

It is fitting to note that Lenin clearly perceived the phenomenon of alienation of the state apparatus from society in conditions which, from today's viewpoint, would certainly be acknowledged as liberal. This also applies to the trade unions and, above all, to the Communist Party.

An important role in the implementation of socialist democratism was to fall to the *trade unions,* and not only on the social and economic plane, but also directly on the political plane. The political function was primarily to comprise effective struggle against the bureaucratisation of the state apparatus, in the interests of the workers. The 1919 Programme of the RKP(b) which we have already quoted defined the role of the trade unions in the following words:[19]

> The organisation-apparatus of socialised industry should be
> based primarily on the trade unions. . . . In accordance with
> the statutes of the Soviet Republic and with established
> practice, the trade unions, extending to all local and central

organs of industrial management, should take into their hands the entire management of the national economy as a single economic whole. Ensuring thus an indissoluble link between the central state administration, the national economy, and the broad working masses, the trade unions should involve the masses in direct participation in the running of the economy over the widest possible field. Participation of the trade unions in the direction of the economy and the inclusion of the broad masses is at the same time the principal means to combat bureaucratisation of the economic apparatus of Soviet power and creates the possibility of making production subject to real popular control.

The powers accorded them would formally mean a high position for the trade unions, which were generally represented in state and party authorities at all levels and were consulted by the planning organs, fulfilled control functions (in the 1930s in the USSR they were even acknowledged formally as an organ of state control in enterprises), played the role of ministry of labour at certain periods, managed social insurance funds, and so on. At the same time, with the transfer of state enterprises to economic accountability (in the USSR the transition to the so-called new economic policy – NEP) the obligation of the trade unions to defend the interests of the workers was strongly underlined.[20]

Yet almost from the first years of the revolution a hiatus appeared between their formal powers and reality, and this deepened in the course of time until the unions had completely lost their role as one of the important elements of socialist democratism. At the root of this process, it seems to me, lay that consistent characteristic of the etatist model, the fetishisation of the state as the emanation of the will and interests of the working masses. For this reason too, even in early programme documents (e.g. the work by Lenin quoted above) the position of the trade unions *vis-à-vis* the state is defined quite differently from that *vis-à-vis* economically accountable enterprises, with great emphasis on the slogan 'strengthening proletarian class state power'. Later, official doctrine emphasised the necessity of combining defence of the workers' interests with the interests of production and in the course of further development the former aspect yielded more and more clearly in favour of the latter, until the final triumph of the formula of defence of the workers' interest *through* attention to the interests of production, or the interests of the state as employer and manager of the economy. At any rate, up till the end of the Stalin period public discussions on this subject never raised the question of whether the nature of the conflict between the national economy and household economies, or between the state and the population, did not require the trade unions to concentrate on defending the workers' direct interests, whether such apparent one-sidedness is not an essential safeguard against one-sidedness on the other side, and in general whether the trade unions can play any role in the process of democratisation of the political system without being independent institutions, that is, without pluralist elements in the institutional structure of socialism.

It may then be said that right from the beginning the conception of the etatist model does not also permit use of trade unions to ensure that the working masses enjoy real control over the national-ised means of production. In this field, as in others, deterioration set in, especially from the end of the 1920s in the USSR. Before this, despite limitations of principle, Soviet trade unions succeeded in preserving at least a certain degree of relative independence, expressed among other things in their refusal to accept increases in pay differentials (the gap between the lowest and the highest rates at the time was in the ratio of 1:3). The slogan 'down with *uravnilovka*' (equalisation) during the first five-year plan years[21] and the forceful tightening of the accumulation screw were accompanied by the elimination of the remains of union indepen-dence. From that moment, again with the exception of the initial phase of development in the peoples' democracies, the trade unions became a servile instrument of the state, in particular of the party organs ('transmission from the party to the masses'), which not only set out the general line of union policy but decided every important move, and, which was most essential in practice, decided the appointment of all personnel, both to constitutionally elected bodies and to the staff apparatus. While called upon to combat bureaucrat-isation, in these conditions the trade unions themselves became bureaucratised in a dual sense: internally, as a result of the domi-nation of the hierarchically constructed apparatus over the rank-and-file workers' organisations, and externally as a result of the subordination of the appointed union functionaries to the party apparatus.

To understand the mechanics of the process it is important to grasp the interconnection between relative independence of the trade unions and pluralism, or rather traces of it, in the field of party policy. During Lenin's lifetime such independence went hand-in-hand with relatively liberal relations, as mentioned above, within the communist party, which, even after the famous resolution of the X Congress (1921) forbidding factions, permitted much diversity of view on a number of questions of principle and still used political methods to solve disputes. The elimination of the so-called rightist deviation, the last real ideological-political current which can be distinguished in the bosom of the CPSU, put a stop to this. Similarly in Poland (and, I think, in the other peoples' democracies) the trade unions retained a certain autonomy up to the time of the creation of a single party, modelled completely on the Soviet party of the Stalin period. The same applies to other social organisations, among others those in the villages, which finally were able to remain alive only at the price of losing their character as autonomous associations of civic initiative and becoming narrowly localised fragments of a bureaucratised state structure.

Thus we come to the crucial problem of the political system in the etatist model of socialism – the role of the *communist party*.

The official doctrine does not openly declare the one-party principle; on the contrary, it sedulously presents the peoples' democracies as living proof of the possibility of 'multi-party character'. Yet the accepted formula, 'the leading role of the party', boils down in practice to what is the essence of the one-party system – the political monopoly of the communist party, which puts this monopoly into effect in various forms, among others with the help of other parties which are subordinated to itself but use traditional names.[22] Under conditions of political monopoly of one party, the term 'party' itself becomes inadequate, unless we apply the description 'party of a new type' not to the structure and activity of the communist party, but precisely to its *de facto* position as a mono-party. The 'party of a new type' in this latter meaning is not a horizontally separated group among other equal groups but a vertically separated élite – the vanguard of the working class, according to the official terminology.

The problem of the vanguard nature of the communist party occupies a great deal of space in Marxist literature. The conception of the vanguard appears, among other places, in attempts at sociological justification of the evolution of the political system of the

USSR: the Russian industrial proletariat, numerically small in any case, was so weakened and dispersed as a result of the First World War and the Civil War that the bolsheviks, the argument goes, were compelled to substitute for class power the power of the vanguard of the working class, the dictatorship of the party.[23] We are interested in the problem of the vanguard here only in so far as it is connected with formal or informal party monopoly. From this point of view the vanguard nature of the party means that the ultimate, and in certain respects decisive, test of the democratism of the political system is relations within the party.

We mentioned above the relative political freedom within the communist party during Lenin's lifetime. The peculiar coexistence of this situation with a monopoly position 'externally' did not, however, last long and the first instrument which served towards its liquidation was the extreme way in which the resolution of the X Congress forbidding factions was interpreted: in a relatively short time all forms of organisation, even temporary, for the purpose of working out a platform different from the official one, became classed as violation of the principles of the 'party of a new type'. It was not long before the effects were felt: just as the ban on organisation round a non-bolshevik position paralysed the soviets as institutions of worker-peasant democracy, so too the ban on all forms of organisation round a minority position within the party soon led to the political decay of the party itself. The ban meant the monopolisation of organising power in the hands of those who controlled the official party apparatus. The most important source of their power was their total control of personnel policy – both where it concerned the selection of party and state functionaries and the composition of formally elected party bodies at all levels. The maintenance of the principle of election of party committees and their responsibility to congresses and conferences of party members was gradually transformed into an empty formality because of the decisive influence the apparatus at a higher level exerted on the personal composition of the electing bodies. 'Democratic centralism' was shorn of its adjective in practice, and the constitutional direction of dependence was reversed: the congress no longer elected the Central Committee; but the leadership of the CC, with the help of its apparatus, chose the congress, conferences and lower-level party bodies. This created, among other things, the possibility of complete control of the means of information in the broad sense, both through the formal censorship and also – which is most important – by deciding appointments to positions in the press, radio, publishing houses, propaganda organs of the party and social organisations, etc. The great discussions inside the party with Trotsky had already shown that a minority had no chance to present its views on a more or less equal basis. Later, even this type of discussion, in which the sides were unequal, was totally eliminated, and the apparatus felt itself sufficiently strong to simply remove dissidents from the ranks of the party, liquidating all centres of independent political thought in turn, without regard for the relationship between the conceptions they crushed and real needs. The fact that the party subsequently adopted certain conceptions previously branded as oppositionist (this applied particularly to elements in the Trotskyist position on the question of industrialisation and the sources of accumulation) and that this had no positive consequences for the former oppositionists, showed adequately that the most essential thing was not merit, but the iron principle that the political line is laid down exclusively from above. This principle has been scrupulously preserved to this day.

The crushing of the so-called rightist deviation (headed by Bukharin) at the end of the 1920s and beginning of the 1930s, which coincided with the beginning of the first five-year plan, the formulation of the central system of functioning of the economy and the 'great turn' in the village, concluded an important stage in the evolution of the party. By that time, the argument on whether the working class or the communist party wielded the dictatorship had become pointless, not only from one side, but also from the other. The party – if we understand it as a union of party members – had ceased to be the leading political force, the subject of power. This obviously does not mean that it had lost its importance in the state system of the etatist model of socialism. On the contrary, it is, and remains, the most important component of this system, holding the entire edifice together; yet not as the origin of policy, but rather as the instrument with the help of which a narrow ruling group exercises control over all areas of life and at the same time preserves its own ideological legitimacy – something impossible to achieve by relying exclusively, for example, on the administrative and police apparatus. Such a transformation in the role of the party was bound to increase the weight of the criterion of discipline enormously, with regulation of the composition of the party from above and the transition from a cadre party to a mass party. The party as an organising instrument must have at its disposal a most extensive network of representatives who need not necessarily be ideologically committed, and certainly must not acknowledge the principle of precedence of ideology and independent opinion but must be unconditionally at the disposition of the leadership.

It is precisely this conception of the role of the party as an organising instrument rather than a political actor *sensu stricto,* which is expressed in the relationship of the party apparatus to the state and economic administration.[24] The party apparatus is basically a component of the state and economic apparatus, but it is, at each level, the superior component. The area and degree of intervention by the party apparatus in the decisions of the state and economic administration can be subject to change, but always embrace matters of principle, in particular – which we repeat yet again, in order to emphasise the importance of this factor – matters of personnel, reserved officially (the *nomenklatura*) for decision by the party apparatus. There are differences also in the degree to which symbiosis of the party and state apparatus may be observed; in the Stalin period there was no concern for appearances (the practice of joint resolutions of party committees and the corresponding state authorities, in addition to which, at least in the case of the Central Committee, it was virtually always 'represented' by the apparatus), while later – apart from exceptional cases – an effort was made to mask this phenomenon, which of course is of no substantial importance. It became the rule also for the party and state apparatus to be personally linked, both in the form of overlapping positions *ex officio* and in the transfer of functionaries from one apparatus to the other.

The symbiosis of the party, and the state or economic apparatus, brings into question the basis of the view that the role of the party apparatus consists, among other things, in representing the general, overall point of view as distinct from the local or sectoral patriotism of the other links in the administration. It may be that this difference was noticeable in the initial phase, after which the trend was clearly – and for perfectly understandable reasons – towards similarity of attitudes.

In brief, the etatist model of socialism *etatises the party, too.* The most direct manifestation of this is the mutual penetration of the party apparatus and the state apparatus of repression in the narrow

sense, i.e. the political police. This phenomenon intensifies exceptionally rapidly as an ineluctable result of the evolution of the
system. Beginning with the elimination of freedom of opinion
(which gives rise to the need to employ confidential sources of
information, among other things in personnel policy), through the
transition from political to police methods of combating all manifestations of an independent position, and then even of political
thought itself, to the use of mass terror in carrying out actions such
as collectivisation and 'the liquidation of the kulaks as a class' – all
this was conducive to the close cooperation of the state administration, the party apparatus and the political police, the latter
expanding to an absolutely unprecedented scale, never actually dis-
closed. In this connection one often finds discussions of the question: what is the direction of dependence between the party
apparatus and the security apparatus, or who is subordinate to
whom? This seems to me the wrong way to pose the question, since
both apparatuses are interlinked instruments in a system and are
subordinated – especially at the top of the hierarchies – to one and
the same monopolistic power centre. This situation of course does
not exclude the conflicts which always appear between different
links in an apparatus; hidden from public opinion, these conflicts
often turn into bitter struggles between cliques. The impression that
the security organs are superior to the party apparatus could have
arisen from certain experiences in the peoples' democracies, but this
was mainly due to the fact of the political control centre governing
both apparatuses being located in the Kremlin.

We should like at this point to digress for a moment from the
chronological and subject limits we have set ourselves. If by the
beginning of the 1930s the process of making the party into a uniform body and transforming it from the subject into the instrument
of political dictatorship was complete, what then – from the point of
view of the dictatorship – was the rational basis of the Great Purge?
This gigantic operation in the 'war against the people' – as
Evtushenko once wrote – affected, after all, not only the survivors
of former opposition groups, but also, and perhaps even primarily,
the mass of loyal comrades, defenders and supporters of Stalin,
people who were ready to serve the system zealously, but whom the
authorities chose on their own initiative to sacrifice. This problem
has fascinated many students of recent political history, but has not
yet received a satisfactory interpretation. An interesting aspect of

this problem is brought out, in an indirect and unintended way, by the official Soviet interpretation of the Chinese 'cultural revolution'. Mao Tse-Tung is accused above all of breaking up the Chinese Communist Party and striving to create a new one, built from above. It seems to me that, *mutatis mutandis,* this was also the point of the Great Purge, as one of the final acts which brought the etatist form of socialism to its extreme Stalinist form of the 'cult of personality'. At the beginning of the 1930s the party was purged of oppositionists, but it still numbered in its midst, and also at the highest levels of the party apparatus, in the closest circle of power, people who owed their position to their own revolutionary activity, had independent connections with the international communist movement, had a fully formed ideological basis, etc. They were supporters of Stalin, and with him had ruthlessly smashed the opposition – but they were not created by Stalin. One crack remained, therefore, in the structure of complete dependence, which was a potential danger not only in the personal sense but also as a factor limiting the freedom to make drastic changes in policy and ideology; and without this freedom the system of Stalinist dictatorship would have remained incomplete. Khrushchev's speeches at the XX and XXII Congresses show that this is how the link between the course of the XVII Congress (1934) and the genesis of the plan for the Great Purge, using the murder of Kirov as provocation, should be interpreted. The Great Purge, which in a short time liquidated a series of successive strata of the apparatus, brought analogous results to the Chinese 'cultural revolution': it broke up the existing personal structure of the party and state apparatus, including the security apparatus, and replaced it with new people who owed everything to the dictator and the methods of operation used by him. One also needs to take into account that, in view of their scale and the atmosphere at the time, these changes, which were directly political in character, produced an enormous 'multiplier effect', opening up possibilities of rapid advancement to millions of people, a whole generation. Of course, the machine, once set in motion, ran out of control, but even the effects of this, although originally unintended, nevertheless generally conformed with the interests of the system; they spread fear and demoralisation, broke characters and heightened the feeling of external threat. For this reason, just as in the case of the 'dizzy with success' of collectivisation, intervention from above against excesses came sufficiently late not to prevent a *fait accompli*; the same thing was repeated on a different scale later, in the years following the Second World War, both in the USSR and in the peoples' democracies.

As stated at the outset, the purpose of our characterisation of the etatist model was limited, and we were not aiming to produce an exhaustive picture of that type of socialism which has developed in the USSR and the peoples' democracies. The construction of the model, bringing out – or at least that has been the author's intention – those features which are essential from the point of view of the criteria of socialisation of the means of production, was designed to answer the question: does the etatist model meet these criteria? Assuming that the criteria adopted are appropriate and that this generalised comparison with reality is correct, the answer is unequivocally in the negative: *the etatist model of socialism does not meet the criteria of socialisation of the means of production.*

On the one hand, the means of production, with minor exceptions, are centralised directly in the hands of the state, which occupies a monopolist or virtually monopolist position in all areas of economic life and ruthlessly dominates the individual members of society both in their role as workers and as consumers. On the other hand, this 'special machine for the exercise of state power', probably the most powerful history has seen, has been taken completely outside the political control of society as a result of the extermination of even the slightest trace of political pluralism; in the system of appointments to political positions, in the possibilities of organisation, in the expression of opinion, bureaucratism has attained such a degree and extent as to justify (even abstracting from the extreme forms of the second phase of the Stalin period) using the description *totalitarian dictatorship*.[25] The centralistic economic monopoly and total political dictatorship, which are mutually interconnected and supported by a powerful apparatus of physical coercion, clearly cannot create the premises for that 'union of free men working with common means of production and consciously expending their personal individual labour power as a single social labour power' of which Marx dreamt. If, in addition, we look at the way the etatist model has developed over time, it can be seen that the retrograde evolution of the political system has clearly weakened the democratising influence of the 'initial thrust' made at the time of the overthrow of the power of the bourgeoisie.

The factor which we have called genetic became weaker not only as a result of the simple passage of time but also, and in a certain period primarily, as a result of the elimination from political life or of outright physical extermination of many active politicians and whole sections of the revolutionary movement; it is no accident that the period of the Great Purge in the USSR coincided with a drastic ideological turnabout, which in large measure meant the replacement of revolutionary legitimacy by state-nationalist legitimacy.

The socio-economic factor in democratism became weaker also because of the tendency towards consolidation of the divisions which, again apart from, if we may call them so, natural reasons (the effects of differentiation of incomes always influence the starting conditions of the next generation) resulted to a certain extent from the phenomenon which may be called *socio-political stratification*. This is a question of the consequences of differentiation of material situation depending on level in the political hierarchy, consequences which rapidly began to show themselves after the ending of the 'heroic period' when the earnings of members of the communist party could not exceed a defined level (the 'party maximum'). The campaign against *'uravnilovka'* brought a rise in remuneration at managerial levels which, combined with their easier access to these positions, created in practice a situation of material privilege for party members, and in particular for party functionaries. Position in the party hierarchy gradually began to become the determinant of position on the incomes ladder – formal and informal (special shops, health centres, rest homes, housing privileges, etc.); the latter – which were particularly demoralising because they were surrounded by the shamefaced mystery of the 'yellow curtains', guarded buildings and whole areas behind walls – were graduated like a truly feudal hierarchy, on a scale which was sharply progressive at the highest levels. Against the background of the generally very low standard of living of the population, the privileges, although in absolute terms not comparable with the incomes of the great capitalists or the managerial élite, had an essential material importance, and a still greater negative psychological effect. This had undoubted ideological costs, but also, from the specific point of view of political totalitarianism, irreplaceable advantages, since it corrupted the apparatus by linking the most diverse elements in the material well-being of the functionary with the position he occupied, the confidence shown in him and the 'rights' ascribed thereto.

Comments on the negative feedback effect of the evolution of the political system on the socio-economic factor obviously cannot constitute an evaluation of the changes in the structure of income distribution nor, still less, a characterisation of the processes of stratification, especially from the point of view of class criteria. Such a characterisation, which is linked with the question of the subject of public ownership (who owns the means of production, in the economic sense, if society is not the owner?), is among the most difficult problems in the analysis of the etatist model of socialism in terms of Marxist categories; to attempt it would be beyond the limits of our discussion.

Neither shall we take up a position on the frequently and passionately discussed question of whether the political system of the USSR (and subsequently of the peoples' democracies) was objectively determined by the set of special external circumstances – transition to socialism 'in a state of immaturity' – which, first, did not guarantee the effectiveness of the adoption of democratic forms of transformation of property relations and, second, required industrialisation of the country in a short period of time. There can be no doubt that the situation in which nationalisation is carried out by force and the state takes on the function of 'primitive accumulation' creates fertile soil for the alienation of the state apparatus from a society which is reluctant to accept the great, at times even drastic, material and social burdens imposed on it; feedback arises which is unfavourable for democratism. Does this mean that a backward country to which socialism is introduced without a democratic mechanism and which is subsequently subjected to the tremendous strains of rapid accumulation, was and will inevitably be condemned to totalitarian dictatorship?

The answer seems to me by no means obvious and requires the most meticulous theoretical and historical study. The solution of this great and tragic dilemma is not, however, essential for our problem, if we are to keep it within well-defined limits. We are not, after all, concerned with answering the question 'why', but simply the question 'does' the etatist model of socialism meet the criteria of socialisation of the means of production, and if not, what consequences does this have for the system and its future. The answer to this question is of considerable importance independently of whether the relations that were created were inevitable or whether they could have developed differently.

The statement that the etatist model of socialism does not fulfil the criteria of socialisation of the means of production needs, however, to be expanded slightly in respect of the *peoples' democracies, where certain specific features appear.* From the point of view of our problem the most important specific feature is the fact that despite the dissimilarity of the historical situation and the individual differences between the countries, their political system in a very short time became completely similar in all its essentials to the system in the USSR, and indeed to the worst form of that system. The initial period, in which there might still have seemed to be possibilities of different, more democratic solutions, came to an end in 1948-9. Thereafter there remained only purely formal elements, albeit raised in the official theory of the state to the rank of important specific features, like for example the pseudo multi-party structure already mentioned. The Soviet solutions were transplanted, obviously, in their final version – based on the 1936 Constitution – and thus with no return to the system of soviets of Lenin's time, which also facilitated their adaptation since it permitted them to be formally linked with the traditional institutions (parliament, direct elections, universal franchise, etc.). It is highly characteristic that the state system of all these countries was made *de facto* uniform without regard to the sometimes enormous differences in the influence of their communist parties; for example, in Czechoslovakia the system introduced was analogous to that in Poland, although the Communist Party of Czechoslovakia won nearly 40 per cent of the total vote in the genuinely free elections of 1946 whereas in Poland the communist party was not even in a position to risk presenting itself to the voters separately and under its own name.

The adoption of this identical system in dissimilar conditions had further adverse effects in the peoples' democracies and in particular had negative repercussions on the subjective attitudes of the population towards the changes in the system:

(a) Because, in comparison with Russia in 1917, of the generally higher level of economic development and social diversity of the peoples' democracies, the rate of industrial progress was relatively lower and its positive results were more weakly felt by the population and were politically less effective.

(b) The majority of the countries called peoples' democracies did not indeed have longer years of experience of parliamentary democracy behind them, yet none the less the degree of development of democratic institutions – freedom of the press, freedom of coalition, independence of the judiciary, etc. – and also simply the general level of civilisation in relations between people, was incomparably higher than it had been in Russia; the cultural links with the West were also stronger. The iron corset of totalitarian dictatorship, coinciding with the peak period of the 'cult of personality', terror and dogmatism, was bound to be more strongly felt in these conditions. At the same time the much shorter period for which the system had prevailed limited the effectiveness of the 'educational' function of ideological mystification and thus permitted the preservation of greater perceptiveness of the disparity between the slogans and reality.

(c) The weakness of the internal roots of the socialist revolution in the majority of the peoples' democracies caused even the general foundations of the system to be seen as imposed from outside, not to speak of its Stalinist forms, which a substantial majority of the population regarded as a brutal instrument of foreign domination. There can be no doubt today that in relation to the peoples' democracies Stalinism was just such an instrument, and thus in the postwar period it assumed an international significance at state level. Nor was it by chance that the first great conflict between socialist states concerned on the one hand the USSR and, on the other, Yugoslavia – a country in which the transition to socialism had been carried out in large measure with the support of internal forces.

(d) The factual domination of the Soviet Union over the peoples' democracies, multiplied in some cases – particularly Poland – by factors of a historical and psychological nature, made it difficult to use nationalistic ideology as an instrument for political attraction of the masses. Disappointment with the system could not be compensated by Great-Power status, and any appeal to national feelings was watched in the USSR with suspicious vigilance. This required the communist parties of the peoples' democracies to perform a balancing act between unconditional acceptance of the leading role of the Soviet Union in all areas of life and emphasis on national interests, sovereignty and state integrity. In such countries as Poland and Czechoslovakia the most important factor in maintaining this balance was the German question, and, above all, invocation of the threat of territorial claims by West Germany.

The factors mentioned seem to justify the thesis that the disintegrating consequences of the etatist model were stronger in the peoples' democracies than in the USSR, although their regimes – even at the peak of the Stalin period – had to reckon more with the conditions limiting their political freedom of action and, at least to a certain degree, had to modify the drastic nature of their methods, both in respect of the economy and of the scale and brutality of the terror.

3   The self-management model

By the self-management model we understand a generalised form of the attempt to solve the problem of socialisation of the means of production which is expressed in the theoretical conception and the experience of Yugoslavia. Presentation of the conception of the self-management model is that much easier than in the case of the etatist model because it requires far less reconstruction from historical practice by the author and can be based to a large degree on authentic interpretation in official programme documents.[26] Even the use of the term 'self-management model' to describe the Yugoslav solution is fully consistent with the terminology of the League of Communists.

This abundance of programme material is certainly connected with the fact that the Yugoslav conception was born as a challenge to the experience of the USSR, which was the only one that existed at the time and was recognised as the classical example; it therefore required clear formulation and broad theoretical justification for both internal and external use. The history and sociology of the 'Yugoslav schism' would themselves be a most attractive subject for research on the evolution of socialism, which, however, we must pass by completely. Neither shall we deal with the interrelationships between the self-management model and the specific features of Yugoslavia as a multi-national country with a federal structure and a mass of resultant problems. This last restriction undoubtedly involves some risk from the point of view of the possibility of evaluating Yugoslav experience, which after all cannot be examined in abstraction from this important element in its real conditions. However – as we indicated at the outset – we are primarily interested in the self-management model as an alternative to the etatist model, which justifies focusing our attention on general problems common to both types but solved by different means. This purpose creates a variety of difficulties which, who knows, may offset with a vengeance the relative ease of presentation of the theoretical conception.

Let us begin with a negative statement: in the self-management model socialisation *does not boil down* to transition of the means of production into the ownership of the socialist state. The otherwise awkward beginning with a negative observation – rather than a direct statement of what socialisation consists of in the self-management model – can in this case be justified by the essential feature of the whole conception, which treats socialisation of the means of production as a process rather than a once-for-all act.[27] In distinction from the etatist model this is thus *a dynamic conception of socialisation.*

The beginning of the process of socialisation is the overthrow of the political rule of the bourgeoisie and the creation of a socialist state (the dictatorship of the proletariat) which takes over ownership of the basic means of production, organises the economy on the principle of planning, and – in the spheres of income distribution, personnel policy, education, culture, etc. – carries out a policy of revolutionary transformation to implement the slogans of social justice, development of productive forces and raising the standard of living and cultural level of the broad masses. The characterisation of the socio-economic essence of the stage of revolutionary transformation in the first period after the attainment of power which is found in Yugoslav doctrine, as expressed in the Ljubljana programme, does not differ in principle from the Soviet doctrine presented above. The official documents of course use different terminology but there can be no doubt also that the justification of the socialist character of the system which arose in Yugoslavia as a result of the victorious revolution contains the factors which we have named, respectively, genetic and socio-economic.[28]

On account of this, means of production nationalised by the socialist state are regarded as in social ownership. But – and here we encounter the first dissimilarity in comparison with the etatist model – this is *indirectly social* ownership, and thus a lower, somewhat embryonic form of social ownership. The indirectness consists in the fact that the means of production, as well as the national income produced and the 'socialist surplus product' (the surplus for the purpose of accumulation and satisfaction of general needs), are not under the direct disposition of the creators of this income, the associated producers in the Marxist sense, but under that of a state acting in their name. This is indeed a socialist state, which has arisen as a result of mass revolutionary activity, but despite that it is a *state* and thus a separate apparatus of government, which at best represents society, but cannot be identified with it. We have emphasised more than once already that the state, being the owner of the means of production, is bound to appear towards workers and consumers as a separate party – as an employer hiring workers on specific conditions and consequently also as the distributor of incomes. The sense in which socialisation is a process stems from the gradual elimination of this indirectness, from the transition from state ownership to 'more and more direct social ownership, under the more and more fully direct disposition of the liberated and associated working people'.[29] According to Yugoslav doctrine, social ownership *sensu stricto* is *direct social* ownership, which not only abolishes monopoly of ownership and – which goes with it – monopoly of political and economic power by an individual or a narrow group of private owners, but also by a socialist state. It is precisely on this that the accent falls in the definition of socialism: 'Socialism is a social system based on socialisation of the means of production, in which social production is directed by associated direct producers. . . .'[30] It follows from this that state ownership is not only, first, a lower form of social ownership but, second, is social ownership only in so far as it is consistently developing towards direct social ownership. The institutional form of direct social possession of the means of production is producers' self-management; hence our term 'self-management model'.

Progress in the process of socialisation of the means of production, in the sense adopted above, requires the fulfilment of a number of conditions, among which the development of the material forces of production plays a not inconsiderable part. An especially important role (and a particularly interesting one from the point of view of the central problem of this book) does, however, fall to political conditions. Their analysis of these conditions, their attempt to show them in motion, and their strong emphasis on the point that under socialism, too, development must take place by means of overcoming endogenous socio-economic contradictions, are the source of one of the most important elements in the historical contribution of the Yugoslav communists, who strove to draw some conclusions from the experience of the etatist model. Quite apart from any substantial evaluation of the solution they proposed, the fact is worthy of note that the SKJ became the first ruling communist party to raise so acutely the problem of development of the system through conflict and to oppose so decisively the deep-rooted view which statically linked socialisation with the takeover by the socialist state of ownership of the means of production. Of course the ideology of the SKJ also serves as a total rationalisation of the party's actions at all times (among other things, of its past policy, all phases of which had to be objectively justified), but the direction adopted evidently requires greater attention to be devoted to the real contradictions between productive forces, production relations and the political superstructure, than does the ideology of the etatist model of socialism.

In the Yugoslav formulation, after the attainment of power socialism enters the *etatist phase* ('statism'). The necessity of passing through this phase is general, applying to all countries, including those which are industrially highly developed and possess a powerful, well-organised working class that is conscious of its interests. The etatist phase, however, is particularly essential – and longer lasting – in the case of countries which are less developed economically and socially, since the socialist state must first create the material conditions for transition to the next phase; this is mainly a matter of industrialisation and the associated change in economic and social structure. We have here an attempt to lay down concretely the way of transition to socialism in 'conditions of immaturity'; the consequence of immaturity is the greater role and duration of the etatist phase, which in turn becomes the source of exacerbation of the contradictions of development.

The basic contradiction of the transition period[31] consists in the fact that on the one hand the state is an essential instrument for progress in the *process of socialisation,* and indeed the main task of the truly revolutionary state (dictatorship of the proletariat in the real sense) consists in working towards the transition from the etatist phase to the phase of socialisation *sensu stricto.* On the other hand, however, the state – including one which has arisen as a result of spontaneous revolutionary movement by the masses – cannot manage without an *apparatus of compulsion,* not only and not so much in the form of an administration in the ordinary sense, but in the form of institutionalised organs of power; against this background there arises a tendency for the ruling strata to become separated and independent, so that it gradually strives to subordinate to itself (in Yugoslav documents the term monopolise is frequently used) various aspects of social activity and, in particular, disposition over the economic surplus. The contradiction also grips the party; on the one hand, as the vanguard organisation of the mass of the people, its participation in the exercise of power counteracts the tendencies to alienation of the state and transformation of it into an instrument of domination *over* labour; on the other hand, the role of the party in the state creates a real threat of bureaucratisation of the party itself, and in particular of symbiosis of the party and the state apparatus, which leads to especially negative consequences, among other things in the ideological field.

The solution to the contradiction clearly cannot consist of simple elimination of one of its poles, since each of them has an objective basis. It is rather a matter of creating the most favourable possible premises for *progressive* movement – in the direction of the phase of real socialisation of ownership. This is the direction dictated by the needs of economic development, which in the long run would be retarded by state forms of domination over labour (just as it is retarded by private forms of domination under capitalism) and the processes of bureaucratisation which are inseparable from this type of domination. But the spontaneous operation of economic requirements cannot suffice, in view of the forces making for petrification which are linked with the interests of the apparatus as it becomes alienated. Hence the role of the party, the organisation which, at any rate in the initial period, is relatively least bureaucratised, mostly closely connected with the authentic aspirations of the masses. For the party to fulfil the role of inspiration and active promoter of the process of socialisation it must keep out of the exercise of state power in the narrow sense to the maximum extent, must not permit itself to become fused with the state apparatus and must overcome the tendencies to become bureaucratised itself. For this reason, too, in the Yugoslav conception the party should not govern directly, should not become – as in the etatist model – a super-organ of power over the corresponding links in the state apparatus at all levels. The party should retain fully the features of an ideological and political organisation, representing the historical interest of the mass of the people, an interest consisting in liberation from all – and thus including state – forms of domination over labour. Separation from direct acts of government prevents the identification of the party with the state apparatus and allows it to preserve its own perspective and the necessary critical attitude towards the organs of political and economic administration. The *reform of the party* carried out at the beginning of the 1950s was designed to correspond to this formulation, which was expressed outwardly in the change in its name (from Communist Party of Yugoslavia to League of Communists of Yugoslavia).

Diagnosis of the contradiction of the etatist phase leads to a therapeutic conclusion: the withering away of the state. This at first glance is an ultra-orthodox conclusion, just as some elements in its development in the SKJ programme are ultra-orthodox, in particular those which strive to demonstrate that withering away means also preservation by the state of many important functions – also in the economic field – since they allegedly lose their political character; the malicious could find here a further reverberation of the pseudo-dialectical sophisms of Stalin about 'withering away through strengthening'. But it is not these elements that set the tone of the Yugoslav conception; the decisive point in it is the concrete postulate of gradual *limitation of the role* of the state in favour of self-management institutions: [32]

> with the development of the socialist democratic system there is a reduction in the role of the state government in the direct management of the economy, in the sphere of cultural and educational activities, health, social policy, etc. Management functions in these fields pass to a growing extent to the various social self-management organs, either independent or linked in an appropriate democratic organising mechanism.

It is a matter, then, of gradual elimination of the state as an intermediate link between working society and the means of production in the broad sense, of gradual liquidation of the two parties in the mechanism for combining labour power with means of production, the hiring party and the hired party, the employer and the employee. Understood thus, the withering away of the state is to counteract the perpetuation of different social roles in relation to the means of production.

Therefore, the self-management model consists not in including worker self-management as one of many components in the system, but in giving it the key role – economically, socially and politically. The process of socialisation of the means of production and evolution towards the Marxist vision of free associated producers is nothing other than the development of worker *self-management*.[33]

Before we pass on to discuss the Yugoslav conception of worker self-management, a few general remarks are in order.

The idea of self-management is not new; it has long appeared in various versions of socialist programmes, and, on the other hand – among other things after the Second World War – it has been adopted in some capitalist countries as one of the instruments of social solidarity. This latter aspect is seen particularly in the Gaullist plan to introduce universal worker participation in the management of enterprises.[34] Equally old are the reservations and opposition to the idea of self-management, even in its lowest form – participation. Abstracting from the reservations connected with the whole problem of the etatist model *versus* the self-management model (which we shall deal with fully below), the controversy mainly concerns two questions: (1) social attractiveness, (2) organisational rationality.

Those who have doubts about the social attractiveness of self-management cite the insufficient interest of workers in taking on the role of joint entrepreneurs; workers do not see any advantage in burdening themselves with additional efforts, with difficult tasks which exceed their competence and are the obligations of management. In conditions of free trade unions distaste for a position of solidarity may be associated with this, as also may be fear of loss of bargaining position. At the same time there is the fact, which we have cited already, that worker self-management is among the most popular slogans in periods of upheaval, and if it later loses its attractiveness this can presumably be ascribed in large measure to negative experiences caused by factors independent of the workers. All this shows that much depends on the traditions of particular countries and the conditions created for self-management. At any rate, while noting the controversy, it does not seem to me that doubts about its social attractiveness could by themselves suffice for rejecting the idea of worker self-management.

The problem of organisational rationality is raised more frequently and has greater substance. The possibility of rational division of labour between professional managers and experts and the corresponding worker institutions is questioned and the complications introduced by disrupting the structure of dependence, the increased time taken by collective decision-making, etc. are emphasised. It is hard to deny that the introduction of self-management into a management system may to some extent cause substantial complications. However (1) their extent depends on skill in solving concrete organisational problems, and (2) modern management theory attaches less weight to clarity of structures and much more to ensuring effective participation of workers at different levels, and in particular to reducing the sharpness of the division between managers and executants. The formation and stimulation of positive, creative postures demands not only that the whole workforce understand its target, but also that it identify itself with the aims of the organisation. This cannot be achieved without the real possibility of influencing decisions about the target itself, without various forms of consultation and sounding of opinion among the workforce, which eventually merges into the concept of self-management as an element in the management system. If we are talking about purely administrative inconvenience involved in the collective mode of decision-making, then – quite apart from the question of worker self-management – precisely this mode is becoming more and more widespread in the West as an inevitable result of the corporate character of enterprises, state interventionism, and the growing importance and complexity of the implications of the most important strategic decisions. Galbraith[35] correctly treats the committee mode of decision-making as one of the essential features of the modern economic organisation. It may be argued that this applies to highly competent teams, committees of experts, rather than to universally elected workers' organs. The force of this argument is considerably less, however, than it might appear at first glance. Worker self-management, at the least, is not bound to represent the extreme of incompetence in contrast to specialists; on the contrary, it may even create more favourable conditions for the use of experts than a purely 'managerial' organisation does, particularly where it is a matter of ensuring that the documents submitted for decision really present a wide range of variants. Of course this requires correct and precisely defined forms of functioning of self-management, and above all a division of decisions into operational and strategic (concerning fundamental questions of enterprise policy) which is appropriate to the concrete situation. In sum, it seems to me, the objection of organisational irrationality can be refuted, and the extension of the idea of participation under various systems and at various, including extremely high, levels of industrial organisation is, if not proof, at least a weighty contribution to this assertion.

In a socialist economy worker self-management is additionally favoured by certain specific factors connected with the postulates touched on in chapter 1 concerning developing the posture of joint manager of the means of production in the consciousness of the workers. This applies to the role of self-management in solving conflicts about income differentials and in interesting workers in the long-term results of their enterprises' activity. Experience shows that the first of these problems – implementation of the principle of distribution according to work in a way which would permit the differentiation of pay required to stimulate productivity while at the same time preserving the limits set by the feeling of social justice – cannot be solved by administrative methods from above; self-management may ease the situation considerably and contribute to finding compromise solutions better suited to the concrete conditions and accepted by the workforce as their own rather than imposed. The same applies to the second problem, the conflict between the need to take decisions which will have consequences lasting for a longer and longer period and the limited time horizon of the manager who is simultaneously a public official. The self-management solution offers a greater possibility of interesting the whole workforce in long-term results, which in turn opens up the possibility of replacing the time horizon of the non-owner manager, which is limited by considerations of individual stability, by the considerably broader time horizon based on the continuity of the collective.[36] Obviously, it would be fallacious to count on the automatic operation of these effects of self-management, since (1) use of the self-management form still does not prevent the creation of élites in enterprises, who exert an influence on the distribution of incomes and weaken or even destroy the interest of the whole collective in the results of the enterprise's operations, and (2) if the system of economic incentives is wrongly constructed strong *collective* preferences can arise for short-term results.[37] Despite this, the opportunity which the self-management solution creates seems to me indubitable, and not just temporarily but, primarily, in the long run. Real self-management at enterprise level should have enormous educational significance for the development of socialist attitudes to work and ownership at a general level. For this reason, too, we regarded the absence of the premises for worker self-management and economic democratism as a negative feature of the etatist model.

Returning from these general remarks to the Yugoslav conception of worker self-management as the foundation of the socialist system, it must be recorded that, both in theoretical works and in the official programme documents of the SKJ, the difficulties we have discussed above are recognised. The basic position, however, is expressed in the conviction that overcoming these difficulties is only possible through the operation of self-management, which generates in the course of its development additional feedbacks between increased authority over a growing area and workers' attitudes. Hence the pressure for consistent elimination of features of the etatist phase, transfer of more and more new spheres of activity to self-management, and creation of the economic and political premises for making the authority granted effective.[38] In the practical experience with the evolution of the Yugoslav system this tendency is reflected in the following areas:

(1) In the increase in the powers of self-management organs within enterprises. From 1950, when plants were formally transferred to management by their workforces, the self-management organs have gradually gained greater influence over a number of key decisions, among them the appointment of managerial personnel, including the director (general manager). Towards the end of the 1960s the director of the enterprise was already being appointed by the workers' council, and the only restriction concerned the list of candidates presented by the selection commission, which examines the applications by means of a public competition (the selection commission consists of equal numbers of representatives of the local council, the commune and the workers' council). The self-management organs have generally ceased to be hampered by obligatory regulations, have the right to issue their own internal regulations on the basis of statutory delegation (in this connection some theoreticians speak of the development of a separate type of 'autonomous' law), etc.[39]

(2) In the extension of the area of operation of self-management. In general self-management forms are associated with the

classical sectors of material production; industry, agriculture (state), construction: trade, too, does not create any special problems from this point of view, but transport and communications do. Despite this, self-management in Yugoslavia has been extended to these sectors, too, and also – in a more or less consistent manner – to education, science, culture, health services, banking and insurance. The intentions are understandable: confining it to the sphere of production would endanger the universality of the self-management model and split the working community into a self-management and an administered part, contrasting them one against the other; on the other hand this type of maximalism probably intensifies rather than diminishes the difficulties, even when the principles of worker self-management are not applied to administration *sensu stricto,* the administration of justice, the armed forces or the security organs.

(3) In the granting to self-management enterprises (and, with the extension of the area of self-management, to non-productive bodies) of special rights in the parliamentary system at all levels. Apart from the chamber filled by direct universal elections, at each territorial level (commune, county, republic, federation) there exists one or a number of chambers representing worker self-management organisations in specific fields of life (production, education and culture, health services and social policy). We shall pass over completely the complicated structure of elections to these chambers and the rules of functioning of the representative organs; but it is essential to emphasise the tendency to give self-management a role as a general political factor too, and the members of self-management organisations something in the nature of a double vote: apart from a vote in the elections to the chambers filled on the normal territorial principle they participate – indirectly – in filling the chambers representing self-management.

(4) In the creation and enlargement of the economic foundations of worker self-management. This crucial problem requires a broader discussion, to which we now move on.

The economic foundations of the process of socialisation of the means of production in the self-management model derive from the primary status of the idea of self-management, the characterisation of the role of the state in the etatist phase and the demand for gradual transfer of disposition over the surplus to the direct producers. This can only mean to postulate *the most far-reaching possible decentralisation* of economic decisions, which in principle – with the exceptions mentioned below – should be taken by self-managing enterprises. This concerns in particular decisions about the division of the surplus earned between consumption (workers' incomes) and investment and about the use of the investment allocation. This is the only way one can expect to implement the thesis that socialisation ultimately consists in liquidation of the situation where disposition over the means and results of production is based on *external compulsion* towards the direct producers. As long as the whole or the predominant part of the surplus is at the disposition of the state, the etatist phase continues; elements of etatism disappear, and elements of socialisation grow, commensurately with the change in the proportions in favour of self-managing enterprises. In other words, the economic essence of the process of socialisation consists in limitation of the direct economic activity of the state and extension of the field of self-management decisions.

Of course this is a general tendency, which comes up against various concrete obstacles and cannot lead – at least in the foreseeable future – to total elimination of disposition over the means and results of production by the state. One of the most important factors justifying redistribution of part of the surplus through the state budget is the necessity of liquidating economic backwardness in general and the backwardness of certain regions in particular (the influence of the transition to socialism in 'conditions of immaturity'); associated with this is the question of financing a number of social services ('the principle of solidarity'), although Yugoslav theoreticians interpret the role of the state in this field in very diverse ways. There can be no doubt, however, what the general trend is, and it is confirmed in practice. From this point of view we can distinguish the following four stages in the development of the Yugoslav system of functioning of the economy: (1) the centralisation stage – up to the beginning of the 1950s; (2) the stage of introducing self-management and the first elements of decentralisation, while reserving a number of key economic decisions to the central state organs, particularly in the regulation of the distribution of incomes in enterprises and in the field of investment – up to 1956; (3) the stage of extension of the powers of self-management to the sphere of distribution of the incomes earned in enterprises, but with the state still retaining the dominant role in investment decisions – up to 1965; (4) from the 1965 reform, the stage of transferring decisions about expanded reproduction to the level of enterprises, which are to dispose of the predominant part of investment funds, leaving in the hands of the state (though not necessarily at federal level) mainly the resources clearly designated for particular general purposes (these include the subsidy for the backward regions).[40] This division into these stages bears, as usual, the image of a simplified stereotype, but it does reflect the general outline of the trends of development.

A radical decentralisation of economic decisions which is treated as the correct line of development must involve allowing the market mechanism to operate on a considerably wider – one could say qualitatively different – scale than in the conception which the author of the present work calls 'the decentralised model' or more precisely 'the model of a planned economy using a regulated market mechanism'.[41] This conception is based on distinguishing three groups of economic decisions: (1) fundamental macro-economic decisions, mainly concerning the direction of social and economic development; (2) partial decisions (of sectors of production and enterprises), mainly concerning current operating problems of the economy; and (3) individual decisions (of households), relating to choice of profession, place of work, expenditure patterns, etc. Decentralisation in a planned economy, in this conception, can only apply to the second group of decisions, since the third is decentralised in the nature of things (in conditions of free choice of profession and place of work and choice of consumption pattern) and the first must be centralised if it is to be a planned economy. The decentralised model of functioning of a socialist economy consists, then, in decentralisation of the second group of decisions, in replacement of the method of hierarchical directive planning (see the description of the system of functioning of the economy in the etatist model) by the method of indirect steering, with the help of which lower-level bodies ('sub-systems'), planning autonomously are directed on to the general course defined by the central plan for the 'system' as a whole. The market mechanism plays an essential role in this conception, but it must be precisely a *regulated* mechanism, appropriate to the role of steering instrument, in accordance with the principle of primacy of the central plan.

The conception of the decentralised model of functioning of a socialist economy lays down that creation of this type of market mechanism demands the fulfilment of three conditions: (1) retention

at central level of the basic long-term decisions on the speed and
directions of economic development (the investment ratio, direct
allocation of the basic portion of investment funds), on the general
proportions of distribution of the income to be consumed (in particular between personal and public consumption) and on priority
social and political objectives and the resources to realise them; (2)
setting the 'rules of behaviour' of 'sub-systems' at central level, i.e.
setting their objective functions so that by maximising them (connected with material incentives) they contribute to maximisation of
the objective function of the 'system' as a whole; (3) ensuring the
parametric character of the economic magnitudes entering the
calculations of 'sub-systems' (prices, interest rates, tax rates,
exchange rates, etc.) by assembling a set of economic instruments at
central level which permits direct determination or effective influence and control of these magnitudes.

The reader will of course be aware that he has been given here a
far from adequate and extremely schematic description of the conception of the decentralised model of functioning of a socialist
economy. But this scheme is to serve only to bring into relief the
essential features of the mechanism of functioning of the economy
within the self-management model. And so it must clearly follow
from what we have discussed above that the self-management
model – in its pure form, without the compromises which are constantly forced in practice – must eliminate from the model of functioning appropriate to it all those limitations which we regard as
inseparable from a *regulated* market mechanism in a planned economy. If the process of socialisation is to consist in the development
of direct social ownership by associated producers, the area of
direct allocation of resources by the state must diminish and thus
what we call the basic, central-level, macro-economic decisions can
be at most a relict, but not however a principle, setting the frame of
operation of decentralised enterprise decision-making and the functioning of the market mechanism. Similarly, it would be contrary to
the basic assumptions of the self-management model to impose
'rules of behaviour' on enterprises from above; these rules must
result in a natural way from the supreme principle of self-
management of the collective. As for economic magnitudes, it is not
their parametric nature itself that is contrary to the assumptions of
the self-management model, but the method by which this is
ensured; prices, interest rates, etc. must be parametric in relation to

F

enterprises not as a result of being set by state organs (that would mean intensification of etatism again) but as a result of market competition.

Thus the principles (the model) of functioning of the economy corresponding to the assumptions of the self-management model of socialism are based on the commodity character of the links between collectively managed independent enterprises. The SKJ programme states this clearly, although cautiously and with limitations regarding the time when it applies: [42]

> At the present level of development of productive forces the laws of commodity production operate in the economic system of Yugoslavia too. As long as commodity production is necessitated by objective conditions violation of the law of value and other laws of the market does not strengthen but, on the contrary, weakens the socialist elements in the economy, hampers the initiative of individuals and enterprises, retards the development of productive forces and gives birth to forces outside the sphere of production which forcibly subordinate it to themselves.

To the extent that the role of commodity relations has increased in practice, particularly after the inauguration of the 1965 reform, which meant a decisive step beyond the framework of our 'decentralised model', the interpretation of the programme formulation cited above has been becoming more definitive. Here is a passage from a resolution of the IX Congress of the SKJ: [43]

> The League of Communists acknowledges that under contemporary conditions socialist commodity production is the only possible form of rational expansion of productive forces, and an objective prerequisite for the development of self-management and direct socialist democracy. For this reason it is necessary energetically to pursue the policies of the reform [of 1965] towards a fuller assertion of more developed and freer forms of socialist commodity production, opposing any subjectivism and statist denial of the effects of its economic laws.

Yugoslav theoretical writings frequently 'dot the i' by defining the socialist economy simply as a commodity economy. [44] This definition seems to remove the problem of the limits, framework and area of commodity relations altogether, or at any rate eliminates it from the range of alternatives of conscious, social *choice* of principles of functioning of the economy. If socialist production is by definition production of exchange values, then the question of choice, and thus of which instruments to approach it with, does not exist. In these conditions the objective function of producers is uniquely defined in this sense, that the objective of the operation of a given productive unit appears autonomously rather than being subordinate to the overall objective of the national economy. With acceptance of a definition of the socialist economy as a commodity economy the hierarchical structure of objectives, of which Lange[45] wrote, must in the nature of things disappear, as also the principle of primacy of production of use value, in relation to which the production of exchange value may be an effective means, but not an objective. The total effect in this case is the sum of partial effects, just as the total outlay is the sum of partial outlays. It is hard to visualise if and how an economy which is consistently treated as a commodity one can take appropriate account of external economies and diseconomies, since this conception itself contains the relationship between part and whole, 'system' and 'sub-system', and thus must also involve an overall objective function and the capacity of making direct optimising calculations from the point of view of this objective.

In a commodity economy *sensu stricto* the rules of behaviour of economic units derive from the logic of the market mechanism. This means, first, that there is a permanent tendency to transfer resources from less profitable to more profitable uses (in terms of the costs borne by enterprises and market prices, both current and anticipated in the not-too-distant future). It means, second, that the position of the national economy as a whole (the 'macro-economic equilibrium' as some economists call it) becomes merely the resultant of the activities of individual economic units. The price system under these conditions is formed according to the relationships between supply and demand, and the question to what extent market prices reflect the relationship of *social* opportunity costs (i.e. opportunity costs from the point of view of the national economy as a whole) loses all sense, since social opportunity cost – as something different from the opportunity cost expressed by actual market magnitudes – is not included in the narrowly conceived framework of the commodity economy.[46]

Of course, we have been speaking all the time of a *socialist*

commodity economy as distinct from the capitalist type of commodity economy. The subjects of commodity relations here are not
private owners but associated producers, workers' collectives. This
fact has a bearing on the concrete form of the objective function in
the enterprise: in the self-management model this cannot consist in
maximisation of profit per unit of capital, but in maximisation of
income per member of the self-managing collective, i.e. per employee.
Theoretically at least this is precisely the naturally formed objective
function of which we spoke above. The equilibrium point of the
enterprise is also set in terms of it, as distinct from the equilibrium
point of the capitalist enterprise operating under conditions of free
competition (we shall return to the significance of this equilibrium
point). Some Yugoslav economists have also tried to link the
natural tendency to maximisation of net income per employee with
the specific conception of 'normal price' in the self-management
model, the so-called income price.[47]

The growth of the area and freedom of operation of the market
mechanism increases its influence on the process of distribution of
national income, both as regards the sources and proportions of
incomes for consumption and the part of income assigned for
expanded reproduction.

On the incomes of the population (for simplicity we shall treat
them as equivalent to consumption) Yugoslav doctrine stands firm
on *the principle of distribution according to work*. It is hard to say
whether this principle is regarded as transitional (to 'distribution
according to need') on a historical scale, since the question simply
does not appear, either in programme documents or even in economic literature, and at no time has it been linked with the process of
socialisation. It is precisely the fullest possible practical implementation of 'the principle of distribution according to work' that is
regarded as one of the most essential preconditions of progress in
the process of socialisation. The stress on the principle of distribution according to work cuts in two directions, against two groups
of undesirable phenomena: first, against non-labour, and in particular parasitic, incomes; second, and this is specific to Yugoslav
doctrine, against incomes which are determined 'arbitrarily' – i.e.,
by the state administrative organs – without economic verification
by the market rules of functioning of the self-management model of
socialism. These rules influence both the distribution of incomes
within the enterprise and that between enterprises and sectors of

economic activity, and finally the distribution between enterprises and branches ('sub-systems') and society as a whole ('the system'), represented by the organs of the state.

At the level of *distribution within enterprises* the rules of functioning of the economy in the self-management model should find expression in democratism in setting wage rates and differentials and in better adjustment of these to concrete conditions, compared with a centrally laid-down network of wages and bonuses – always assuming, of course, that real self management is operating.

Considerably more complicated problems arise at the level of distribution of incomes *between different enterprises and branches*. The question is clearly one of the link between the economic results of enterprises (or associations of enterprises) and the level of workers' incomes. This link appears in any system of material incentives which takes account of the overall results of an enterprise's operations, no matter what way these results are expressed (volume of output or profit, results relative to plan or in absolute terms, etc.). None the less, a number of elements in the self-management solution, in particular the tendency towards radical restriction or simply elimination of basic macroeconomic decisions at central level, and ensuring a major role for market competition, make the scale of the problem appreciably greater here and its effects on the unity of personal and social interest considerably more complex. On the one hand, heavy dependence on the overall results of the enterprise, which obtains its revenue not by virtue of arbitrarily granted limits and funds but by effective selling, and is thus subject to the test of the market, extends the sphere of interest of the workers as joint owners of the means of production and thus becomes a factor in practice in forming the feeling of a connection between individual and the general interest.[48] On the other hand, dependence of personal incomes on ultimate financial results in conditions of market competition introduces many intermediate links which make the workers' material advantages quite remote from their visible work input. In this situation differentiation of incomes between workers in particular enterprises and branches is subject to the influence of factors related to market uncertainties. The principle of linking workers' incomes to financial results derives from the general assumption of mutual interest and thus also mutual responsibility of employees, not only as workers but also as joint owners, joint entrepreneurs. In a certain sense the whole conception of socialism contains this type of principle of mutual interest and mutual responsibility, since the level and rate of growth of an individual's income is to depend not only on his personal work input but also on economic efficiency on a national scale. The application of this principle to the enterprise level is, from a certain point of view, only a difference of scale and may be treated as a way of making the dependence more concrete and comprehensible. For evaluating the consequences of this transition to the enterprise or branch level, however, the degree of general social control over the overall external conditions in which specific collectives operate is not without significance. In the self-management solution the degree of such control is relatively small, whilst the dependence of workers' incomes on the financial position of their enterprise, and thus on the market situation, is very considerable.

The problem of the distribution of income in the self-management model becomes particularly complicated as the enterprise is left a larger and larger part of the total pool of investment resources and decisions about their use are transferred to this level. To all intents and purposes the need arises for a new interpretation of the principle of distribution according to work. As long as – as in the decentralised model of functioning of the economy – the basic mass of investment resources is at the disposition of the central organs, it can be assumed that decentralised investments are for the purpose of expanded reproduction within enterprises (modernisation, increasing production capacity in the given line of production, etc.); in other words, the future benefits from productive accumulation of part of income still accrue to the given collective which controls the additional or more efficient means of production. This assumption no longer holds in a situation where the predominant part of the social accumulation fund is under the disposition of self-managing enterprises. The changes in branch and territorial structure which are normal in the process of development demand the transfer of resources, and thus, in these conditions, demand opening up to existing enterprises the possibility of investing outside, in other enterprises, in other regions, at times even with no connection to their previous line of activity. The forms may be various – direct investment, long-term mutual credits, or through banks, etc. – but they do not alter the socio-economic problem: the resources invested must bring income to the workers of the enterprise possessing the surplus for accumulation, but with no new input of work by the collective concerned. Permitting this possibility means greatly broadening the interpretation of the principle of distribution according to work: the essence of it is extended to 'past', accumulated labour, too. There is no need to stress how deep the effects of this type of phenomenon can be on the distribution of income, differentials, the proportion of 'current' work to 'dividends', etc.

Another problem connected with the consistent transfer of disposition over the surplus to self-managing enterprises is the question of the resources for satisfying general social needs. If we pass over administrative and military requirements, which are obviously solved by means of the tax system, there remains the question of financing the so-called *public consumption,* which absorbs a rather substantial part of the surplus. Acceptance and implementation of the principle of disposition over resources earned by the workers' collective concerned leads either to financing a considerable part (for there can be no question of financing the whole) of services directly by charges, or to clearer supplementation of the general system of services by an element linking an appropriate part of services to the financial contribution made by the collective of a particular enterprise.

In the light of the role in the self-management model of decisions by self-managing enterprises on the distribution of income – for the processes of expanded reproduction, for the structure of wages, the satisfaction of general social needs, etc. – particular importance attaches to the possibility of counteracting the threat of monopoly (or, to be precise, oligopoly) in the market. Differentiation of incomes and, what is more, of the conditions of expansion, too, can now follow not only from the fluctuations of the market, which at times cancel each other out in the longer run and at other times simply demand greater ability to adapt (which has positive effects from the point of view of the national economy), but also from unequal market power, with the well-known negative effects. The danger of monopoly is connected with the way prices are formed. It is true that monopolistic behaviour does not automatically disappear with direct state control of prices, since a very large enterprise will manage to exert pressure on the controlling organs, but the danger is incomparably greater and more real when the movement of prices is left to the free market mechanism.

In Yugoslav writing it is generally assumed that these dangers

82   *East European socialism*

can be counteracted, within the general conception, by creating conditions of effective competition. Two groups of methods are
ascribed a particularly essential role in this: (1) liberalisation of
foreign trade, giving broad possibilities of increasing imports to
break domestic monopolies;[49] (2) implementation of the principle
of free entry to specific fields of economic activity, with which is
connected the possibility of splitting up too large enterprises, or
deconcentration.[50] Both points, however, are bound to present
great difficulties (balance of payments, economies of scale and
irrational duplication, especially in a relatively small country) and
sometimes even conflict, as for example in the case of a necessity to
concentrate production because of the demands of the world
market. This last factor may be the reason why, after the inauguration of the 1965 reform – as distinct from the previous period,
when even some artificially forced deconcentration occurred – a
tendency rather towards integration of excessively small enterprises
has been visible; integration has to take place completely voluntarily, on the initiative of the enterprises themselves (self-
management decisions) without the use of administrative methods.
But whatever the methods and forms of integration, it can hardly be
expected to favour freedom of competition and counteract signs of
monopolisation of the market. Nothing else remains, presumably,
but appropriate intervention by state organs.

Thus, from one of the possible aspects, we have come to the
problem of the place and role of *the central level of economic
decisions* in the self-management model. Does what we have said so
far about the conception of socialisation by means of gradual elimination of the state as an intermediate link between associated
workers and the means of production mean that Yugoslav doctrine
postulates the aim of total elimination of an economic central authority and of any elements of redistribution of income on a national
scale? To avoid misunderstanding it must be emphasised that this is
not a question of a 'transition period' in which the necessity for the
state to exercise direct economic functions *still* exists, at times on a
large scale – particularly because of the backwardness of a country
or of specific regions. The question is of a general character, and
concerns the general theory of the self-management model of socialism.

At the abstract level the answer we find in authoritative interpretations of the Yugoslav conception is definite: the self-

management model does not assume and does not postulate the elimination of central economic decisions, central planning, co-ordinated economic policy, etc. The view that self-managing enterprises constitute group ownership is categorically rejected. The concept of social ownership, which – as we have seen – is so strongly linked with direct disposition over the means of production by workers' collectives, also includes the whole of society as the owner.

The positive content of this type of formulation is not easy to decipher; it is more clearly seen from the negative aspect, that is, what social ownership *must not be*: it must not be monopoly either of the individual or collective, nor of the state. As we read in the SKJ Programme:[51]

> Production and distribution, as also disposition over the social product, are influenced in defined ways by both the social community and the specific producer. These relations are not absolute – they contain a contradiction; yet they must undoubtedly develop gradually in the direction of greater and greater direct influence by working man and greater and greater conformity with the needs of society as a whole.

At another point, though applying more to the conditions of the 'transition period', we find:

> From these conflicts there follows the necessity for the independence of producers in production to be limited by particular centralised economic institutions and functions of society and the state, and at the same time for the power and the economic function of central social and state organs to be limited by the independence and self-management of producers and the basic factors of socialist material development.

Where is the possibility seen of maintaining a dynamic equilibrium between the conflicting factors developing towards 'greater and greater direct influence of working men and greater and greater conformity with the needs of society as a whole'? In gradually divesting general economic functions of their political character, in 'depoliticisation' of central economic direction: 'as the political power, the state is less and less directly involved in productive activity'.[52] And what, in turn, does 'depoliticisation' consist in? In the general economic functions of the state, the role of central economic authority, not deriving[53] from political power, nor from economic monopoly, but from the fact that the state itself changes, i.e. in this field it becomes, and must become, more and more a system of territorial-political self-managing organisations of producer-consumers and their socio-economic community of interest at different levels, from parish to federation. . . .

The true social content of this process [the development of social ownership *sensu stricto*] is the development of self-management of producers in production, self-management of the masses working in parish, county, republic and federation, and clear delimitation of rights and obligations between all these organs.

This somewhat lengthy string of quotations seems justified in so far as it helps to eliminate distortions in the presentation of an extremely complex theoretical construction, which endeavours to solve the conflict between maximum self-management for associated producers and the perceived need for planned direction on a general economic scale. This conception is an attempt to reconcile two negatives generally regarded as mutually exclusive: socialisation of the means of production is not equivalent to nationalisation, but neither is it equivalent to collectivisation (in the sense of transformation into group ownership). The conclusion from the passages of the SKJ Programme cited, and also from numerous works by Yugoslav theoreticians, is that self-management must be both an element of economic democracy and also a basic element of political democracy. The linking of self-management with the system of representative organs (mentioned on p. 72) takes on a new significance really here – it is to become an inseparable component of the category *direct* control of the means of production by associated producers. Direct social ownership is no longer to consist only in self-management decision-making at enterprise level, but also in joint decision-making on a broad scale (parish, county, republic, federation) through the medium of a specific political system which is democratic because it is self-managing or, *vice versa,* is self-managing because it is democratic. From the point of view of the criteria we have introduced this means at the least that in the self-management model too we cannot evaluate the reality of socialisation of the means of production without subjecting the *political system* to 'the test of democratism'.

If we have correctly interpreted this theoretical construction it would follow that in this conception the self-management model has to be integrated on a national scale, subject to two conditions: (1) that the integrating function is fulfilled by organs which are themselves an emanation of self-management, state organs of a specific type, which are a form of voluntary association and not an external force in relation to 'free associations of producers'; and (2) that the area of centrally regulated problems is relatively small, particularly in respect of direct allocation decisions. Both conditions must be fulfilled together: it is regarded as impossible to maintain the proper character of the central organs in a situation, for example, where the basic part of resources for the purpose of expanded reproduction is taken out of the control of self-managing enterprises, or – using the terminology frequently encountered in Yugoslavia – is taken out of the economic sphere and made the object of 'arbitrary political decisions'. In principle the central economic authority should limit its intervention to: (a) working out forecasts of general development trends; (b) counteracting signs of 'imperfection' of the market and the threat of monopolistic behaviour; and (c) correcting market processes in specific cases when the market either does not work at all or operates in a way obviously contrary to long-term social objectives (the development of extremely backward regions, acute social problems, etc.).

Can the term 'planning' be used for this type of central coordination, which must in practice involve some sort of medium- and short-term economic policy? As usual, the answer depends on the definition of the term, but a positive answer would have to mean that we are limiting planning mainly to a general guiding role and a factor correcting the basic allocation function of the market mechanism in particular situations.

Thus the self-management model does not contain the postulate of elimination of the central economic level, but it does contain the postulate of radical limitation of its function, to the role of coordinator of the autonomous operations of self-managing economic units. If we try to summarise and compare the principles of functioning of the economy proper to the self-management model of socialism and the 'decentralised model' mentioned above, we must say that the difference consists not only in different proportions of centralisation and decentralisation, but also in opposite kinds of interrelationships between 'the system' as a whole and 'sub-systems': in the 'decentralised model' the central level sets the area of autonomy of 'sub-systems', whereas here the self-managing 'sub-systems' relinquish a portion of their rights in the name of coordination of their operations. This recalls slightly the distinction in constitutional law between a federal state, in which 'competence of competence' belongs to the federation, and a confederation of states, in which it belongs to the individual members.

In our presentation of the self-management model we have tried as much as possible to avoid reference to practical Yugoslav experience – both in view of our intention to present the model in a pure form, and because these experiences are associated to a certain degree with the earlier phases of development, when the system of functioning of the economy did not extend far beyond the framework of the construction which we have called the 'decentralised model'. Similarly, in our evaluation, to which we now move on, we try to confine ourselves to the methodological plane of models, i.e. to make a theoretical evaluation, and only occasionally bring in generalisations with an empirical basis. This corresponds to the limited role given to the self-management model in the book as a whole – namely that of providing contrast.

In accordance with the criterion of socialisation of the means of production we have adopted, let us try to answer the question whether and to what extent the self-management model solves the problem of democratism in the management of the economy understood in the broadest sense. In a certain way this evaluation is harder than it was for the etatist model, in which, because of the concentration of the means of production directly in the hands of the state, the whole problem boils down to an analysis of the political system and its economic implications. In the self-management model the question of the democratism of the political system *sensu stricto* can only be separated out after weighing up the real significance and limits of direct economic democracy. For this reason we begin our brief concluding analysis with an evaluation of self-management and its role in transforming society into the owner of the means of production.

Self-management as an institutional form of management of enterprises with autonomy (the two things, as we have seen, are closely connected) can become a democratising factor in relations in the economic sphere itself directly in two aspects: internal and external.

The *internal* aspect consists in involving workers in the management of their enterprise. If this becomes a reality, the disalienating – or integrating – consequences are manifold and so obvious that there is no need to enumerate them. The root of the problem however is this 'if', which is far from automatically fulfilled by even the boldest institutional solution. This aspect of Yugoslav experience is presented in widely differing ways in the literature, and the differences in evaluation frequently reflect simply the far-from-uniform practice. Élitist and technocratic tendencies appear on the whole everywhere, but they gain the upper hand mainly where they do not encounter a mature workforce, particularly the manual workers' section, where there is a lack of ability for self-organisation, capacity to appoint leaders, etc. One can expect, then – assuming suitable economic, institutional, political and ideological preconditions – that with the growth of the general level of culture and consciousness of the workforce these features will grow, leading to a rise in the degree of reality of self-management. From this point of view, and provided that we understand socialisation as a process, the basis exists for positive evaluation of the self-management solution.

The *external* aspect consists in the limitation of the economic omnipotence of the state by the introduction of pluralistic elements into the sphere of economic decision-making. The relationship between households and the national economy here can no longer be reduced to the relationship between households and the state, since many relatively independent decision centres arise. This also applies to purely economic matters, including in the field of income distribution, as well as to broader problems, particularly those of personnel. Taking into account that this type of decentralisation, transferring economic decisions to a significant and growing extent to self-managing enterprises, reduces the role and simply the numerical size of the bureaucratic and also the party apparatus, the degree of subordination of the individual to the state diminishes. The limitation of the monopolistic position of the state in the economic field is bound to take on a political significance too. It would be a mistake to ascribe to economic pluralism the capacity to provide a definitive solution of the problems of political democratism, but a certain influence undoubtedly exists and should not be disregarded.[54] This influence becomes greater, the more economic decentralisation is accompanied by the development of real worker self-management in enterprises (when an important social factor is added to the economic factors), but it can be felt even when the growth of enterprise independence is mainly turned to advantage by managers to strengthen their own position.

The role of economic self-management as a democratising element in production relations is nevertheless *relative* – as the field of economic decisions of self-managing bodies is extended, so the field of decisions of the state narrows. This gives rise to a dilemma: to recognise that the role of this factor is limited (which does not mean insignificant) or to give it priority and adopt the appropriate economic solutions. It should be unequivocally clear from our discussion that the self-management model – although it cannot be accused of eliminating the central economic level – resolves the dilemma in favour of the second alternative. But if so, and if the hypotheses we formulated in chapter 1 are correct, then the self-management model comes into collision with the objective tendency towards growth of the role of central planning, or any active planning based on the supremacy of macrocriteria and long-term economic calculation extending far beyond market criteria and signals. It could be said that the self-management model – conceived as a consistent whole – is an attempt at solving the problem of socialisation of the means of production not by giving public ownership certain specific features which make it social ownership (see chapter 1) but by limiting the public character of ownership. From this point of view it is symptomatic that in Yugoslav literature one continually comes across the contrast between economically justified decisions and political decisions, where the adjective 'political' has a clearly pejorative tinge and is a synonym for arbitrariness and irrationality. Whilst basic macro-economic decisions are in the nature of things political decisions since they set and assess the objectives of the economy, they establish the general criteria and the framework which give economic calculation a definite character, but do not in the least reduce its significance thereby.[55] Political decisions can obviously be arbitrary and mistaken, but this does not mean that they should (and can) be eliminated at any price in favour of partial decisions based on free market criteria; it does on the other hand demand the minimisation of arbitrariness and error – but this is already primarily a problem of political system.

An interesting illustration of the collision between the striving for maximum extension of the field of economic decisions of self-managing enterprises and the objectively determined need to ensure the supremacy of general economic criteria is offered by the effects of abandoning central setting of the objective function of 'sub-systems'. We mentioned this problem in our characterisation of the differences between the 'decentralised model' and the principles of functioning of the economy in the self-management model, which does not permit imposition of rules of behaviour for enterprises from above. As a result the natural objective function of the self-managing enterprise becomes maximisation of net income per employee. However, such an objective function affects the equilibrium position of the enterprise, i.e. the determination of the optimal (more accurately, the desired) levels of output and employment. Assuming that, with given fixed capital, the set of actual alternative levels of output and employment includes a section with increasing marginal costs, theoretical reasoning will easily bring us to some very categorical negative conclusions. It can be demonstrated that under these conditions the enterprise maximising net income per employee will tend to be satisfied with lower levels of output and employment than, *ceteris paribus,* the enterprise maximising profits; such an enterprise also shows a stronger tendency to use more capital-intensive and more labour-saving techniques of production, and in certain circumstances can even react paradoxically to an increase in prices, reducing rather than increasing output and employment.[56] Of course, our assessment of even the purely theoretical value of this type of conclusions depends on our view about the adequacy of the assumptions made; attempts to translate the conclusions into practice should be approached even more cautiously. Yet the fact cannot be questioned, that the objective function under discussion does create the tendency, which in certain circumstances can prove dominant, or at least substantial, in practice. From the macro-economic point of view the tendency to prefer economy of living labour at the price of a lower degree of utilisation of productive capacity or more capital-intensive investment, would only be justified in conditions of shortage of labour and surplus of capital; in other situations 'sub-systems', from this point of view, should behave differently, and thus should be guided by a different objective function. In this sense abandonment of the supremacy of the macro-economic point of view, of *regulation* of the market mechanism, in favour of the allegedly natural rules of behaviour of collective commodity producers, can have negative general economic consequences. It would be too hasty, clearly, to simply associate the high and lasting unemployment in Yugoslavia with the systemic solutions discussed above. Nevertheless, there can be no doubt that a system of functioning which impels enterprises to maximise net income per employee does not, to put it most cautiously, favour the relief of unemployment. It must be emphasised here that we are posing the problem on the economic plane; enterprise rules of behaviour which are contrary to general economic requirements lead to a reduction in employment because employment is not advantageous *for them,* with the given objective function, not because it is macro-economically irrational. This has nothing in common with the phenomenon of absolute over-employment, maintained in certain circumstances from social considerations.

There are many symptoms of the collision between the self-management model and the objective tendency towards growth of the role of central planning. They relate to various different fields, both narrowly economic – primarily the coordination of long-term investment decisions and the associated general equilibrium of the economy – and also social (employment, income differentials, payments from the social consumption fund, etc.).[57] We shall not analyse them in detail as that would demand concrete investigation of Yugoslav experience, which has all along been conditioned by a variety of external circumstances among other things, and in addition by the specifically Yugoslav nationalities question. It is sufficient to state (1) that official circles are aware of many of the symptoms mentioned (particularly at the time of periodical 'self-examination') and (2) despite general doctrinal faithfulness, in the everyday functioning of the economic mechanism there is time and again a return to instruments of direct management by the central level. These instruments operate in a specially characteristic way in the field of prices, which had been freed from administrative control long before the 1965 reform; in reality, however, brief periods when price movements were determined by the market mechanism quickly gave way to renewed regulation, and of the most drastic type at that (price freezes). A similar phenomenon may be observed in the field of wages (personal incomes), and also foreign trade, where the declared principle of enterprise disposition over its own foreign currency earnings was never properly implemented. There has perhaps been least intervention in Yugoslavia in the system of indicators of effectiveness, or the definition of the objective function of enterprises, which in turn, however, has probably strengthened the need for increased intervention in the market, since it was one of the sources of disequilibrium and inflationary processes.

It is hard to evaluate the effectiveness of the various forms of direct intervention, but the fact that they did not stem from the system, but from a temporary need for symptomatic treatment of acutely inflamed conditions, inclines one towards scepticism. Indirect confirmation of the correctness of this sceptical evaluation is provided by the reform of 1965, the necessity of which was due not only to considerations of principle and conformity with the socialisation programme but also to pragmatic reasons – the need to overcome a number of economic difficulties allegedly caused by inconsistent adoption of the true principles of functioning of the self-management model, particularly in the field of disposition over resources for accumulation. But the period since the reform provided no evidence that these expectations have been fulfilled; on the contrary, the symptoms of lack of stabilisation have become deeper, which has caused restraint in the tempo of changes (among other things in the relative shares of enterprises and territorial-political organs in the 'surplus'[58]), and also return to administrative instruments, once again presented as extraordinary temporary measures. The continual zigzags in the implementation of far-reaching economic reforms, which are after all supported whole-heartedly by the political leadership and official ideology (and therefore do not face the obstacles encountered by reforms in the USSR and the peoples' democracies), can hardly be interpreted otherwise than as testimony of contradiction between current doctrine and objective needs and possibilities.

The changes in the position of worker self-management as a result of the 1965 reform can also hardly be regarded as unequivocal. On the one hand, the field of decision-making of enterprises themselves has been extended, but on the other the necessity of concentrating production by merging enterprises and the necessity of enhancing the role of the banks, which had somehow to compensate for the weakening of state control over the processes of accumulation, acted in the opposite direction; they removed the centres of decision further from the workforce and compelled resort to frequently multi-level systems of indirect representation of self-

G

managing units. This latter phenomenon by itself need not be in the least anti-democratic, but from the point of view of a doctrine which stresses the importance precisely of democracy directly at the place of work it may raise a question mark.

The same problem, but on an incomparably larger scale and with a fundamental importance, appears in the question of *the democratism of the political system* in the self-management model; we have actually posed it already, when describing the place of the central economic authority in the Yugoslav conception, but now in our summing-up we must return to it briefly.

The leading idea of the self-management model – as a form for implementing the postulate of socialisation of the means of production in the narrow sense – consists, despite all reservations, in the most far-reaching possible limitation of the economic functions of the state and the transformation of the economy into an association of associated self-managing producers of goods and services. In accordance with this idea, the essence of democratism of the 'association of free producers' stems from the 'depoliticisation of the economy', leaving the centre a role which is basically residual and at any rate does not threaten the sovereignty of 'sub-systems'. The foundation of democratism in the self-management model is that the way the means of production are used is decided directly at the place of work by self-managing workers' collectives; an essential, though secondary, supplementary element, which can only operate in conjunction with the first, is indirect participation by self-managing units in taking decisions about matters *delegated* to the political organs at different levels, including the centre.

Meanwhile, as the whole of our discussions hitherto should have shown, the economic preconditions for such a general solution are lacking. Because of the necessity of maintaining the principle of supremacy of 'the system' *vis-à-vis* 'sub-systems', the interrelationships are, as it were, reversed: workers' self-management can be an essential element – and also politically – but a secondary, supplementary one, which can only operate in conjunction with political democratism at the level of the state as a whole. Thus, to cast our conclusion in the form of a slogan, it is not 'depoliticisation of the economy' but 'democratisation of politics' that is the correct direction for the process of socialisation of nationalised means of production.

Here in fact we could stop – from the point of view of the purpose which analysis of the self-management model was to fulfil in our discussion as a whole. If the self-management model points to no other solution of the problem of socialisation than that which we established as a result of our analysis of the etatist model, if the question is still ultimately solved on the plane of democratism of the political system, then evaluation of the degree of democratism of the concrete system of political relations in Yugoslavia would only be necessary here if the Yugoslav system were an independent object of research for us rather than only a basis for comparison. The few sentences which we nevertheless devote to this theme below are dictated, firstly, by fear of being suspected of avoiding taking any position, and secondly, by a desire to emphasise certain factors which may prove helpful later in analysing the evolution of the etatist model in the post-Stalin period.

Thus, on the one hand, emphasis should be placed on the additional influence, which has been mentioned so often, of autonomy of enterprises and workers' self-management on the democratism of political relations through limitation of the monopolistic position of the state and thus of the possibility for use of and the effectiveness of political and economic pressure against individuals or groups. Thanks to this, some elements of pluralism arise, which make it easier to take an independent position, at least in certain categories of questions. In this respect the situation in Yugoslavia is undoubtedly better than in the USSR and the peoples' democracies (even in the post-Stalin period, not to speak of the earlier years) – although it should be remembered that other factors may weigh here too, including those connected with international relations.

On the other hand, it must be stressed strongly that autonomy and self-management of enterprises, and also the complicated constitutional-legal construction designed to create the institutional forms for building self-management indirectly into the structure of the higher levels of authority, have in practice proved insufficient to bring about a deeper change in the political system. The scope for open formulation of independent opinions and for legal opportunities of effective restraint of autocratism is certainly broader than elsewhere in Eastern Europe, but limits which cannot be transgressed appear as soon as matters regarded (arbitrarily) by the authorities as fundamental are involved. Hence, among other things, the at first glance surprising phenomenon of apparently bitter economic discussions which nevertheless carefully avoid the foundations of the self-management model or even the form which they take at present in the 1965 reform – although it is well known that there is opposition in many circles to the directions taken by the reform, from both purely economic and social considerations. The Yugoslav political system does not admit opposition, does not give the opportunity for presentation of an alternative solution to the problems of the socialist road of development or for soliciting social acceptance of any such alternative, does not create conditions where individuals or groups of people win the right to take political decisions by means of genuine competition for the votes of the electorate. As a type of system, the Yugoslav political system belongs to the same category as the Soviet system. This therefore means that it does not meet the demands of the criterion of socialisation we have adopted.

4   Conclusions from the analysis of the two models

Our analysis of the etatist and the self-management models, although to some extent abstract in character, seems to permit us to draw a few joint conclusions, which should help us to take the correct direction in our further discussion – from the point of view of the main theme of this work. This applies in particular to the evaluation of the evolution of the etatist model of socialism in the post-Stalin period.

These conclusions, as concisely as possible, can be summarised in the following points:

(1)   Using the criterion of socialisation which we have adopted ('society *has* effective disposition over the means of production'), the answer to the question whether socialisation of the means of production *sensu stricto* has been achieved in the socialist countries of Eastern Europe in the period examined must be in the negative – for both models. Yet recognition that this answer is correct still does not create a sufficient basis for rejecting the Marxist theory of the objective necessity of socialisation of the means of production as a law of historical development. Such a tendency may after all assert itself in further evolution, which would have then to be towards socialisation – under the threat of continual exacerbation, to the point of violent outbursts, of the contradiction between the needs of the development of productive forces and relations of production which did not meet the criteria of socialisation. From this

aspect verification of the hypothesis of the necessity of socialisation still remains a central problem, defining the plane of further analysis.

(2)   Acceptance of the preceding conclusion, however, permits us *ipso facto* to recognise as verified the thesis that if we give the category social ownership a different content from public ownership, then we must at the same time recognise that socialisation takes place as a process rather than through a once-for-all act. The static conception of socialisation thus falls, and in particular that form of it which identifies socialisation with nationalisation by a socialist state.

(3)   Implementation of the idea of worker self-management has an essential significance for progress in the process of socialisation, both directly – by democratising relations in the economy itself – and also indirectly by introducing elements of pluralism into the whole social and political system, including into the system of personnel selection. Yet decentralisation of the system of functioning of the economy, which is a precondition for self-management, cannot go beyond certain limits defined by the economic and social rationality of central planning, by the growing need in the modern world for internalisation of external costs and benefits, by the requirements of maintaining the supremacy of the point of view of the 'system' as a whole over that of 'sub-systems'. Recognition of this line of reasoning as correct leads logically to acceptance of the thesis that socialisation does not invalidate nationalisation but includes it as a subordinate – necessary but not sufficient – feature.

(4)   It follows then from our whole analysis (and, which is worth emphasising particularly, from analysis of *both* models) that the problem of socialisation turns on the question of the democratic evolution of the state, of the political system. This is what determines, among other things, the preservation and enrichment of the effects of the 'first push' – the revolutionary social and economic change of the initial phase of socialism.

Notes

1   'Socialist ownership of the means of production involves both the use of the means of production in the interests of society as a whole and effective democratic participation by production and other workers in the management of the means of production'. *Pisma Ekonomiczne i*

Społeczne 1930–1960 (*Economic and Social Papers 1930–1960*), Warsaw, 1961, p. 135.

2 'On political economy and the relationship between economics and politics under socialism', in *Economics and Politics of Socialism*, London and Boston, 1973.

3 The well-known Czech economist Ota Šik has dealt with the problems of interest at a general, theoretical level in his book *Ekonomika, Zajmy, Politika* (*Economics, Interests, and Politics*), Prague, 1964.

4 See M. Kalecki, *Zarys teorii wzrostu gospodarki socjalistycznej* (*An Outline of the Theory of Growth of a Socialist Economy*), 2nd ed., Warsaw, 1968, ch. 8; English translation *An Introduction to the Theory of Growth in Socialism*, Oxford, 1969.

5 The term 'democratism' instead of simply 'democracy' is to emphasise that this is not only a matter of constitutional principles but also of the extent to which they are implemented in practice, of real 'democraticness'. Of course, we do not attach any fundamental importance to the distinction between these shades of meaning.

6 Similar terminology is widely used in Yugoslav theoretical literature, which has undoubtedly exerted a certain influence on the views of the author of this book. I wish, however, to point out that the terms etatist and self-management are not used here in precisely the same way as in the Yugoslav literature, and certainly do not lead to the same interpretation of the two types of socialism.

7 *Contemporary Economic Systems, A Comparative Analysis*, ed. J. B. Lippincott, Philadelphia-New York, 1964.

8 March 1919. See *WKP* (*b*) *w rezolucjach i uchwałach zjazdow, konferencji i plenarnych posiedzen komitetu Centralnego* (*Resolutions and Decrees of Congresses, Conferences and Plenary Sessions of the Central Committee of the RCP(b)*), Ukrainian ed., 1949, vol. 1, p. 291.

9 In particular, a passage from the article 'The immediate tasks of Soviet power' is well known and often cited in this context.

10 Lenin, *State and Revolution*; *Selected Works*, Moscow, 1936, vol. 4, p. 84.

11 See W. Brus, *The Market in a Socialist Economy*, London and Boston 1972, and also the summary in 'Die Entwicklung des sozialistischen Wirtschaftssystems in Polen' ('The development of the socialist economic system in Poland'), *Hamburger Jahrbuch für Wirtschafts- und Gesellschaftspolitik*, 1965.

12 'The Cooperatives'; *Selected Works*, Moscow, 1936, vol. 8, pp. 226–30.

13 Czesław Bobrowski, *Formation du système soviétique de Planification*, Paris, 1956, p. 83.

14 The legal side of this distinction is scrupulously preserved in the socialist countries, at any rate in Poland. But clearly we are concerned here not with the legal but the socio-economic aspect of the problem.

15 See p. 20.

16   Lenin, *State and Revolution*; *Selected Works*, Moscow, 1936, vol. 7, p. 82.

17   In the place of representative bodies stemming from elections, Lenin and Trotsky set up the Soviets as the only true representation of the working masses. But as the political life of the whole country is suppressed, the life of the Soviets too is bound to become more and more paralysed. Without universal elections, without unrestricted freedom of the press and of assembly, without free advocacy of views, the life of every public institution dies, becomes a sham life, and the bureaucracy remains the only active element. No one can succeed in avoiding this law. Public life is slowly being buried, a few dozen party leaders with inexhaustible energy and limitless idealism direct and manage, ultimately a dozen eminent heads among them are the leaders and the elite of the workers are called to an assembly every now and then to applaud the speeches of the leaders and to express unanimous agreement with the resolutions proposed. Basically then it is a clique system – a genuine dictatorship, though not the dictatorship of the proletariat but the dictatorship of a handful of politicians, i.e. dictatorship in the bourgeois sense, in the sense of the Jacobins. What is more, such relations are bound to favour a return to barbarism in public life: attempts at assassination, murder of hostages, etc. (Rosa Luxemburg, *Die Russische Revolution*, in *Politische Schriften*, Frankfurt am Main, 1968, vol. 3, p. 136).

18   'The Proletarian Revolution and the Renegade Kautsky', *Selected Works*, Moscow, 1936, vol. 4, pp. 113–217.

19   Op cit., p. 292.

20   The state enterprises will to a large extent be put on a commercial basis. In view of the urgent necessity of increasing the productivity of labour, of making every enterprise pay its way and make a profit, and in view of the inevitable rise of departmental jealousy and excessive departmental zeal, this circumstance will inevitably create a certain antagonism of interests in matters concerning conditions of labour between workers and the directors and managers of the state enterprises or the government departments in charge of them. Therefore, as regards the socialized enterprises it is undoubtedly the duty of the trade unions to protect the interests of the working people, to facilitate as far as possible the raising of their standards of living and constantly to correct blunders and excesses of the business organizations resulting from the bureaucratic distortions of the state apparatus. (Lenin, *The Role and Functions of the Trade Unions under the New Economic Policy*, *Selected Works* (*The Essentials of Lenin in Two Volumes*), London, 1947, vol. 2, p. 761.)

21   See Stalin's speech to economic managers, 'New conditions – new tasks in economic construction', *Works*, Moscow, 1955, vol. 13, pp. 53–82.

22   It must be pointed out, and not for the first time, that this does not
     mean that the forms are immaterial. A pseudo multi-party system
     can in certain circumstances facilitate the appearance of a real multi-
     party system, or at least elements thereof. But this already takes us
     beyond the etatist model.
23   See I. Deutscher, *The Unfinished Revolution*, London, 1969.
24   The concept of the party apparatus – and, by analogy, of the state or
     union apparatus – embraces both the professional functionaries who
     are secretaries or members of party executive bodies and also func-
     tionaries who are not members of formally elected bodies but
     are employed in so-called political positions. Thus, from the institu-
     tional aspect the party apparatus is the executive organs (bureaux,
     secretariats, executives) which are the *de facto* party authorities
     at the given level, plus the personnel subordinate to them (excluding
     technical personnel).
25   The description of certain forms of state socialism as 'totalitarian
     dictatorship' may arouse emotional objections – even though it
     should be obvious that this is not the same thing at all as equating
     the aims and historical role of these forms of state socialism with,
     for example, those of fascist-Hitlerian totalitarianism. These mis-
     understandings and objections could be avoided simply by using the
     term 'dictatorship', but in Marxist terminology this concept characterises
     not only and not so much the way in which power is exercised as the
     essence of the state. Hence the need for the term 'totalitarian dic-
     tatorship', understood *literally* as a state system in which *all* legal
     manifestations of political life are totally subordinated to the mono-
     polistic centre of power. The term '*extreme forms* of totalitarian
     dictatorship' refers basically to the two decades from the middle of
     the 1930s to the middle of the 1950s, that is, to the so-called period
     of the 'cult of personality'.
26   We shall base ourselves primarily on the *Programme of the League of
     Communists of Yugoslavia*, adopted at the congress in Ljubljana in
     1958 (the so-called Ljubljana programme), and, where specific features
     of the later phase of development are concerned, on the documents
     of the IX Congress of the League of Communists of Yugoslavia
     (March 1969). A useful survey of the evolution of views on, and the
     stages of change in, the economic system, within the general con-
     ception of the programme, is provided by Branko Horvat, 'Yugoslav
     economic policy in the post-war period: problems, ideas, institutional
     developments', in *American Economic Review*, vol. 61, no. 3, part 2,
     supplement, June 1971.
          This obviously does not mean that the characterisation of the self-
     management model in this book should be treated as a mere re-
     capitulation of the corresponding official documents. The attempt at
     a synthetic presentation which is made below contains the author's
     own interpretation, for which he alone bears full responsibility.
27   In Polish economic writings this particular feature has been especially
     strongly emphasised by Edward Lipiński – see *Teoria ekonomii i*

aktualne zagadnienia gospodarcze (*Economic Theory and Current Economic Problems*), Warsaw, 1961, essay on 'Alienation', p. 190 ff.

28   The undisputed leading role of the working class in state power, with the communist party at its head, that is, a specific form of dictatorship of the proletariat, and similarly the conscious and consistent orientation towards socialisation of the basic means of production, have given the new popular-democratic Yugoslavia a socialist character from the very beginning, despite strong survivals of the old social relations and the immaturity of the young socialist forms (*Program SKJ*, ed. Kultura, Belgrade, 1958, p. 103).

29   Ibid., p. 123.

30   Ibid.

31   Clearly the concept of the transition period in the conception of the self-management model is used in a different sense than in the conception of the etatist model. Here we are concerned with the transitional nature of the essence of socio-economic relations and thus with the transition from the embryonic form of social ownership (state or indirect social ownership) to mature social ownership *sensu stricto* (direct social ownership based on self-management). It may be worth pointing out that the category transitional is understood in a similar way by some Western Marxists (e.g. Paul Sweezy), who describe the East European socialist countries as 'in the transitional phase' (ownership of the means of production no longer private capitalist but not yet socialist); this position does not in the least go hand in hand with acceptance of the Yugoslav solution – on the contrary, many of them criticise it even more sharply than the solution which we have called the etatist one.

32   *Program SKJ*, op. cit., p. 112.

33   A terminological note: both in Yugoslavia and in other countries the term '[manual] workers' self-management' is used, which is not of course accidental. It is a question of emphasising the special role played by the actual transformation of the working class (manual workers) into the class owning the means of production. In some countries attempts have been made to give this expression in regulations guaranteeing manual workers the appropriate preponderance in self-management organs, which in certain conditions may be justified. But self-management of course embraces the whole labour force, and thus white-collar workers too, including engineering and technical personnel. In Yugoslavia, self-management also applies to institutions in which the labour force consists exclusively or almost exclusively of white-collar workers. Ultimately, the changes in the structure of employment which are already taking place, and will become more marked in the future, will make the qualifying adjective '[manual] workers' more and more anachronistic. There will always remain, however, the problem of the relation between the labour force and the management of the enterprise or section. In sum, the term 'worker self-management' seems an adequate description, though it is no part

of the author's intentions to employ this term (which we shall use below) to contrast '[all-] worker' with '[manual] workers', nor to diminish the continuing importance of the question of assuring manual workers an appropriate role in the management system.

34   The distinction between worker self-management (French – *auto-gestion*) and *participation* by the labour force in management is relatively easy in theory: self-management means that the highest authority rests with the labour force, which, in some form or other, decides, among other things, the appointment of managers; participation in management means that the labour force becomes one of the members of the managing bodies, and the extent of authority enjoyed by the particular members differs in different systems. In both cases the labour force acts mainly through its representatives.

      The theoretical distinction does not always fit with the names used in practice. For example, in Poland since 1956 the term 'workers' self-management' has been used although the authority of the labour force only reached the level of participation in management in certain periods of social pressure. In Yugoslavia it is emphasised most heavily that it is a question of actual *self-management* and the creation of conditions such that real relations correspond to the description used.

35   J. Galbraith, *The New Industrial State*, Harmondsworth, 1968.

36   See W. Brus, *The Market in a Socialist Economy*, op. cit., pp. 3–4, 155–6.

37   D. Granick draws attention to this in 'Some organisational problems in decentralised planning', *Coexistence*, no. 5, 1966.

38   From this point of view the resolutions of the IX Congress of the SKJ in March 1969 deserve special attention, particularly 'The socialist development of Yugoslavia on the principles of self-management and the tasks of the SKJ' and 'The ideological and political foundations of the further development of the SKJ'.

39   See B. Horvat, op. cit., pp. 99–102.

40   See Jovan Djordjevic, 'A contribution to the theory of social property', *Yugoslav Thought and Practice*, no. 24, 1966.

41   See W. Brus, *The Market in a Socialist Economy*, op. cit., chs 3, 5; and also 'Die Entwicklung des sozialistischen Wirtschaftssystems in Polen. Bemerkungen zu einigen allgemeinen Problemen' ('The development of the socialist economic system in Poland. Remarks on some general problems'), *Hamburger Jahrbuch für Wirtschafts- und Gesellschaftspolitik*, 10, 1965. From now on the term 'decentralised model' will be used in the narrowly defined sense as one of the types of functioning of a socialist economy. To avoid misunderstanding we must point out that the concepts 'decentralised model' and 'centralistic model', or 'free market mechanism' relate to a narrower sphere of problems (the system of functioning of the economy only) than the concepts 'etatist model' and 'self-management model' which conceptually embrace the whole of production relations.

42   *Program SKJ*, op. cit., p. 149.

43   Resolution of the IX Congress of the SKJ, 'Socialist development in

Yugoslavia on the basis of self-management and the tasks of the
League of Communists', March 1969, I, 5, translated in *Socialist
Thought and Practice*, Belgrade, no. 33, January–March, 1969, p. 48.
44 See among others the papers and discussions at the scientific conference devoted to the centenary of *Capital, vol. I, Treci naučni skup
Marks i savremenost* (Third scientific congress on Marx and contemporary society), subject group III, 'Socijalizem i robna privreda'
('Socialism and commodity production'); papers in vol. 4, discussion
in vol. 5, Belgrade, 1967.
45 See O. Lange, *Ekonomia polityczna*, I, 3, Warsaw, 1963, p. 200 ff.
46 The operation of the market mechanism in the conditions described
is frequently conceived in Marxist economic literature in terms of the
operation of the law of value. See, among others, W. Brus, *The Market
in the Socialist Economy*, op. cit., ch. 4, in particular the distinction
between the current and the perspective aspects of the operation of
the law of value.
47 See B. Horvat, op. cit., p. 113.
48 The interpretation of the principle of distribution according to work
in the Yugoslav literature puts a strong emphasis on the necessity of
taking account of *the results* of work (remuneration according to
results, not inputs of work) and in turn only those results which have
gained social acceptance are considered; the most universal and
objective test of social acceptance is that of the market.
49 The problem of international economic relations occupies an important place in the system of functioning of the economy in the
self-management model. Our reference to the anti-monopoly role of
imports touches only one of many aspects of the problem, with which
we shall not deal here in view of the limited aims of our analysis.
50 According to Yugoslav legislation:
　a new enterprise may be founded by an already existing
　enterprise, by a government agency or by a group of citizens.
　The founder appoints the director and finances the construction.
　Once completed, the enterprise is handed over to the work
　collective which elects management bodies. As long as all
　obligations are met, neither the founder nor the government have
　any say about the operations of the enterprise. Enterprises are
　also to merge or to break in parts. If a work unit wants to leave
　the mother enterprise, and the central workers' council opposes
　that, a mixed arbitration board composed of representatives of
　the enterprise and of the communal authorities is set up. In all
　those cases it is, of course, implied that mutual financial
　obligations will be settled. (B. Horvat, op. cit., p. 104.)
51 *Program SKJ*, op. cit., pp. 125, 141.
52 Ibid., p. 128. In this context it is worth quoting the view of Oskar
Lange (*Economic and Social Papers 1930–1960*, op. cit., p. 136),
which in a certain sense is similar:
　The gradual reduction of political direction of economic

processes is the essential expression of maturing of a socialist society. The further socialist society is removed from its capitalist heritage, and from the heritage of the transition period, in which non-economic pressure plays the decisive role, the greater the extent to which the direction of economic processes is separated from the exercise of political power. This process prepares the way for the eventual 'withering of the state'.

Lange also refers here to Engels' and Lenin's formulation of the distinction between 'government of people' and 'management of things and direction of the processes of production'.

53 *Program SKJ*, op. cit., pp. 128 and 125.
54 This conclusion tallies in general outline with those of B. Ward, 'Political power and economic change in Yugoslavia', *American Economic Review*, May 1968, who makes the only attempt known to this writer to investigate the direct interrelationships between the Yugoslavian solution of the principles of functioning of the economy and the political system.
55 See 'Economic calculus and political decisions', in W. Brus, *Economics and Politics of Socialism*, op. cit.
56 See B. Ward, 'The firm in Illyria', *American Economic Review*, September 1958, and *The Socialist Economy. A Study of Organisational Alternatives*, New York, 1967; also E. Domar, 'The Soviet collective farm as a producer cooperative', *American Economic Review*, September 1966, and the comment by Joan Robinson in *American Economic Review*, March 1967. See also W. Brus, 'Zuročeni a bod rivnovahy porniku' (Interest rates and the equilibrium point of the enterprise), *Politička Ekonomie*, no. 10, 1968 (Prague), and Radmila Stojanović, *Veliki Ekonomski Sistemi (Large Economic Systems)*, Belgrade, 1970, ch. 3, section 5. The arguments of Ward and Domar are fundamentally opposed by Jaroslav Vanek, 'Decentralisation under workers' management', *American Economic Review*, December 1969.
57 These symptoms have become, among other things, the basis of a broad critique of Yugoslav theory and practice – both from spokesmen of the official doctrine in the USSR and the people(s)' democracies, and from numerous centres of the so-called New Left. The Yugoslav solution has been particularly sharply opposed by the group around *Monthly Review* (Paul Sweezy, the late Paul Baran and Leo Huberman). In *Monthly Review*, March 1964, an article appeared on Yugoslavia with the characteristic title 'Transition from socialism to capitalism?', vigorously attacking the use of the market mechanism and concluding with the dramatic appeal, 'Beware of the market – it is the secret weapon of capitalism!' Here is not the place to set out in a more exhaustive manner our attitude to the views of the extreme left on this problem, but let us draw attention to two interesting features: (1) vigorous criticism of market-type relations between enterprises frequently goes hand in hand with passionate support of worker self-management which, from the economic point of view is,

to say the least, inconsistent; (2) justified criticism of a tendency to *unlimited* use of the market mechanism and of *abuse* of the idea of linking material incentives with financial results (especially when capital investment and the possibility of taking advantage of a monopoly position are involved) extends to *all* forms of use of the market mechanism, including regulated, and *all* forms of material incentives linked with financial results. The author of the present book has tried to demonstrate the necessity of distinguishing between the justified use of commodity-money forms within defined limits and the hypertrophy of treating socialism simply as a commodity economy (see 'Commodity fetishism and socialism', in W. Brus, *Economics and Politics of Socialism*, op. cit. It must also be pointed out that the later exchange of letters between Paul Sweezy and Charles Bettelheim (*Monthly Review*, no. 7, December 1970) seems to indicate a certain moderation of their position.

58 See Velimir Rajković, 'An appraisal of the implementation of the economic reform and current problems', *Eastern European Economics*, Summer 1970, vol. 8, no. 4, translated from *Ekonomist*, no. 4, 1969 (Zagreb).

3

Changes in the post-Stalin period

This chapter has to answer the question whether the changes in the post-Stalin period provide any basis for modifying our evaluation of production relations in the USSR and the peoples' democracies from the point of view of the criterion of socialisation *sensu stricto*. In our analysis we shall make use of the conclusions formulated towards the end of the preceding chapter, and thus examine the alterations both in the political system and in the system of functioning of the economy, particularly from the angle of the conditions for development of worker self-management; an esssential part of this must be to project these problems against the background of the changes in the degree of satisfaction of the material needs of the population and in the social distribution of income.

In the nature of things chapter 3 is bound to contain somewhat more historical material. Nevertheless the author's intention remains to sketch a synthetic picture based on the general course of real processes. Because we are dealing with processes which do not in the main lend themselves to presentation in quantitative statistical form, Polish experience, which is most directly known to the author, occupies a special position as the basis for generalisation.

Analysis of the evolution in the post-Stalin period covers, roughly, a period of fifteen years – from the middle of the 1950s to the end of the 1960s. For Poland this interval virtually coincides with the Gomułka period: from the turning point of October 1956 (together with the 'prolegomena' of the few preceding years) to the events of December 1970.

1 The starting point

We tried to exclude from our characterisation of the etatist model the extreme forms of Stalinism in its second phase – from the Great Purge to the death of Stalin. It seems to me that this makes it easier to evaluate the evolution of the etatist model in the post-Stalin period. But in order to present this evolution itself, to show what it comprised, we must relate the changes to the starting point, that is, to the political, social and economic situation of 1953 (or of neighbouring years in the absence of information relating precisely to that year). We try below to describe briefly the factual situation in 1953 and then to weigh up certain interrelationships between the phenomena recorded.

The first phenomenon to be noted is *the rapid growth of productive potential*. The general volume of production in all the socialist countries in 1953 significantly exceeded the post-war level. Differences in the rate of growth appeared between individual countries, but the average rate compared well on the international scale (the average annual growth rate of national income for the Comecon countries in 1951–5 was around 11 per cent; it is true that some scholars point to the lesser credibility of official statistical data for this period than for later ones, but it is hard to accept that any likely corrections could change their order of magnitude). There was a major growth in the stock of productive capital and a change in its structure in favour of industry. The rapid growth of investment meant that a further substantial increase in productive capacity could be expected in the future. It can be said that above all doubt the post-war period introduced an essential new feature into the question of the link between changes in system and acceleration of economic growth, since it showed that certain phenomena are repeatable at different periods and in different countries. Nationalisation of the basic means of production, and concentration of decisions on the level of accumulation and the use of the accumulated resources in the hands of the state proved itself an effective instrument for accelerated industrialisation not only in the USSR but in the peoples' democracies too.

Rapid industrialisation was associated with a clear *imbalance* in the development of the capacity and actual output in particular fields. Within industry there was a decisive preponderance of growth of the so-called group A over group B, which approximately reflected the rapid development of output of means of production compared with consumer goods; it is interesting that as a rule this preponderance was more strongly marked in the actual course of events than in plans. Despite this the imbalance within industry was many times less than the enormous differential between industry and agriculture. The catastrophic situation of Soviet agriculture is difficult to illustrate with official statistics, since they were later conclusively repudiated; it can be stated with complete certainty that agricultural production in the USSR at the time of Stalin's death was significantly lower than in 1913 and, what is most important, there was no prospect of improvement in the conditions of continual intensification of all those factors which we mentioned when discussing the problem of etatisation of cooperatives (see chapter 2, section 2). In the peoples' democracies the current situation in agriculture was better than in the USSR, since individual agriculture was still predominant almost everywhere, but it was only relatively favourable and was not just insufficient for requirements but deteriorating from day to day: the screw of accumulation, enhanced by a conscious policy of economic pressure with the aim of inducing the peasants to join the collectives, was crushing agriculture with a burden which was harder and harder to reconcile with the minimum prerequisites of normal productive activity. This was the ultimate effect of the political and police pressure directed against the most economically active strata in the villages. Around 1955 some of the people's democracies (Bulgaria, Czechoslovakia) had already achieved a relatively high indicator of collectivisation.

Even ignoring the special situation in agriculture, *the efficiency of use* of productive potential was very low. This is not a matter of overall quantitative results, which have been mentioned already, but of the relation between results and outlays. The inadequate growth of labour productivity required continual compensation in the form of above-plan growth of employment; material intensity increased while the quality of products was unsatisfactory; the rigidity of the organisational and technological structure obstructed the adjustment of supply to suit the needs of customers, the enrichment of assortment, etc.; industry, although young in years, showed a deep-rooted conservatism and fear of innovation.[1] The industry of the socialist countries in this period contained certain features of a self-reproducing organism: it produced too much for production itself, too little final output, particularly as far as consumption in the narrow sense is concerned.

We shall refrain for the time being from pronouncing judgment on the connection between low efficiency and the system of functioning of the economy. We shall observe only that it was precisely in this period that *centralisation* reached its peak intensity. The actual role of the elements of economic calculation (exaggerated by some students of the Soviet economy on the basis of the situation at the end of the 1930s[2]) was practically reduced to zero, and obligatory output-levels, cost limits, physical control of sales and supply, etc., became virtually the sole instruments of planning and management.

The standard of living of the population at the close of the Stalin period was at a very low level, so the year 1953 became a kind of nadir from this point of view. In this field it is difficult to operate with synthetic indices describing the situation in the various countries at one stroke. For example, in the case of the Soviet Union we cannot speak of a fall in real wages at the beginning of the 1950s in comparison with the end of the period of post-war reconstruction; there was such a fall on the other hand in a number of the peoples' democracies, in particular in Poland (according to official data the index of real wages per non-agricultural employee amounted to 94 in 1953, with a base of 100 in 1950). The level of real wages in the USSR was nevertheless extremely low and according to detailed Western research[3] reached in 1952 barely 66–88 per cent (depending on the prices used in the calculation) of the 1928 level. There were also variations in the income differentials between town and country (in the USSR the difference was considerably greater, to the disadvantage of the countryside).

The index of average real wages for a large aggregate is never a sufficient measure of the standard of living of the population. This applies all the more to the conditions of the Soviet Union and the peoples' democracies in the period under discussion. The point is not so much the slender volume of stocks of more durable consumption goods and savings (which means that the whole burden of supporting a family rests on current income) but, above all, the limited and at times even barely perceptible relationship between the system of prices used in the indices and the real market situ-

H

ation. In conditions of permanent market shortages the opportunities to buy commodities at the prices fixed were limited, sometimes simply non-existent; this opened up the possibility of one of the most curious types of political and economic fiction, namely price reductions in the absence of the corresponding commodities, particularly in districts far from the metropolis. Of course no index included the conditions of life of the people whom we could call 'citizens of Gulag Archipelago' – the inmates of the prisons and the concentration camps; if not for the whole of Eastern Europe, then at least for the Soviet Union, where the number of prisoners at this period was probably in the range of 8–10 millions, this is an aspect which cannot be overlooked in describing the standard of living of the population.

On the other hand, observations of this kind should not cause us to lose sight of the influence of the transformations in social and economic structure, especially if we take the pre-revolutionary situation as our point of reference (1913 for the Soviet Union, 1937–8 for the peoples' democracies). The elimination of open and concealed unemployment and the pauperism of those employed in cottage industry or domestic service, the growth of non-agricultural employment and mass migration from country to town as a result of industrialisation, social and professional advancement and the associated transfer to a higher-paid group, the broader range of services from the social consumption fund, etc. – all this makes general indices of consumption per inhabitant or real income per employee, taking account of the elimination of unemployment and analogous factors and of services from the social consumption fund (this type of index is still the only one published in Soviet statistical yearbooks), higher than the base level even at times which were definitely unfavourable from the point of view of the standard of living. We are not aware of any special calculations of this type for 1953 exactly, but by interpolating or extrapolating from data for other periods it is not hard to reach the conclusion that – in spite of everything – even for 1953 one can find indices which show growth in the standard of living of the population of the USSR in comparison with 1913 or of that of Poland in comparison with 1937–8.[4] These indices express certain historical phenomena, but they have very limited social significance, since they obliterate the relationship between income and work done; they refer to the initial conditions, which came to be felt as anachronistic, particularly against the background of the growth in productive potential and general progress on a world scale. Of course, the time interval plays a part here – comparison with the pre-war situation in the peoples' democracies in 1953 certainly made more sense than the analogous comparison for the Soviet Union with 1913. But in both cases this could not obscure the extremely hard material position at the time which for the majority of employees was summed up by a level of pay which did not provide the social minimum cost of living.

Slightly similar problems face us if we want to describe the situation in the field of *the social distribution of income* at the close of the Stalin period. The general background is one of greater equality than under capitalism, both in comparisons over time (pre-revolutionary capitalism in the present socialist countries) and in comparisons at the same time (contemporary capitalism of the Western type, particularly if we take into account not only the social structure of the distribution of personal incomes, but also of wealth in the field of consumption). We have spoken many times of the social and economic factors making for greater equality, so there is no need to enumerate them yet again. As for illustrations, let us in addition note only the far-reaching equalisation of average incomes of manual and white-collar workers.[5]

Against this general background differentiation of pay does appear and – because of differing family situations and so on – it influences differentiation of material positions and thus brings a tendency to stratification. This is a very complicated process which requires a completely separate evaluation. For this book the essential point is that during the whole of the Stalin period, and particularly in its last phase, stratification of incomes according to political criteria was gathering strength and was closely connected with the levels in the hierarchical party-state apparatus (see chapter 2, section 2). The special privileges of the functionaries of this apparatus meant, among other things, that the social consumption fund, which is often treated as a natural instrument for counteracting the effects of excessive income differentials, became in reality a factor enhancing inequality; with incomparably easier access to the material services from this fund (the higher levels of education, the health service, housing privileges which were so valuable in that period, rest centres, etc.), the functionaries of the party-state apparatus enjoyed a share in them which considerably exceeded their numerical proportion. In addition it should be pointed out that –

despite widespread conviction to the contrary – the overall volume
of the social consumption fund in the last years of Stalin's life was
lower relative to pay and consumption than in the following years.[6]
Also typical of the 'anti-egalitarian' tendencies was the practice in
the USSR of charging tuition fees in the last three classes of general
secondary schools and in higher education,[7] although it was contrary to the constitutional principle of free education. This step
found no imitators in any of the peoples' democracies, which may
support the hypothesis that rulers' revolutionary feeling for equality
is a *sui generis* inverse function of the time that has elapsed since
the moment of gaining power. . . .

As far as *the political system* is concerned, as has already been
implied by previous odd remarks, at the close of the Stalin period it
was characterised by extreme features of totalitarianism, with the
individual dictator at the peak of a pyramid of power. In the Soviet
Union in the post-war period there was no longer any concern even
for certain forms which had previously been scrupulously observed
(e.g. the summoning of plenary sessions of the Central Committee
of the CPSU; from 1947 the CC did not meet once). It is clear from
many later testimonies that not only such organs as the parliament
or Central Committee, but also the closest circle of the oligarchy –
the Politburo – lost their direct statutorily guaranteed influence on
decisions. Unlimited power over affairs and people was in the hands
of Stalin, and the sub-dictatorial authorities at all lower levels, both
within the USSR and in the peoples' democracies, derived their
mandate from him.[8] Of course, this did not mean, and could not
mean, total exclusion of the influence of a certain category of
associates on the dictator's decisions – through the medium of the
supply and control of information. The general factors of increasing
isolation of the centre of power from real social processes and the
specific factor of the unleashing of a new wave of mass terror in the
post-war years lead to the security organs gaining a virtually monopolistic position in the system of supply and control of information
and thus in influence over political decisions. The transformation of
'workers' and peasants' power' into a police state reached the
highest point yet known.

One after another waves of terror struck Soviet society: the mass
arrest of people returning from Hitler's prisoner-of-war camps and
forced labour; the 'combing through' the officer corps of the army –
victorious, but contaminated by contact with the Western world; the

phantoms of the Decembrists; the 'Leningrad affair' – the crushing of that stratum of the party apparatus (and the intellectuals connected with it) which by its conduct in the hardest days of the war had gained authentic social authority and was to some degree able to shine in its own, not just in reflected, light; the deportation of whole nations, summarily accused of collaboration with the Nazis, and also a considerable portion of other nations, who formally enjoyed sovereign rights on the territory of union or autonomous republics but were regarded collectively as politically unreliable (primarily the Baltic countries); the continuous action against non-informers, alleged wreckers and saboteurs in all fields of life, an action gathering in strength with the prolonged hardships and failures – to its apogee in the form following the Tsarist tradition, of accusations of ritual murder, (the Jewish 'doctors' plot', whose protagonists without doubt escaped a show trial only as a result of Stalin's death).[9]

In the peoples' democracies the quantitative extent of the oppression was less, as we said, but the political and moral effects were analogous; in comparison with the history of the Soviet Union from 1917 there was a characteristic 'compression ' in time here, the various waves of terror were laid on top of each other: against people and whole circles actively or only historically connected with bourgeois and social-democratic political movements, against those who had worked in the pre-revolutionary state and economic apparatus, against the richest strata of the peasantry, and finally – almost simultaneously – against some Communist activists, including many prominent party leaders, who were condemned in show trials on the pattern of the Moscow trials of the 1930s.

The extreme form of the 'cult of personality' and mass terror were accompanied by an ideology of apologia for the existing situation, completely ignoring reality, which was connected with the whipping up of an atmosphere of external and internal threat (the theory of the intensification of the class struggle with the progress of socialism). Intellectual life was still more ruthlessly constricted than in the USSR before the war. This applied particularly to science, and not just the social sciences, which, after a short-lived 'breathing-space' during the war (which is little known in the world outside), were put in order by Zhdanov with redoubled brutality, but also to the natural and technical sciences, which now had to renounce 'formal genetics', criticise the theory of relativity, and curse cybernetics as a pseudo-science in the service of imperialism. This renunciation of the opportunities stemming from the real achievements of science, technology and organisation in favour of feverish dreams of a 'secret weapon' promised by charlatans like Lysenko and the creators of the 'Stalin plan for the transformation of nature', in a country groaning under the burden of its inability to satisfy the most elementary needs, was extremely symptomatic of the closing phase of 'the folly of the Caesars'.

Closely connected with the features of the situation in 1953 noted above is the furthest possible *isolation from abroad* – political, economic, scientific and technical, cultural, day-to-day. We shall not develop this theme, which involves among other things the international situation at the time and the objective sources of the 'cold war'. What is worth recalling, as it was unusually harmful from the economic point of view and was instrumental in this isolation, is the anti-cosmopolitan campaign and the attribution to Russians of the principal role in the progress of science and technology in the world. In the sphere of ideology this campaign was an additional spur to the strong increase in nationalistic tendencies.

What was the reason for this particular evolution of the etatist model in the last phase of the Stalin period? At the time – when Stalinism had reached its peak – there was no doubt about the answer. The reason was abundantly clear – it stemmed directly from the objective laws of history. The lagging production of consumer goods followed directly from the ineluctable law, according to which the growth of production of the means of production had to exceed the growth of production in consumer goods; the deflationary price increases in Poland in January 1953 were the result of the operation of the law of value,[10] and the use of force was a necessity defined by the law of intensification of the class struggle. In retrospect, it is hard to accept as chance that in the theoretical pronouncement which was to be the ideological signpost to the future, *Economic Problems of Socialism in the USSR*, Stalin put the objective character of economic laws in the foreground, emphasising the law of faster growth of production of the means of production, castigating the use under socialism of the obsolete distinction between necessary and surplus labour, and advancing the postulate of replacement of commodity exchange between the state and the kolkhozes by the so-called product exchange as the last step

towards – using our terminology – the etatisation of agricultural collectives.[11] Also these examples were consistent with the intention of
continuing the previous line in economic policy (this was confirmed
by the XIX Congress of the CPSU in 1952), and this even more categorical underpinning with the authority of laws, which were supposed to be independent of the will of the people under socialism,
too, gave these intentions the property of mystical perfection.[12]

The practice in the last phase of Stalinism of mystical justification
of the correctness of every action soon lapsed and today hardly
appears in the European socialist countries. One can, on the other
hand, still come across a way of thought which claims its own kind
of *rational justification*, pointing to circumstances alleged to have
caused a necessity to reach for methods and solutions inadequate to
later conditions. Various kinds of interrelationships stand out
prominently here – both purely economic and economico-political.
The first category includes, above all, the well-known thesis that
extreme centralism in planning and management followed inevitably from the extensive phase of development, from the need for a
drastic change in the structure of the economy and concentration on
narrow sectors, from the weakness of personnel at lower levels, etc.;
but these statements are not supported by evidence that in the conditions of the time the problem of the useful limits of centralisation
did not also exist, that uniform solutions were essential although the
relationship between extensive and intensive elements varied in
different countries; or that, even if widespread use of obligatory
output targets was necessary, a better indicator should not have
been sought than gross output, which leads to extravagance with
raw materials and divorces the evaluation of economic activity from
the benefits obtained by the user.

The same thing can be seen with the chain of thought which links
the economic aspects, particularly the standard of living, with political factors. In this formulation the necessity of screwing accumulation up to the maximum possible, and the priority of heavy industry, followed unconditionally from the external threat of aggressive
imperialist attack; if the inadequate development or efficiency of the
productive apparatus did not permit defence to be assured in the
normal way, then extraordinary means had to be resorted to – the
burden on agriculture, the sacrifice of current consumption, etc. The
imperialist threat and the need for effective safeguards is held to
have justified the extreme measures of internal coercion too, and

to have justified the risk of persecuting innocent people, particularly when economic necessities might have given rise to dissatisfaction, thus facilitating imperialist penetration. . . . From this point of view centralisation of economic decisions is presented in a positive light, and so even is the ideology, which, by every means – including the essentially religious cult of the omniscience and infallibility of the leader – was to assist in psychological preparation for the struggle.

This reasoning, too, can be countered by a long line of objections to particular links in it and, especially, to its initial premises, which were actually even subjected to public examination later, to a relatively insignificant extent. To arouse doubts about the basis for these premises it is sufficient even to recall to mind the differences between the pre-war and post-war position of the socialist world: the Soviet Union ceased to be an island in the sea of capitalism and found itself in a 'socialist environment', representing all together around a thousand million people and a substantial productive potential; the military strength of the USSR had been demonstrated in a convincing manner; considerable opportunities existed for influencing world opinion and getting effective political support in case of a real threat. All this should have justified relaxing the screw – in comparison with the end of the 1930s – rather than tightening it, as in fact happened.

It is not worth while, however, going into an analytical polemic against the defenders of the relations ruling in the countries with the etatist model at the close of the Stalin period. Both versions – the mystical-absolutist and the rational-relativist ('necessary in its time') – dissolved like a soap-bubble on contact with what followed almost immediately after Stalin's death, and with no change in any other elements apart from this one.

First, there was a drastic reversal of the trend in the standard of living and real wages. The estimates mentioned above of real wages in the USSR (outside agriculture) already showed an unprecedented increase by 1954; whereas for 1952 the index, taking 1928 as 100, was 66 or 88, for 1954 it was 82 or 113 respectively (an increase in the range of 25 per cent!).[13] In Poland, according to official data, the index of real wages, taking 1949 as 100, rose in the course of one year from 105·8 (for 1953) to 119·7 (for 1954), or about 13 per cent.[14]

Less than half a year after the execution of a severe deflationary move with the blessing of the law of value it proved possible and necessary in Poland to proceed to a new disposition of forces and resources – this time in favour of consumption. Similar phenomena, with greater or less intensity, appeared in other countries (Hungary). In addition, as distinct from the Stalin price reductions, which were spectacular in terms of propaganda but largely ineffective, the growth of real incomes was now accompanied by increased availability of commodities and the general supply situation, though still far from sufficient, to be sure, clearly improved. This was partly the result of concrete economic moves and partly simply the result of the change in climate for the consumption sphere. In housing, too, a change in the situation soon turned out to be possible (above all in the Soviet Union which, after decades of 'objective' impossibility, started a very intensive building programme). Even in the sphere of income distribution – usually the subject of rather long-term changes – a certain movement towards diminishing pay differentials was recorded.[15] And of course, the proportional division of national income between accumulation and consumption changed.

Second, a change in agricultural policy followed. In the Soviet Union (the September 1953 Plenum, and earlier still Malenkov's speeches) the noose strangling the kolkhozes, the private plots, the workers' auxiliary economy, began to be slackened. In Poland, at the threshold of 1954 (II Congress) the important decision was taken to stabilise compulsory deliveries, which played a role somewhat similar to the replacing of confiscation of surplus by a tax at the beginning of NEP: incentives arose to increase output. In Hungary, the first Imre Nagy government attempted to go further (disavowing basically the whole collectivisation programme) but was restrained.

Third, the 'doctors' plot' affair in the USSR, which had fortunately not been completed, broke up, and following it the gates of the prisons and concentration camps began to open, at first slowly, then more and more widely. The tempo of releases and rehabilitation varied (it was slowest in Czechoslovakia) but altogether in a short space of time millions of alleged enemies of the people, agents, spies and saboteurs emerged to freedom.

Fourth, the cold war proved capable of relief. This statement does not mean to ignore the complexity of the post-war international situation and the danger associated with the ideologically inflamed rivalry between the blocks. But we are concerned with the consequence of the undoubted fact that the reduction of tension in 1953 was – to put it as cautiously as possible – 'to some extent' or 'also' a result of change in the USSR's position, a change clearly correlated with the internal transformations produced by Stalin's death. In a short time the Korean war was ended, the state treaty with Austria was signed, the USSR established diplomatic relations with West Germany, etc. The most glaring forms of inequality in the relations between the USSR and the peoples' democracies also began to disappear.

We have confined ourselves to the most important matters, passing over many others, in particular controversial ones over which a struggle has flared up in the subsequent period. This applies among other things to the system of functioning of the economy, although it is worth noting that as early as 1954 a joint resolution of the CC CPSU, and the Council of Ministers of the USSR criticised 'excessive centralisation' of management.

There can only be one conclusion from all this: it was not objective necessities but a definite type of *policy* that was the source of the phenomena comprising the Stalinist deformation, or for those who prefer a stronger word, degeneration; a deformation or degeneration measured, in the author's view, not only or maybe not at all in relation to an abstract ideal of socialism but in relation to the general foundations of the etatist model.

If we accept the above conclusion, the process of evolution of the political system towards extreme forms of totalitarianism which we have described becomes completely coherent. The requirement for a continual increase in extreme forms of totalitarian – in Stalin's case personal – dictatorship itself demands consequently both greater and greater centralisation of decisions and the permanent intensification of terror, the function of which consists not only in control but also in the moral disintegration of society, which is probably the most effective means of subjugation. The psychosis of the growing threat – internal and external – becomes an ideological protection, and the remainder, together with the treatment of personal incomes as a residual magnitude, fits easily with the previously mentioned attempts at rationalisation of the last phase of Stalinism.

Thus the internal logic of the system led inexorably to more and more degenerate forms, spreading to all areas of life. The system cannot be said to have become frozen then; it was changing – but the changes consisted in continual rigidification, ossification of its specific elements, and in growing inability to adapt to the needs of development. If we are looking for a classic example of intensification of the conflict between the relations of production and productive forces and at the same time an example of how much the relations of production under socialism are defined by the ruling political system, the close of the Stalin period is perfectly suited to this purpose. The economic decisions concentrated at the summit corresponded less and less to real needs, even from the point of view of the centre's priorities, not only because of the technical impossibility of controlling and processing the information flows, but above all because the political system caused distortion of information, which was intended not to reflect reality but to create a picture which pleased the dictator; for the same reasons all corrective mechanisms were to a greater and greater extent eliminated. The selection of personnel according to political police criteria of the lowest level led to a catastrophic decline in the quality of management at all levels and, in combination with the increasing bureaucratisation, to complete paralysis of initiative, which was disabled by the lack of any feeling of stability and by fear of responsibility; the mass terror thus brought not only enormous direct losses in the form of physical annihilation of people and the driving of millions (including many people with the highest qualifications) to the depths of camp labour, but also incalculable indirect losses.

The possibility of making use of the technological and organisational experience of more highly developed countries was cut off; the growing isolation went hand in hand with mechanical imposition of Soviet patterns on the peoples' democracies, which – especially in the most developed among them – caused additional complications and waste. On top of all this there was the general interrelationship between the level of consumption and labour productivity: as the end of the war receded further into the past, the more strongly the negative influence of the low standard of living on labour productivity became apparent.

It follows from this that the transformations which were initiated immediately after Stalin's death were economically determined, something which can easily be formulated in terms of the dialectics of productive forces and relations of production. Of course Stalin need not have died in 1953 and the system ruling in the USSR and the peoples' democracies would certainly not have broken up automatically under the influence of growing economic difficulties, even if it had lasted a few years or a decade and more longer. But in retrospect there can be no doubt that the intensifying conflict between the system and economic requirements would have demanded interim control with the help of more and more drastic police measures, but which in the long term could not have prevented the break-up.

It must also be remembered that the processes we have described took place in the socialist countries with the etatist model in very different external conditions from before the war, when capitalism was experiencing the greatest economic crisis in history and its after-effects. After the Second World War the developed capitalist countries – using the instrument of state intervention – succeeded in pushing their economies on to a path of rapid and relatively steady growth, combined with large social and financial gains for the working classes. As early as the first half of the 1950s it became clear that this was not a short-term phenomenon of the post-war market situation and that there was no real basis for expecting an imminent outbreak of a depression analogous to 1929. This had a variety of ideological consequences: the fall in attraction of the socialist countries' high quantitative growth indices, the growing significance – on both sides of the Iron Curtain – of comparison of the living conditions of the working masses, which was bound to have a worse and worse propaganda effect for the socialist side, both externally and – despite the isolation – internally; against the different social and economic background political relations, cultural life, etc. began to be evaluated differently. But the problem was not confined to ideological consequences: the whole future of the competition between the two systems, including its military aspect, became involved.

Here we come to the question of the social forces interested in executing change. With reference to our discussion on the subject of the clarity of the notion of social interest (see chapter 2, section 1) the situation in 1953 must be counted among those where the choice of direction for action, from the point of view of the social interest, presented no difficulty; for the vast majority of society the abandonment of Stalinism was in the highest degree desirable. What, however, is particularly important for analysis of the transformations in the post-Stalin period is the fact that the predominant part of the party and state apparatus, and above all its top levels, must also have been interested in changing the previous situation. If we take

for example the members of the Politburo or the CPSU functionaries of similar rank, they too must indeed have had a distorted
picture of reality, but despite everything they were better informed
than Stalin and at the same time, as they were looking from a higher
point, they grasped better than the lower levels the overall consequences that were threatening if the system were left in undisturbed
form. This thesis is supported by, first, the few supposed attempts to
bring in changes while Stalin was still alive;[16] second – and probably more convincing – the fact that immediately after the leader's
death at least three claimants to supreme power, Beria, Khruschev
and Malenkov, came out or tried to come out with a similar programme, and the struggle between them was not so much about the
content of changes as about who would have the chance to introduce them and use them as a trump card for himself.

There were at least three groups of reasons why at the starting
point of the new period interests of the 'establishment' in certain
sectors coincided – despite strong sympathies for the past – with the
social interest. First, there was justified concern about the fate of the
state and the whole block, with which the position of the apparatus
was connected in an obvious way; the intention of this statement is
not to exclude idealistic motivations *a priori* but simply to observe
that other motives did not come into conflict with self-interest.
Second, was the understandable striving to eliminate the state of
permanent threat to which every functionary – including, and
perhaps above all, those at a high level – was exposed in the system
of unlimited personal dictatorship and mass terror; precisely from
this point of view the revelation of Stalin's practices by Khrushchev
at the XX Congress met the objective interests of the apparatus –
despite the high political price which had to be paid. Third, the
exigencies of the competitive struggle for power. The death of
Stalin ended the period of special 'unity of the party' – in monolithic
and unlimited subordination to the will of the dictator; true, this
had not eliminated struggles between cliques – on the contrary even
– but they had been about winning favour 'above', not about influence 'below', which could even prove dangerous. Now the situation
underwent a change: leaders and candidates for leadership lost their
halo of divine anointment and instead became at least to a certain
degree dependent on support – primarily, obviously, from the various links in the party and state apparatus (principally the apparatus
of direct coercion) but in a round-about way from social opinion

too, mainly of the working class, whose hitherto purely liturgical hegemony began to acquire some significance in the new conditions, particularly when it took the form of open or potential pressure. This peculiar and pale form of pluralism, which did not completely vanish even in periods when one group was predominant (the feeling of immutability of the system never returned after Stalin), began to restore a certain importance to personal popularity, ability to influence the people and thus, in the ultimate reckoning, to coming out against real social needs as well.

At the same time, a short period of time after the death of Stalin was sufficient for the realisation of how limited was the sector in which – we shall formulate it generally and in the negative in order to avoid abuse of the concept of social interest and thus *a priori* pigeonholing – sharp socio-political conflicts in connection with the changes taking place could be avoided. It is hard to say anything certain about symptoms of such conflicts in the Soviet Union (strikes or riots in camps); beyond the borders of the Soviet Union, on the other hand, there followed outbursts whose message was unequivocal: Berlin in June 1953, Poznan in June 1956 and the whole complex of events called the 'Polish October', and finally the Hungarian uprising. These outbursts, in which the main physical force was the workers but a significant part of the party intelligentsia was an ideological one, had – apart from their direct long-term influence on the future course of events – the additional significance of bringing out into the open the main dilemma of the whole of the subsequent period: is it only a question of rejecting the Stalinist deformation while preserving the basic framework of, in particular, the political system; or must evolution involve going beyond the framework of, in our terminology, the etatist model? We shall not be running ahead if we state the sociologically obvious fact that the party and state apparatus – regrouped, indeed, but originating from the previous period and deriving the legitimacy of its position from it – took its stand on the first of the two alternatives: it was for replacement of the absolute petrification of the system by relative, dynamic petrification which permitted adaptation – but without violation of the basic foundations.[17] The struggles and disputes at the peaks of the party hierarchies in the post-Stalin period, both in the USSR and in the peoples' democracies, proceed to a considerable extent around the question of the effectiveness and expediency of different variants of strategy and tactics from the point of view of the simultaneous fulfilment of the two postulates, both broadly in the interests of the power élite, petrification and adaptation. These internal conflicts are on top of the deeper conflict over the second alternative – that of going beyond the framework of the etatist model. Together they make up the complex background without which we cannot make sense of the evolution in the fifteen years after Stalin's death, in particular of the characteristic 'stop-go' movements, the slowness, the zigzags and apparent inconsistencies in policy changes and institutional reforms.

2 Changes in social and economic policy

In accordance with the intention declared in the introduction to this chapter, our analysis of the changes in the political system, broadly understood, in the post-Stalin period is preceded by a sketch of developments in the degree of satisfaction of the population's material requirements, taking into account – as far as possible – shifts in the patterns of income distribution. Our discussion of changes in social and economic policy is limited mainly to this aspect.

One of the principal postulates derived from the critique of the Stalin period consisted in the demand that the sphere of satisfaction of the requirements of the population – consumption – cease to be the *residual* in the division of resources between competing aims. This applied to the plan construction stage, in which consumption was treated in principle as a resulting magnitude, determined after resources have been allocated for other aims higher up on the scale of preferences. It also applied to the plan implementation stage, in the sense that consumption must cease to fulfil the role of an automatic shock absorber for all deflections. An example of this kind of postulated change in approach to the consumption requirements of the population in the post-Stalin period – which was implemented – is provided by Soviet grain policy: in Stalin's time the USSR more than once experienced tremendous difficulties with food supplies, but even in years of severe harvest failure did not import grain but on the contrary – for political reasons – maintained net exports; in later years, on the other hand, they did not shrink from resorting to imports when the level of consumption was threatened (a particularly striking case is the agricultural year 1963–4).

Reality in the post-Stalin period, however, has only partially corresponded to these postulates, and that more in the first phase than subsequently. Consumption has not taken the place of heavy industry or the complex of military-political requirements. Its move to a higher point on the scale of preferences of the central plan has been achieved against opposition and in a zigzag manner. What is particularly interesting is the correlation between progress in this field and direct or indirect pressure of a political type. The relationships which we observed at the starting point of the post-Stalin period appeared later, too, as is shown, for example, by the exceptionally high growth of consumption in all the peoples' democracies in 1956–8, the sharp improvement in the USSR in 1965 (after the fall of Khrushchev) and, finally, the significant change in Poland after the bloody events on the Baltic coast in December 1970 and the subsequent strikes. Conversely, also, absence of pressure, or the conviction that no pressure will appear, as in Poland at the time the prices of foodstuffs were raised in December 1970, has had a negative influence on satisfaction of the population's requirements.[18] Finally, it deserves to be noted that in the post-Stalin period also the growth in the standard of living by way of growth of real wages (per employee) lagged behind the growth of incomes calculated per inhabitant, and not only in countries with large reserves of labour like Poland but also in Czechoslovakia and Hungary in the 1960s. This fact exerted a negative influence on the social feeling of what progress was being achieved.

It is easy to point to general reasons why the implementation of the postulated reversal of the Stalinist attitude to satisfaction of the population's requirements encountered objections and difficulties. Strengthening the position of consumption in the bargaining over the division of limited resources reduces the central planner's freedom to manoeuvre and increases the demands both on the rationality of strategic choices in the central plan and on the efficiency of operation at lower economic levels. If the fulfilment of these demands involves the necessity of making institutional changes which threaten the foundations of the political system in the etatist model, the mechanisms of petrification begin to operate. We do not in the least ignore the purely material difficulties in improving the living conditions of the population in the course of rapid economic development, but there seems no doubt that the conflict emphasised above has exerted an essential influence on the course of socio-economic processes in the socialist countries in the post-Stalin period.

Passing on to a brief characterisation of the specific phases of development from the point of view of the growth of incomes and the associated growth of consumption, it must be said that the tendency initiated virtually immediately after the death of Stalin was visibly strengthened in 1956 – at least in the peoples' democracies.[19] Two kinds of factors coincided at that time: on the one hand – strong political pressure, produced by the intensification of the de-Stalinisation process as a result of the XX Congress of the CPSU, by the events in Poland (Poznan and the later growth of mass movements up till the changes in the party leadership in October 1956) and, in particular, by the Hungarian uprising; on the other hand – the possibility of mobilising considerable reserves, which later proved to be predominantly of a short-term type. The abandonment of some of the obvious mistakes of the past by itself releases reserves. This applied in the first place to agriculture which, at the level of development of the majority of the socialist countries and with the existing structure of consumption, largely determined the standard of living. Despite the different concrete situation in individual countries the general direction of changes in this field was similar: increasing the profitability of agriculture as a branch of the economy and the incomes of the agricultural population by improving relative prices, rationalising liabilities (the system of obligatory deliveries, first of all) and substantially increasing investment outlays. In the Soviet Union a considerable part of the increase in outlays was absorbed initially by gigantic enterprises of an extensive nature (assimilation of virgin lands, maize); in the other countries it was associated more with intensification. Everywhere it was decided to increase the area of operating independence of state agricultural enterprises and producers' cooperatives (in the USSR an important reform was the abolition of the machine-tractor stations and the allowing of the kolkhozes to buy machinery). The inherited neglect was so great that even sub-optimal solutions brought spectacular results. The reduction of the burden suffocating agriculture seemed by itself to work wonders. In all the countries – perhaps to the smallest extent in Czechoslovakia – clear gains were achieved in comparison with the first half of the 1950s.

In Poland the changes in agricultural policy had a special significance since they took place in conditions where private farms were

I

predominant. This position was strengthened both by the fact of liquidation of 90 per cent of the producers' cooperatives previously created (they nevertheless embraced not more than 10–11 per cent of the total area) and by its indirect consequences: the necessity – at least for some time – to assure the individual peasant farms not only the preconditions of stabilisation but also of expanded reproduction. Because of this, economic conditions in the Polish village underwent a radical improvement in relation to the preceding years, although the so-called new agricultural policy of the PUPW never formally renounced the idea of socialisation of agricultural production, which became perceptible again in practice a certain time after 1956 (the privileged position of the state sector and the restrictions on private agriculture in the sphere of mechanisation, the taking over of uncultivated lands, etc.).

Besides the changes in agricultural policy (but not unconnected with them) a great reserve in the first phase of the post-Stalin period was provided by bringing into use productive capacity created predominantly with investment outlays undertaken in the preceding years. This was frequently capacity which should have come into operation sooner, so these were postponed effects – extremely costly overall, but currently requiring relatively minor additional outlays. In Poland and some of the other countries this circumstance was taken advantage of to make an appreciable reduction in the share of accumulation and an increase in the share of consumption in national income. Together with the partial conversion of the armaments industry this contributed to the improvement in the supply to the consumer market. The countries in which political tension was especially high (Hungary, Poland, East Germany) obtained important economic concessions from the Soviet Union (Poland, among other things, in the form of writing off of debts to the USSR, nominally in compensation for the previous excessively low prices paid for her coal exports); to some extent this must also have applied to others of the peoples' democracies. Poland's balance of payments was significantly improved as a result of American credits (totalling over half a milliard dollars in the course of five years) and thanks to the favourable position on the world market for coal. The pressure to create new jobs also declined since the numerically small age-groups born during the war were beginning to enter the labour force.

As a result of the operation of all these factors the peoples' democracies recorded very rapid growth in the incomes of the population in the years 1956–60, mainly in the form of growth of real wages. In 1960 the indices of real wages (1955 = 100) were as follows (to nearest whole number):[20] Bulgaria, 135; Czechoslovakia, 125; East Germany, 143; Hungary, 147; Poland, 129; Rumania, 148. With the exception of Bulgaria and East Germany these indices were considerably higher than for the previous five years, and for all the peoples' democracies (only the Soviet Union showed the opposite trend) much higher than for the following five years when the growth of real wages suffered a drastic setback.[21]

This setback can be very closely connected with the reversal of the direction in which the factors previously enumerated worked. The political pressure which had made the raising of incomes of the population a categorical 'imperative' weakened; stabilisation of the system ensued, in which certain forms underwent change but not the essence of the exercise of power, as before free of democratic social control and therefore able to impose its own preferences. At the same time came the exhaustion of the easily accessible reserves, which had probably anyway been too optimistically evaluated as permanent and capable of extrapolation in to the future.[22] Even before the end of the five-year period 1956–60 a change could be observed towards increasing the accumulation burden on national income. The plans for the period 1961–5 reflected the initiation of a new stage of major industrial investments, but attempted to combine acceleration of the tempo of expansion with further growth of wages. But when in the course of implementation it turned out that the low level of efficiency of the economy – especially in the area of labour productivity, the slow growth of which had again to be compensated by an overplan increase in employment – did not permit simultaneous achievement of both goals, the setback followed, in the first place for wages and social investments. At the same time the five-year period 1961–5 brought a weakening of the overall rate of growth of national income. With the exception of Rumania, this applied to all the peoples' democracies and the USSR. The setback was felt most severely in the most highly developed countries – Czechoslovakia and East Germany.

The hitherto similar course of development of the two successive phases of the post-Stalin period underwent a differentiation in the second half of the 1960s which no longer permits us to discuss all the countries together. A certain group (USSR, Bulgaria, East

Germany) – on the basis of various factors which we are not in a position to analyse here, and in particular with great differences in the level and structure of their economies – displays more favourable indices of growth of incomes of the population. Czechoslovakia, Poland and Hungary (up to 1967 inclusive) continued in principle the previous trend.

As far as Poland is concerned, without going into details, it must be pointed out that – apart from the chronic shortcomings of the system of functioning of the economy – a heavy responsibility for the results of the 1966–70 period rests on the mistaken policy of self-sufficiency in grain, which led to the restriction of meat production and a one-sided and excessively taut investment programme. Characteristic of the political system and its influence on socio-economic processes was not only the fact of arbitrary imposition of an economic strategy but also the manner in which the solution of the crisis that had arisen was attempted: by raising foodstuff prices, and at least a two-year wage freeze. The experience of Poland at the end of the 1960s proved once again that increasing the total volume of incomes of the population by means of the rapid growth of employment cannot be socially accepted as compensating for the slow growth of real wages.

Seen from the angle of realisation of the postulates of growth of consumption and its rise to the position of principal aim of the plan, the picture of the post-Stalin period is therefore clearly not uniform, and comparison of the first phase with the subsequent ones might lead us to conclude that there was a negative trend. Despite this, it seems to me a mistake to overlook or underrate the favourable differences when both periods as a whole are contrasted.

First, the influence of 'the turn to consumer incomes' of the second half of the 1950s is cumulative in the following years in the sense that the raised level serves as the next point of reference.

Second, the problems of consumption, the satisfaction of the population's requirements, have never again been pushed to such a position as in the Stalin period, when basically the only evidence of recognition of the political importance of the problem was the concealment of literally all data which could illustrate the true state of affairs. In this respect the post-Stalin period brought fundamental changes, which provides some measure of assurance against totally uncontrolled relapse. This applies both to wages and prices and to services from the social consumption fund, the role of which increased in the years 1956–70 in comparison with the previous period. The improvement in the housing situation should also be stressed, particularly for the Soviet Union, where intensive building permitted at least partial escape from simply catastrophic conditions.

Third, the growth of incomes – which as a whole undoubtedly took place, although it was insufficient in relation to possibilities and aspirations – created for a certain group of the population the possibility of saving, and thus of gradually building up a stock of consumer goods. This is a phenomenon with very interesting and manifold consequences. If the incomes of a family reach a level at which the possibility of a 'margin for accumulation' arises, further growth in its standard of living ceases to depend exclusively on income growth, and continues in the form of gradual build-up of a stock of durables – even with non-growing incomes (as long as they permit a surplus over the costs of satisfying narrowly current requirements to be maintained). The material form taken by increasing stocks of consumer goods varies – from a larger number of shirts up to 'status goods' such as cars and private houses, which can partly fulfil a capital function; but every form can in principle play a part in raising the standard of living (or the life style, as some economists call the magnitude which takes account of the wealth component too). The psychological consequences are twofold. On the one hand, even with unchanged incomes the level of 'what I own' can increase from period to period, which is measurable and palpable evidence of growing affluence; this raises the relative importance of the stabilisation factor. On the other hand, the accumulation of private consumer good stocks extends aspirations, among other things – and sometimes mainly – as a result of comparison with others. In the post-Stalin period this type of phenomena and the associated problems, including political ones, are intensifying.

Fourth, despite all the meanderings of agricultural policy, the post-Stalin period has brought a radical improvement in the position of the agricultural population, who constitute a considerable part of the total population. As regards Poland, whose experience in this area has a number of specific features, it is probably no exaggeration to say that not until after 1956 did the majority of private farmers begin to reap any fruits from the industrialisation of the country. Whilst previously such effects as social advancement and the movement of rural youth to non-agricultural occupations, migration to towns, etc., were offset by the stagnation and even decline of the incomes from peasant farms and the accompanying depreciation of their capital, in the new conditions the opposite phenomena appear more and more often: the continuous and rapidly growing demand for agricultural products increases profitability (especially of intensive cultivation of industrial crops, and of market-gardening and fruit-growing), and consequently often raises the value of agricultural productive capital, including land. In addition this also influences the position of emigrants from the villages who have rights to property, and also that of the so-called peasant-workers, for whom even a partially exploited small agricultural holding becomes a substantial source of income. These processes are taking place, despite the fact, which we underline yet again, that the situation in the Polish village is far from idyllic, and the unsolved problems of the direction of development and social and economic structure of agriculture are growing.

It still remains to examine the growth of incomes in the USSR and the peoples' democracies against the comparative background of the capitalist countries. This comparison does not in the least demonstrate the superiority of the socialist side in the 'competition of the two systems', particularly as far as indices of real wages are concerned. Data for the fourteen countries in table 242/303 of *Rocznik Statystiki Międzynarodowej* (published by the Polish Chief Statistical Office) for average real wages, excluding agriculture in 1967 (1960 = 100) are reproduced in Table 3.1.[23]

TABLE 3.1

Austria	143	Bulgaria	126
Belgium	143	Czechoslovakia	112
Denmark	134	Poland	114
France	126	Rumania	132
W. Germany	144	Hungary	116
USA	114	USSR	135
Great Britain	121		
Italy	137		

The data quoted demonstrate that the definite progress achieved in the socialist countries in the years after the sacrifices to industrialisation did not unfortunately amount to a seven-league jump on the world scale. This is in general confirmed by comparisons with

1955 too, though these can only be made for a few countries on the basis of the tables cited. The corresponding index of real wages for 1967, taking 1955 = 100, is shown in Table 3.2.

TABLE 3.2

Belgium	168	Bulgaria	173
France	142	Czechoslovakia	140
Great Britain	159	Poland	146

It follows from this that even the relatively favourable years did not reduce, or at best only reduced to a minimal degree, the disparity in the *level* of real wages between the socialist countries and the developed countries of Western Europe. The relative levels of real income per inhabitant would appear more favourable (because of the high growth of employment in the majority of socialist countries), but it is difficult to speak of radical changes in the proportions. One case studied in detail – the comparison made by the statistical offices of Poland and Austria of the level and structure of consumption in the two countries – gives rather the opposite picture, although it may be a little atypical: in 1964 average consumption per inhabitant in Austria was 80 per cent higher than in Poland. Taking into account that at the same time average consumption per inhabitant in Czechoslovakia was around 45 per cent higher than in Poland, the superiority of Austria in relation to Czechoslovakia would amount to near 25 per cent, which, if it shows anything, hardly shows diminution of the gap in comparison with the pre-war period.

Let us pass on to changes in the pattern of *income distribution*. This problem is exceedingly difficult to present quantitatively, particularly in the present state of special studies, and we shall examine it from one point of view only: the possibility of establishing a connection between the evolution of income distribution in the post-Stalin period and possible processes of stratification.

In New Left circles in the West one frequently encounters the opinion that the post-Stalin period increased income differentials and consequently brought about a deepening of vertical social stratification. Opinions of this kind are usually accompanied by contrasting the later phase of development, aimed at strengthening economic incentives, with the allegedly more egalitarian past.

Reality, however – in so far as it can be assessed on the basis of meagre and fragmentary data – does not support the thesis of increasing income differentiation in the post-Stalin period by comparison with the preceding period. As far as differentials in remuneration for work are concerned, the conclusion of the authors of the UN Economic Commission for Europe study already cited is rather the reverse.[24]

> The available statistical information suggests that there has been a general tendency for the spread of wage – and salary – earnings (measured by the inter-quartile deviation or the quartile ratio) to narrow over the period under consideration, particularly in the aftermath of the wage reforms initiated in the mid-1950s.

The differences on which the above rather cautious conclusion is based are very minor, and it is hard to attach very much weight to them. But at any rate they are a sufficient basis for the verdict that differentials did not increase. This is also the conclusion which follows from all the material relating to Poland which is known to this author: both the relative earnings of manual and white-collar workers and the proportions within each category remain relatively stable within particular sections of, or the whole of, the period in which we are interested.[25]

What is the size of these persistent differentials? It follows from the material in the article by W. Krencik, cited above, that if we consider all earnings in Polish industry in 1970, including the numerically small extreme groups (those earning least, who make up 1.3 per cent of the total, and those earning most) the range of differentiation for manual workers is 1:14; elimination of these extreme groups immediately reduces the range to 1:6, and restriction to 90 per cent of the total employed reduces it to 1:5. For white-collar workers the upper group is somewhat more, and the lower group somewhat less, numerous; but the general proportions remain basically similar. The range of differentiation of earnings is thus undoubtedly considerable, the more so if in addition we take into account differences between branches and regions.[26] But earnings differentials are only one of the factors influencing differences in the level of well-being of households (measured by incomes per head); these differences depend on many other factors as well (including the proportion of services enjoyed from the social consumption fund), and above all on the number of persons who have to be maintained by the earning members of the family. Family budget studies in Poland, and in other socialist countries, show that this last factor has the greatest significance; at the same time they also show that the gap between the highest and lowest income groups in the post-Stalin period was relatively stable (comparisons with the previous period cannot be made since in 1950–5 family budget studies were dropped). It follows from this that in extreme cases, when, at one pole, a large family has one person working and receiving low earnings and, at the other, a small family has highly-paid workers, we have very substantial differences in well-being. In such cases the equalising role of the social consumption fund should be specially pronounced. As we have pointed out, data relating to Poland (and also the USSR) show that the weight of the social consumption fund in the incomes of the population fell during 1950–5, and displays a gradual but systematic increase in the post-Stalin period.[27] A representative study carried out in Poland in 1964 showed that the gap between the highest and the lowest income group, which amounted to 1:6·97 on the basis of incomes from work per person, declined to 1:5·22 when services from the social consumption fund were taken into account.[28]

Despite the fact that the thesis of growing earnings disparity in the post-Stalin period is not justified, and the changes which would have to confirm it in fact display rather a weak tendency in the opposite direction, the problem of the effect of the pattern of incomes on the development and persistence of social divisions seems indeed more acute. This is the result, in our view, of the following reasons. First, the very fact of maintenance of income differentials over a longer period (leading to substantial differences in well-being) has stratifying effects, among other things through its influence on the starting conditions of the younger generation, which makes it a peculiar kind of inheritance. Second, with growth of the overall level of incomes, maintenance of the same differentials brings the upper layers more quickly and fully to the position where it becomes possible to build up a stock of durable consumer goods, which produces cumulative effects. Third, all these phenomena appear against the background of the natural evolution of the conditions of social and professional advancement, with the widespread dramatic jumping up the ladder which was characteristic earlier inevitably coming to an end in the later phases of development.

The connections between the structure of incomes and the processes of stratification are thus very complex and cannot be reduced to growing disparity in pay. Similarly, coagulation of social divisions cannot be counteracted just by the simple formula of equalisation of pay, but requires a comprehensive long-term policy capable of reconciling different and often mutually conflicting aspects. This is a typical example of the absence of obvious solutions which would reflect the social interest in a totally unambiguous manner.

In our general characterisation of the etatist model we stressed that a feature of it is the interrelation between material situation and position on the hierarchical ladder of the power apparatus. In this respect the post-Stalin period brought no fundamental modification, although the forms changed somewhat, and so, too, in some cases, did the relative weight of the advantages obtained. In the course of de-Stalinisation, the extent of conspicuous material privileges (the hated 'yellow curtains') was limited initially, the more radically the more strongly mass social pressure was voiced. Later a significant part of these privileges was restored, generally in a more discreet form. This is one of the factors which does in fact weaken the equalising role of the social consumption fund.

The really new features in the distribution of incomes, on the other hand, appeared when the post-Stalin period brought a certain revival of the private sector. We have mentioned the consequences of the change in agricultural policy in Poland, consequences which from the point of view of the pattern of income distribution extend far beyond the peasantry itself. To a lesser extent as far as the size of the social group is concerned but to a greater degree as regards income differentials, this also applies to the private sector outside agriculture (more precisely we should perhaps say the non-peasant private sector, since in Poland a part of the private capital not originating from agriculture is invested in very lucrative market-gardening or livestock-rearing enterprises). While avoiding hasty generalisations about the whole of the private sector, it can be stated without any doubt that a certain part of it attains very high incomes, completely incommensurable with the upper income groups in the state economy or administration (including high-level functionaries). This is to a considerable extent the result of the inflexibility of state and cooperative enterprises, which allows private capital to invest in fields which are generally highly and rapidly profitable – the more so when new – and which in the nature of things appear in a dynamic but 'supply-determined' economy. To this must be added the chronic inability to regulate the incomes of private initiative by fiscal policy, which – at least in Polish practice – lurches from one extreme to the other: either it is in fact passive and an ineffective instrument for regulating incomes, or it is unilaterally restrictive, with harmful effects on the general interest. At any rate, it is a fact that possession of financial resources, land, fixed assets, etc., in these circumstances can be an advantageous starting point for private accumulation and for climbing to a relatively high level on the social incomes ladder, or at any rate one which towers above the surroundings. This fact exerts a far from minor indirect influence on the life style and aspirations of a large part of the population.

This type of phenomenon occurs – though on a smaller scale – in the other countries too, and is associated not so much with the size of the private sector (e.g. in East Germany the non-agricultural private sector has long played a considerably greater role than in Poland) as with the inefficiency of state regulation and control.

Finally, we must not overlook the influence on the actual pattern of income distribution exerted by economic crime, which is favoured by the bureaucratisation of the economy and public life. As the unique studies of this subject carried out in Poland have shown, redistribution of incomes as a result of corruption in the course of time strengthens the processes of vertical stratification, since it leads to a distinctive concentration of criminal activity in organised groups, often connected with various links in the state apparatus.[29] Clearly, apart from its direct material effects, this phenomenon produces enormous moral damage.

To sum up, positive changes in the material situation of the population in the USSR and the peoples' democracies undoubtedly ensued in the post-Stalin period, and not at the price of increasing income differentials. Their quantitative scale, structure and sources were, however, of a kind which could not relieve the social tensions and create the preconditions for harmonious development, particularly because of the natural growth in the complexity of the problems as a higher economic and cultural level was attained. Certain categories of conflict, which in Stalin's time were effectively overwhelmed by the burden of concern with satisfying the most elemen-

tary needs (including personal safety), and were also partly ideologically dispersed by the more lively recollections of the past then
and by faith in the early conquest of all obstacles, now came to the
surface. This applies among other things to the broad consumption
aspirations which produce a critical response even to real benefits if
they are not regarded as commensurate with the efforts devoted to
economic growth and with the accepted norms and other elements
of the social consciousness formed by the concrete historical conditions. The problem is similar with attitudes to the pattern of
income distribution – both from the point of view of social justice
and of economic rationality.

In order, then, that our brief sketch of the changes in social and
economic policy in the post-Stalin period should properly fulfil the
role of background to the analysis of the evolution of the methods
of government we must be fully aware of the distinctly diverse
character of the results obtained and the sources of conflict associated with them.

3   Modification of the methods of government

We begin by analysing the changes in the methods of using force, or
direct political coercion. The differences between the Stalin and
post-Stalin periods in this field are too well known to need detailed
presentation here. We are mainly concerned with deriving links
between the changes in methods and the social and economic
aspects of the post-Stalin evolution of the etatist model.

At the most general level the post-Stalin period is characterised
by the abandonment of mass terror which may be conventionally
called 'preventive'. Terror of the Stalin type was not confined to
groups or individuals really – or even potentially – inclined towards
opposition, but struck at entire large circles, frequently including
people who were utterly loyal to the regime, and were ready to serve
it with complete and often fanatical devotion. Ignoring the possible
interpretation of this type of terror as a pathological feature of the
consciousness of the dictator and his closest surroundings, a more
rational explanation seemed to be the desire to obtain precisely this
'preventive effect' – prevention not only of indications of opposition
to a given policy but also *a priori* to any other line taken by the
ruler in the future – by the creation of a state of universal fear
embracing all levels of the social scale (including all links in the

apparatus of power) and all fields of activity. Precisely for this reason Stalin's terror also, and at certain phases above all, 'could and had to' strike at his own supporters. The ruler's action was not a reaction to a definite ('anti-state') action of the citizen. On the contrary, both at the time of the Great Purge in 1937 and at the end of the 1940s and beginning of the 1950s, 'the intensification of the class struggle' followed an initiative from above, implemented in accordance with a certain conception, of which some of the main elements were the principles of designating the victims. This statement (or, for those who prefer it, hypothesis) does not contradict the numerous observed manifestations of spontaneity of mass terror, since it was not a matter of absolute but of relative precision in relation to the aims laid down. More than once spontaneity was an essential element in the operation, among other things from the point of view of the possibility of devolving responsibility for the so-called excesses.

The abandonment of the Stalinist forms of terror covered several stages : the first was the release of prisoners, the next the political disavowal of mass terror as a method of government (at the XX, and later the XXII, Congresses of the CPSU), combined with the – much delayed – public rehabilitation of victims; as we have already said, the tremendous importance of the at least partial exposure of the Stalinist terror mechanism consisted, among other things, in its significant reduction of the probability of a return to the condemned methods, which increased the feeling of personal safety, particularly in the party-state apparatus, including very high levels of the hierarchy.

Finally, the third element which developed in practice in the post-Stalin period, and which from the point of view of a long-term evaluation is of the greatest importance, was a fairly radical change in the methods of using the apparatus of compulsion to maintain the existing political system. This is not the place to analyse all the components of this change, which embraces among other things the very cautious restoration to suspects, defendants and the convicted of certain fundamental rights, long regarded as obvious in civilised countries, but presented at times in the socialist countries as an outstanding triumph of 'socialist legality'. Without denying the importance of procedural legality and the length of sentences and the way they are carried out – particularly in comparison with the complete lawlessness of the previous period, it nevertheless seems to

me that the most important new feature, the most important change
in *policy* on repression is the renunciation of mass terror, which we
have called 'preventive', in favour of the method of directed, 'selective' striking at individuals and circles displaying or suspected of
political activity regarded as dangerous to the regime. This is a
change in principle, although obviously the area of activity subject
to persecution and the scale of police supervision over all fields of
life are enormous and bear no comparison with the situation under
what is contemptuously described as formal democracy. But in spite
of everything, penal repression[30] now is generally incurred 'for
something' and not 'for nothing', as in the Stalin period. It is difficult to exaggerate the importance of this change for the population;
only a minimal part of society is sufficiently active and involved, in
normal situations, to risk the severe consequences threatened by
conflict with the authorities, who treat all unauthorised political
activity, or even the shadow of it, as anti-state. The transition from
'preventive' to 'selective' terror thus opens up broadly the previously
rare chance of a peaceful life, subject to not treading on forbidden
terrain. This is an extremely attractive chance, especially for the
generation which has been tormented by the previous period and
has learnt to regard autonomous political aspirations with scepticism. Acceptance of these realities, which can relatively easily be
justified to oneself on the basis of the favourable differences
between the new and the past features of the system, and which is
assisted from outside by intensive appeal to general national and
state interests, is one of the most important factors in the political
reality of the socialist countries in the post-Stalin era. In the long-
term future conformism as the *political* foundation of the system is
bound to produce conflicts, the consequences of which we shall
analyse in further discussion. But for the time being this state of
affairs brings undoubted advantages to the rulers. For this reason,
too, not only does the view that power in the socialist countries
since Stalin has also been based on mass physical terror seem to me
an oversimplification, but so, too, does the perception of serious
tendencies at the highest levels of power towards a return to the
terror of the past. Experience proves that in the new conditions a
sufficient degree of intimidation can be achieved with the help of
selective terror, and, particularly, that extremely brutal blows are
prepared by the broad system of daily surveillance and – which was

so characteristic of Poland in the last phase of the Gomułka regime – by the use of political provocation.

It seems easy to indicate the economic implications of the abandonment of the Stalinist forms of physical coercion. On the one hand, the change in forms was dictated not only by political but also by economic reasons: the necessity of overcoming the negative effects of mass terror on labour productivity, the utilisation of specialists, the adoption of more rational economic, organisational and technological solutions, etc. On the other hand, the improvement in the material way of life of the population was an essential precondition for the new forms of political coercion – in the first phase of the post-Stalin period simply through its function as a temporary instrument for relieving tension by satisfying the most pressing needs, in subsequent phases by creating the basis of the longings and aspirations for stability, which were often officially criticised as the wrong aim for a society in the nature of things supposed to be the dynamic vanguard of progress, but which were quickly accepted as the ones relatively most favourable for the permanence of the system of government. From the point of view of the average citizen the rejection of the policy of preventive terror created the necessary conditions for the development of a feeling of relative personal safety without which it would be hard to make use of the opportunities opened up by the economic changes discussed above.

Besides these general interrelationships we must also note in the case of Poland such specific factors as the restoration of a feeling of personal safety to the broad circles of people, particularly of the intelligentsia, who were associated during the Second World War with the political and military organisation of the government in exile. This was the initial condition both for the direct utilisation of many hitherto debarred people with high professional qualifications and for increasing the effectiveness of the stress put on national solidarity in ideology.

In the *ideological field*, too, the post-Stalin period is characterised by a number of new features with substantial direct or indirect significance for economic processes. True, the principle of ideological dirigisme remained intact, as did the striving for effective control of intellectual life and its subordination to the state; but the methods for implementing this were rationalised. Stalinism – as we have tried to show – as it continually extended the area of control with the passage of time, made it more and more universal, all-embracing – from modern history to physics. Hand in hand with this, the processes which can be described by the term *activisation* of party direction of science, culture and the arts, were intensified: more and more rarely was it confined only to delimiting forbidden zones; more and more frequently a positive contribution was demanded – creative work according to the rules set from above, propagation of certain essential theses as the only correct ones, etc. Just as in other fields, so in this, the post-Stalin period marked a transition to considerably more selective measures. The obvious economic damage inclined the authorities to renounce direct intervention in substantial problems in the exact and technical sciences, and the whole ideological anathema was removed from organisational disciplines. There remained only the problem of direction of subjects in accordance with the preferences of the economic plan, but that is another category of problem, which appears everywhere where there is the question of translating the results of research into the language of practical applications.

Policy towards the arts, and particularly literature, followed distinctly different courses in individual countries, but here, too, a general trend can be observed – in the direction of limitation of the plane of intervention and use of orders forbidding things rather than orders to do things. In principle the times of blind imposition of 'socialist realism' in painting, the excommunication of jazz and the condemnation of all more modern literary and theatrical forms had come to an end. Modern forms of expression proved to be free of explosive properties and could be regarded as at worst politically neutral – as opposed to contents, principally of literature, which were subject to close control.

The selective policy of party direction in the social sciences began to develop in a very characteristic way. The experience of Poland illustrates the far-reaching growth of freedom in techniques of research, including those only recently questioned from considerations of principle. In economic theory, mathematical formalism is breeding without hindrance, often on the basis of assumptions explicitly contradicting those of Marxist theory, as, for example, in the case of the well-known Cobb-Douglas production function (we are not concerned here with the question of the usefulness of the Cobb-Douglas function, but only with recording the fact that ideological consideration plays no part in evaluating this). Philosophical works written from openly idealistic positions are exhibited on the shelves of bookshops and their authors enjoy – often deservedly – public authority and official support. The authorities are convinced that this does not in the least threaten the foundations of the system, and brings political advantages (the attraction of some circles of the intelligentsia) and ideological advantages (it makes it easier to bandy nationalistic slogans about). As far as this last point is concerned, it is connected with the continuation and intensification of the phenomenon, which appeared clearly in the Stalin period, of initiation and inspiration from above of primitive presentism in the study and teaching of history.

On the other hand, wherever the social sciences touch in a non-conformist manner on problems regarded as fundamental from the point of view of the political system – that is, primarily, problems of socialist society and its future evolution – restrictions and intervention have remained ruthless. Thus it is only an apparent paradox that what is most sharply condemned is any attempt to apply the methods of Marxist analysis to socio-economic and political reality in the USSR and the peoples' democracies. This did not necessarily mean copying the forms of the Stalin period (the general conditions had changed anyway); various forms are used, but tending to eliminate 'unreliability' quite effectively and to ensure the monopolistic character of the official positions. The same applies to the area of freedom of speech on questions of current policy (the character of the so-called 'general national discussions' has not in essence changed in comparison with the Stalin period).

Briefly, in the field of ideology the post-Stalin period brought a turn towards a peculiar kind of pragmatism, in many respects reminiscent of the attitude of the Anglican church as mentioned by Marx,[31] except that in the case of the party in the socialist countries it is a matter of the inviolability of its monopoly of power.

The post-Stalin period was also marked by the controlled *weakening of isolation from the outside world*. This can be called gradual 'opening up to abroad'. On this plane, too, the changes in comparison with the Stalin period have taken varied courses in different countries, and have zigzagged over time, but the general tendency towards the weakening of the wall of isolation from abroad can be stated above all doubt, both as regards relations between individual countries of the socialist camp and relations with the third world and the developed capitalist countries. Such

K

heterogeneous reasons have operated here that it is difficult even to try to enumerate and classify them within the framework of our attempt at a general characterisation of the process. On the economic side the most essential role was played by the indispensable need for more foreign trade and for gaining access to the experience of technically advanced countries, especially in the face of the deepening technological gap in many important fields. In the case of the capitalist countries, the catalyst was the obtaining of a greater degree of autonomy *vis-à-vis* the Soviet Union by some of the peoples' democracies, which created or extended the margin for political and economic manoeuvre.

Despite the fact that this 'opening up to abroad' was always limited and always politically controlled,[32] it had far-reaching consequences – cultural, social and economic. On the one hand, the definite revival of contacts with abroad tended to accelerate the modernisation of methods and structures of production, the introduction of new forms of satisfaction of consumer requirements, and even fundamental changes in the way of life; all this undoubtedly to some extent smoothed out the contrast in style of life between the socialist and the developed capitalist countries, a contrast which, when the possibility of direct comparison was opened up, in the first phase proved enormous, and frankly depressing. On the other hand, the 'demonstration effect' turned into yet another strong and persistent factor arousing needs and aspirations, which faced the ruling system with higher and higher demands, and not just in the economic but in the political field too.

The changes in the methods of using compulsion, the new forms of ideological dirigisme, the opening up to abroad, are phenomena which it would be a mistake to underestimate. Together with the improvement in the material situation, they constituted essential differences between the Stalin and post-Stalin periods, differences which were undoubtedly also expressed in a universal social feeling, particularly in the first phase of the new stage. None the less, the changes of which we have spoken have not infringed the ruling *political system*; on the contrary – they were to serve to maintain it, as more effective, more adequate instruments for 'dynamic petrification'. Using the to some extent schematic but at times useful distinction between the content and the form of social phenomena, we could say that in the post-Stalin period changes ensued in the *forms* of exercise of power which were important for the daily lives of many millions of people, without changes of principle in the *content* of the political system, which consists in *monopolisation of power* in the hands of the narrow directing group in the communist party. With reference to our discussion about the 'starting point' of the post-Stalin period, it must be said that, despite short-term disturbances of equilibrium, the fundamental interests of the 'establishment' from this point of view are achieved.

In the USSR and the peoples' democracies not even partial political pluralisation was permitted in the post-Stalin period. In all its basic elements the structure of actual relationships remained unchanged:

(a)   domination of the apparatus and executive organs (the executive) over the formally elected organs in the vertical state administration (the government over the parliament, the presidia of local councils over the councils, etc.), in the trade unions, in the party;

(b)   appointment of party, state and trade union bodies by the corresponding higher levels of the apparatus through the imposition of candidates and the transformation of election procedures into a formality;

(c)   close compliance with the specific conception of the 'leading role of the party', i.e. subordination of all other institutional systems to the party apparatus, in particular through complete control of personnel policy, exclusion of all independent political initiative and the possibility of free association, etc;

(d)   monopolisation of the media of mass communication, both through selection from above of personnel in the press, publishing, radio and television, and 'normally' through universal preventive censorship.

In sum, therefore, there was no violation of the reversed 'dependency vector' – 'the bottom' depending on 'the top' – which causes every link in the power structure to be aware of its responsibility not to its formal electorate but to its superior link, and to adapt its manner of operation and object of information to this *de facto* structure of subordination. This means consequently that the authorities can – if they regard it as expedient – with no institutional obstacles or limitations, enforce obedience both by means of economic pressure (on the basis of their monopoly over jobs) and by police means. The changes in the methods of ruling noted above fit within the framework defined by the postulate of permanent maintenance of these possibilities, and if such changes prove too dangerous in crisis situations they are suspended. This is demonstrated by the experience of Hungary in 1956 and especially vividly by that of Czechoslovakia in 1968. The 'Prague Spring' set in, and was developing within the framework of the existing institutional system, without going beyond the limits of the law and order of the post-Stalin period; but because this system gradually began to acquire a political content extending beyond the framework of the etatist model, brutal force was used, veiled within the intervening countries by a mendacious propaganda campaign which could be conducted only in conditions of complete monopoly of information.[33]

This does not mean, of course, that the instruments of political rule can be identified with instruments in the technical sense – to be taken down and put back on a shelf at will, depending only on their current usefulness. They are a social fact, which has grown up on a definite basis, and which has to be reckoned with. Hence the surely characteristic phenomenon that even in crisis situations there is never a total retreat to the former methods, and as the danger recedes efforts are made to return as quickly as possible to the instruments proper to the post-Stalin period. It seems, then, that not only the rule, but the exceptions, too, confirm the objectively determined direction in which the methods of governing have evolved in the post-Stalin period, just as they confirm the existence of limits which this evolution has not crossed.

From the point of view of the problems being examined here Poland deserves a place of its own. Poland was the country which in 1956 awakened hopes for real democratisation of the political system, since it could seem as if a mass social movement – by bringing Gomułka to power – had won a victory, and the new leading team in the PUPW – as distinct from the case of Czechoslovakia in 1968 – was not overthrown, but accepted (after brief clashes and vacillations) by the Soviet Union. In reality, October 1956, contrary to rather widespread opinion, marked the end of the current of democratisation and began the reverse process: elimination of everything regarded as a threat to the system of totalitarian dictatorship.[34] Because this process was carried out by internal forces, it proceeded more gradually, without violent disturbances, which makes it more difficult to observe the 'normalising' mechanisms; it was thus in a certain sense a clinical process, particularly in that the cycle reached its end in the form of the crisis of 1970.[35] We shall not, obviously, go into a detailed analysis of Polish experience – we wish only to draw attention to a few characteristic features.

The first sector in which the direction of changes was halted and then reversed was the party apparatus. After a short-lived period of reduction of the number of departments and personnel of party committees at all levels and replacement of functionaries by non-full-time bodies, a renewed and rapid build-up of the apparatus ensued, both in terms of numbers and of functions. After the III Congress of the PUPW (1959) the previous state was in principle restored, which among other things confirms the interrelationship between the political and economic aspects of the process (the return to increased accumulation and retardation of the rate of growth of real wages).

Any elements of real election promptly vanished, too – including on the basis of differences in political position – in the process of appointment of party bodies. There followed the gradual but meticulous elimination of persons involved in the democratisation movement from the party and state apparatus, the military and the security organs. As far as the latter are concerned, as in the case of the party apparatus, the temporary reduction in numbers and limitation of functions soon gave way to a renewed build-up and expansion of their field of activity – without, in general, copying the methods of the Stalin period, it is true, as we have said, but with the unequivocal aim of absolute maintenance of the monopoly of power. The security organs, deeply penetrating all links in the system, including the flow of information, began to play a greater and greater political role, especially as internal struggles at the peak of the party hierarchy grew; this was demonstrated with singular clarity by the events of March 1968.

The hopes that representative bodies, principally the Sejm (Diet), would be able to use their formal constitutional powers were quickly shattered. Once again the real role of these bodies proved to be decided not by their register of prerogatives but by the real dependence arising in the course of their appointment. The 'Polish October' appeared to bring the first breach in the actual process of appointment of deputies and members of councils thereto, since it introduced the principle of a greater number of candidates than the number of seats; this was supposed to create an embryonic chance of election – within the compass of the same, single list of candidates drawn up from above, but at least according to personal criteria. But even this was evidently too much (besides, personal preferences could take on a political shading) and was countered by the slogan 'voting without crossing out', which in practice meant the automatic 'election' of the candidates at the head of the lists.[36] The history of Polish electoral law can thus serve as a classical example of the effects of setting an ossifying mechanism in motion, which succeeds in sterilising the formal-legal solutions of their essential content. This does not of course mean ignoring the role of the formal-legal factor in the political life of the socialist countries, in particular as a stepping-stone to a campaign for observance of citizens' rights and freedoms. By itself, however, outside the context of the real relationships, this factor does not mean very much and does not provide a basis for any evaluation. From this point of view Polish experience with electoral law can be instructive not only for students of the processes taking place in the socialist countries, but also for people who, when seeking ways of democratising a political system, confine themselves to postulates of change in constitutional regulations, electoral law, etc. The introduction of more than one candidate per seat can even seem a shocking change in the first instance, whereas in reality – if other elements in the system remain undisturbed – nothing changes, apart from the possible use of an additional propaganda trump by the authorities.

An important demand of the renewal movement in the period before October 1956 was the opening up of new channels of information – both for the rulers and for society – by the appointment of independent teams of experts who would openly formulate evaluations and proposals. One example of implementation of this demand, shortly before Gomułka came to power, was the appointment of an Economic Council as a consultative organ of the government. And again, more or less from the beginning of 1958, the fate of this institution can serve as a textbook example of the elimination of a foreign body whose introduction was contrary to the logic of autocratism. The Economic Council withered away, not because it did not give advice, but precisely because it did give it, and the greatest stumbling-block was its independent evaluations of the economic situation and prospects (initially published, later only communicated to the government). The Economic Council ceased to exist after a few years as a result of ... inaction, i.e. the Chairman of the Council of Ministers simply did not continue its mandate, without making this fact publicly known, although the Sejm adopted a resolution calling for its appointment. In another case – the so-called general national discussion on the draft plan for 1966–70 before the IV Congress of the PUPW – Michał Kalecki's attempt to submit his own constructive proposals produced a reaction which forced the author to give up his position of scientific adviser in the Planning Commission.[37] From then on the government did without independent expert advice, being content with the most obviously servile paeans of praise for every single policy.

From the point of view of full restoration of the political monopoly in Poland after October 1956 the least problem, relatively, was presented by the trade union organisation. The bureaucratised union apparatus had fought against the demands for democratisation and particularly for genuine autonomy of the trade unions, which made the workers not so much aim at reform of the union organisation as counterpose their own authentic representative bodies – workers' councils – against the unions. Therefore the process of 'normalisation' in this field consisted primarily in limiting the role of the workers' councils and subordinating them to the trade union and party apparatus.[38] Peasant self-government, too, was soon restricted and subordinated to party, state and cooperative administration.

The process of 'normalisation' was most complex and long drawn-out in the intellectual field. Some of the intelligentsia, particularly the party intelligentsia, understood better than other social groups the general significance of the democratisation of political relations and the regressive character of the processes initiated after October; as well as this, these problems were often directly connected with their own professional activity. Hence the articulated opposition to the closing of the first cracks in the system of dictatorship, which had been opened up in 1956; it was this opposition – if it came from party circles and was based on Marxist analysis – that was officially described as revisionism, expectation of a 'second stage' (with the unspoken insinuation of 'a capitalist stage'). For more than ten years the possibilities of independent social activity by intellectuals and their main field for defending them – freedom of speech – were narrowed step by step. The official censorship and administrative forbidding of journals and the activities of student and intellectual clubs of course played an essential role in this process. But these were not the only, nor even the most effective, means: as in other cases the most effective one proved to be internal personnel penetration, and initially rather subtle, but later arrogantly open, preference and discrimination according to criteria of political obedience and moral conformism. Even before Polish higher educational institutions were formally deprived of their autonomy, its *de facto* erosion set in as a result of the transformation of election of academic authorities into a procedural act not very different from nomination. Phenomena of this type appeared even more clearly and quickly in other institutions and professional organisations (there was less need to reckon with traditions and social prestige). With the passage of time political and economical pressure were combined to a greater and greater extent with purely police pressure.

The final contest took place in March 1968, which can hardly be regarded as an accidental moment. On the one hand, sharp social and economic conflicts were growing in the country and, particularly in the face of the Czechoslovak events, threatened the existing political system. On the other hand, the increased pressure on intellectual circles produced a protest movement which could be used for provocation. For this reason, too, the student movement was suppressed with exceptional brutality, and in its wake all public manifestations of intellectual life were made to conform to pattern. The defence of the monopoly of power was in addition interwoven with an intra-party struggle: the blow at the circles which represented the last remnants of a critical view of reality strengthened the position of the group known as the 'police faction' in the heart of the PUPW leadership.

The police action in the March 1968 period was supported by a concentrated political propaganda attack. The aim of this attack was to isolate the student movement and the intelligentsia from society, particularly from the workers in large-scale industry; for this purpose the full force of the mass media was used to blow up a mendacious story of the malicious inspiration of the student demonstrations, and, above all, a great campaign of antisemitism ('anti-zionism') which had a dual function to fulfil: to eliminate the not very numerous but politically active Poles of Jewish origin and – as usual in such cases – to veil the true nature of what was being done in an obscurantist commotion. In conditions where public opinion cannot make itself clear it is not easy to assess how far these aims were achieved; however, a certain degree of disorientation was brought about, all the more so as the 'March' campaign was soon coupled with the campaign in support of the intervention in Czecho-slovakia with its appeal to anti-German animosities. At any rate the authorities succeeded in their intention of pacifying intellectual and particularly academic circles, which were purged of 'trouble-makers' and subjected now to open and direct control by the mass nomination to academic positions of people on whom the auth-orities could rely.

Assessing the course of events in Poland in retrospect, there seems no doubt that the stage described by the cryptogram 'March' was the harbinger and at the same time the catalyst of the crisis which reached its peak in the workers' demonstrations on the Baltic coast in December 1970. The March blow obviously did not solve any real problems. On the contrary – it only exacerbated the conflicts and multiplied the force of the eventual convulsion, since the closing of the last possibilities of political criticism gave the PUPW leadership a feeling of unlimited freedom for autocratic action. This explains, among other things, the astounding decision – astounding in the degree of its political aberration – to make widespread increases in food prices before the Christmas holi-day, a decision which was the last straw and, together with the bloodshed of the reaction to the workers' protest, created the neces-sity of an immediate change in the core of the ruling team. This is naturally a detail, without which the crisis would still have appeared, perhaps in somewhat different forms – but it is an exceed-ingly characteristic detail.

Analysis of the consequences of 'December' for social and econ-omic policy in Poland (and in the other socialist countries) and also, in the longer run, for the more general problems of the political system, does not fall within the compass of this book. It needs to be emphasised, on the other hand, that the change in leadership of the PUPW opened the previously closed sluice gates for a critical evalu-ation of the system – true, as usual in such cases, directed at the past period, but nevertheless exceptionally instructive precisely from the broader point of view.

Evaluations of political and social relations which had until recently been treated as marks of revisionism appeared publicly in 1971, even in documents from the most authoritative party bodies also.[39] A picture emerges from these – incomplete and unsystem-atic, but telling enough – of the total dictatorship which had developed anew in Poland as a result of the post-October process of 'normalisation'. And since, even taking into account the specific features deriving from the personal characteristics of Gomułka, it is hard to accept that Poland was any worse than the USSR or the other peoples' democracies (perhaps with the exception of Hungary towards the end of the 1960s), the official post-December evaluations make an interesting contribution to the general characterisation of the post-Stalin evolution of the political system in the etatist model and thus also support the conclusions based on the criteria of socialisation we have employed.

4 Economic reforms

The fundamental tendencies and conflicts in the evolution of the etatist model in the post-Stalin period, and in particular the striving to raise the level of economic efficiency, were widely reflected in the zigzagging history of reforms in the system of functioning of the economy. While it would indeed be hard to agree with those scholars who regard the course of reforms in the system of functioning of the economy[40] as the best indication of the changes taking place, it is none the less – as followed even from our analysis of the self-management model – an extremely important field which deserves separate treatment.

We have already mentioned that the first voices of criticism of the extreme centralisation of the system of functioning of the economy were raised soon after the death of Stalin in connection with the urgent need to improve the material situation of the population. It probably seemed to the leadership of the CPSU and the other parties initially that it was sufficient to make themselves aware of the needs, to censure the shortages and issue appropriate orders, combined with a certain reallocation of resources.[41] But it quickly transpired that these moves brought mediocre results, which made it necessary to put on the agenda revision or at least a new interpretation of some of the sacred canons of direction of the national economy. One of the harbingers of change was the Soviet decree broadening the powers of enterprise directors (1955). In the theoretical field forerunners of the new currents began to appear earlier, against the background of the discussions on the law of value, inspired by Stalin's *Economic Problems of Socialism in the USSR*, but subsequently directed, far from its source of inspiration, towards criticism of hyper-centralism. But the clearer practical implications of these discussions only appeared when the changed political situation created the preconditions for a broader discussion on reform of the system. An essential role was played here by the removal of the taboo on the Yugoslav experience. It would be a mistake though to ascribe too great a significance to this last factor (which the opponents of reforms were only too pleased to do, in their efforts to discredit them as 'imitation of Yugoslavia'). The conceptions of reform were born out of critical evaluation of the real economic processes in particular countries and, in the first phase, with no possibility of connecting them with Yugoslav experience. To put the matter in its correct proportions, emphasising the role of Yugoslavia does, however, seem important since first, the very fact of the appearance of an alternative solution which, from a certain moment – the spring of 1955 in fact – could not formally be denied the name of socialist, was in itself a turning point; second, apart from one's evaluation of that solution as a whole, it contained concrete features aimed at the universally perceived shortcomings of the centralistic system.

The years 1955–6, in a number of socialist countries, brought more or less bold and well-developed conceptions of reform of the system of functioning of the economy. The first articles by Liberman in Soviet journals, the works of Gyorgy Peter in Hungary, and finally the rapidly growing and extending discussion circles in Poland – all these attempts, despite differences in their theoretical level and in the extent to which they worked out practical proposals, were marked by a clear similarity of basic direction. Without going into details we can indicate the following common or similar postulates in the different conceptions of reform.

(a) Reduction of the degree of centralisation of economic decisions, and extension of the area of independence of the lower units in the nationalised economy (enterprises or groups of them); reduction of the role of vertical hierarchical links in favour of horizontal links (between bodies at the same level), etc.

(b) Elimination or at least radical restriction of the number of detailed indicators for evaluating the activity of enterprises and of the system of direct allocation of factors of production (in physical terms or in the form of narrow limits for each enterprise) in favour of strengthening the role of the so-called synthetic indicators (mainly profitability) and at least partially linking the inflow of means of production and labour with the financial results of enterprises.

(c) Linking remuneration with the economic results of enterprises (or even of a set of enterprises) if not as the only then at least as one of the fundamental principles of the incentive system.

Not universally, but fairly frequently, the creation of institutional conditions for employee participation in the management of enterprises (worker self-management) was postulated.

Even this most cursory summary of the common points in the proposals advanced in the middle of the 1950s testifies on the one hand that a substantial transformation of the system of functioning of the economy was involved and, on the other, that – apart from individual extreme opinions without greater influence – these postulates did not go beyond the framework of the centrally planned economy.

These postulates were substantial in the sense that to implement them would have meant replacement of the complex methods used thereto to direct the economy with another set of methods;[42] the use of these methods required new 'rules of the game' for individual cells in the economy and new instruments to operate with at the central level (shifting the burden from direct orders to indirect regulation – through prices, tax policy, credit policy, etc., on the basis of an appropriate system of incentives). In this connection it was correct to describe the proposed direction of changes as the introduction of certain elements of the market mechanism into the planned economy.

Simultaneously, and not only in the sphere of ideology or the tactics of presentation, but also in the programmes of reform actually worked out (where such programmes appeared), there was the emphasis on the intention of strengthening central planning, among other things by freeing it from the centralistic *semblances* of precision, efficiency and universality, semblances which were becoming more and more dangerous for the real capacity to plan the course of economic processes. These intentions were expressed in the differentiation of the extent of centralisation and decentralisation demanded for long-term (principally investment) decisions and short-term decisions (taken mainly for the given production apparatus), in limitation of the area of autonomy of the lower links to within the framework created by central directive decisions, in definition of the 'rules of the game' (the objective function) of enterprises from above according to a criterion linking their sectional interest with the interest of the national economy as a whole, and in efforts to ensure the parametric character – for enterprises – of the basic economic magnitudes (primarily prices) entering into the calculation of costs and results while at the same time assuring the central organs of economic policy an influence over them in accordance with their overall preferences. This was undoubtedly the predominant type of formulation in 1956, and not only in the USSR, where isolated voices rather were heard, and carefully wrapped up in the protective cotton wool of conventional phrases at that, but also in Poland, where discussion was proceeding freely at the time and in other countries in which similar tendencies appeared (e.g. the statements of F. Behrens and A. Benary in East Germany).

In the document which probably best reflects the consensus of opinion at the time in Poland on the question of reform of the system of functioning of the economy, namely the *Theses of the Economic Council on Certain Directions on Change in the Economic Model*, it is assumed as a starting point that:[43]

> the deepening of central planning and raising it to a higher level is one of the principal directions for the correct development of our economy. The improvement of planning is served not by a multiplicity of indicators, highly detailed elaboration and formal balancing, but by more penetrating economic analysis and, where precise economic calculation is not possible, by well-grounded estimates of how economic phenomena will develop.

The prominent representative of Soviet mathematical economics, and at the same time one of the most consistent theoreticians of economic reform, V. V. Novozhilov, later tried to express the same ideas in an even more forceful way, replacing the term 'decentralisation' by the term 'indirect centralisation':[44]

> Direct centralisation of the solution of economic problems consists in actually taking decisions in the central planning office. Indirect centralisation . . . consists in setting parameters for the calculation of costs and effects, with the help of which local organs . . . would be able to find the variants best corresponding to the general economic plan. . . . Indirect centralisation is essential both in socialism and in communism, as it has the extremely positive

feature that it subordinates *all* local decisions, without exception, including the most detailed, to the plan.

To sum up, then, the principal current in the reform movement of the end of the 1950s declared itself fundamentally and unequivocally in favour of the centrally planned economy, seeing the liquidation of the centralistic system and the introduction of its own kind of market mechanism as an instrument for improving socialist planning and creating the preconditions for optimising behaviour on the scale of the national economy as a whole. The dominant formulation was the one which the author of the present book later attempted to generalise in the form of 'the model of the planned economy making use of the market mechanism ('the decentralised model')'.[45] On the other hand, the doctrinal position which sees the principal path of systemic changes in *unlimited* decentralisation of the economy (as in the self-management model of socialism) hardly appeared at all.

We have dwelt longer on this aspect of the programme of the advocates of reform in the system of functioning of the economy since it provides the essential background for analysing the reasons for the collapse of the 'first wave of reform' (as we shall call the attempts made in the second half of the 1950s – as distinct from the 'second wave of reform' which followed more or less a decade later). This analysis is extremely instructive precisely from the point of view of the interrelationship between political and economic factors in the process of evolution in the post-Stalin period.

Let us note first of all that reform in the sense referred to above was a failure everywhere, despite very different conditions in individual countries. First of all it came to nothing in the USSR, where the direction of change which was probable initially was reversed at the turn of 1956–7 and led to something completely different, namely Khrushchev's administrative decentralisation. Partly because of this there was not even any talk of practical attempts at reform in such countries as Rumania and Bulgaria or East Germany where the purely intellectual initiatives were nipped in the bud. No reforms were implemented in Hungary, of course, after it was crushed. But what is most curious is that economic reform suffered defeat in Poland, too, where the renewal movement of whose programme it was one of the leading postulates seemed to be victorious.[46]

Among the reasons for the failure some part was played by doubts or even negative evaluations of reform from a pragmatic point of view: a certain number of economic officials considered that reform would not increase the efficiency of the economy but, on the contrary, would weaken it. To what extent this view was determined by the social position of the people who derived not only their position but also their way of thought from the period of Stalinist centralisation it is obviously hard to say. The conservatism which is normal in such cases, and the inertia, were bound to make themselves felt, which does not in the least mean that every sign of scepticism should be regarded as unjustified and every reform proposal *a priori* as rational.

Despite the complexity of the reasons for the failure of the first wave of reform one can conclude, it seems to me, that the most fundamental causes were political: fear that to enter on the road of real and complex reform of the system of functioning of the economy would mean at the same time undermining the political system, either directly, or more indirectly by initiating a process of gradual erosion of the existing monopoly of power.

The direct fears stemmed – especially in Poland – from the fact that the postulate of economic reform had been, as we said, one of the components of a political programme aiming not just at overcoming Stalinist deformations but going beyond the framework of the political system of the etatist model. The party leadership and broad circles of the apparatus saw a threat precisely from the workers' councils. The workers' councils, which in some enterprises had arisen from the spontaneous initiative of the workforce and were regarded by many advocates of reform as an essential element in the economic changes,[47] evoked immense dislike in the apparatus as a threat of 'dual power'. This must also explain the fact that in Hungary, as well as in Poland where there were no grounds for drastic action, the campaign against workers' councils, their autonomy and, which is most important, their attempts to develop upwards, even in a section of a branch of the economy, was one of the leading sectors on the 'normalisation' front.

The fears of indirect effects were connected with the question of the long-term influence of economic reform on political relations. To a certain degree such an influence does appear, as was shown, among other things, by our analysis of the self-management model. Genuine decentralisation, in the nature of things, even if carried out within a limited framework, weakens dependence on the central apparatus. The transition from direction by detailed, specific and easily changed orders to steering with the help of more general and stable rules reduces the degree of voluntarism since it makes isolation of specific cases more difficult and compels adherence to a defined procedure for possible changes. The transfer of a certain category of economic decisions to lower levels and the linking of part of remuneration and possibilities of expansion to the financial results of the enterprise increases the responsibility of directors, and, consequently makes it necessary to increase their prerogatives, too, in certain fields previously reserved for the political factor, above all in personnel policy. This could really be an important factor in the emancipation of a relatively large and significant social group. It is difficult to say, of course, how far the guardians of the party's political monopoly[48] were kept awake at night by the vision of a 'managerial revolution', and how far on the other hand their opposition was aroused by the general prospect of introducing at least embryonic elements of pluralism; but there can be no doubt that fears of the political effects of the process set in motion by complex changes in the economic system were a severe obstacle to the first wave of reform.

In Poland the retardation of reforms after October 1956 proved effective among other things because the new ruling team was at the time politically stronger than the old, which had to withdraw under pressure from the demands advanced by the masses and from active demonstrations. True, in July 1957 the model theses of the Economic Council were formally approved, but in practice nothing was done, unless we count the transformation of the so-called central managements of branches of industry into so-called associations, which was supposed to be an example of the replacement of bodies of an administrative type by economic bodies, but turned out to be merely a change of labels. After a certain time a gradual return began to many (though not all) of the old methods. To a certain extent the retreat applied to each of the fields covered by the legal acts mentioned previously:

(a)   the list of compulsory indicators for the enterprise, which was limited towards the end of 1956, gradually began to lengthen;

(b)   the workforce representation's independent disposition over the factory fund was restricted by setting a ceiling on payments to employees, an obligation to designate a prescribed part of the fund for house-building, etc.;

(c) worker self-management was forced step by step into the normal system of institutions fulfilling the role of 'transmission' from the party to the masses, at first informally and later – when the situation was regarded as ripe – through a change in the law.

This last question deserves a few additional words as it is the one most connected with the struggle against all embryonic political pluralism, which the peaks of the party hierarchy clearly saw, among other things, in the workers' councils. The law of the end of 1956 not only gave workers' councils extensive rights in the management of enterprises but also, in so far as this is possible in a legal act, created favourable conditions for implementing the principle of self-government; the workers' councils were the only self-management organs, they were elected in a democratic manner (without the imposition of candidates from above), they were responsible to the workforce rather than to bodies at a higher level, etc. From the first moment it was clear that if the councils were to fulfil the function of real representation of the workforce and of an organ of self-management properly very substantial difficulties would be encountered, which it would require great patience, goodwill and help to overcome. It may be that even with these conditions met not all the hopes that were associated with them would have been fulfilled, but then at least the experience of the Polish attempt at worker self-management would have provided a valid basis for drawing conclusions of a general nature.

The reality, unfortunately, was different. On the one hand – which is an interesting contribution to the role of window-dressing in the etatist model of socialism – the party constantly declared its positive attitude towards workers' self-management, and even, just as with the other elements in its programme, actually excluded all criticism of principle. On the other hand, everything was done to deprive the workers' councils of real significance, and to subordinate them to the party and union apparatus. In the first place the role of self-management organs depended on the growth of enterprises' powers; the retardation of the reform thus meant that the economic basis of self-management was removed. Added to this there were the effects of the general political 'normalisation', which was manifested in this field of changes in the personal composition of the workers' councils: replacement of members appointed in 'the

L

period of storm and stress' by people brought into self-management through new elections, this time controlled by the district party organs and trade union bodies. But the extent of control must still have seemed insufficient, for soon the institutional structure of self-management was radically changed: on the basis of the new law of 1958 the principal organ became the so-called Conference of Workers' Self-management (KSR in Polish), which included, apart from the workers' council, the party committee and the trade union factory council *ex officio*, and after a certain time representation of the youth organisation, technicians' organisation, etc., as well. The membership of the presidium of the workers' council, which is supposed to represent workers' self-management in the periods between sessions of the KSR, includes *ex officio* the secretary of the party committee and the chairman of the local organisation of trade unions. The purpose of this complicated organisational network was obvious: to outnumber the workers' council, which was the only body elected by the workforce and was deprived of any higher level superstructure, by the party and union authorities, who were subordinate to hierarchically constructed apparatuses and completely dependent on them – politically, materially and disciplinarily. Only such 'guarded' workers' self-management was considered safe and was then showered with a mass of powers and functions, as thunderous as they were empty – on account of the loss of any autonomy and prestige as an authentic representation of the workforce. There is no need to underline how much damage, not only temporary but long-term, too, the idea of worker self-management suffered in Poland as a result of this.

The retardation of economic reforms in all the socialist countries which had undertaken them in the middle of the 1950s (Czechoslovakia in 1958) was accompanied by attempts at theoretical justification. The arguments against decentralisation and the introduction of elements of the market mechanism into the system of functioning of the economy can be grouped in the following categories.

(1)   Purely dogmatic assertions of the fundamental contradiction between central planning and an area of use of commodity-money forms which goes beyond the centralistic model.

(2)   Criticism of decentralisation from the point of view of the objective tendencies of economic development, which was accompanied by the increasing scale of production and investment and the growing role of scientific and technical preparation, etc.; against

this background the postulates of decentralisation and extension of enterprise autonomy were presented as a return to a past which had been rejected even by modern capitalism.

(3) Rationalisation of the centralistic model on the basis of the achievements of modern information theory and techniques; computerisation, which would vastly accelerate the flow of information to a centre with enormous processing capacity, would eliminate the deficiencies in the existing methods of directive planning and make resort to any elements of decentralisation and market mechanism superfluous.

The specific weight of each of these groups of arguments was different. *The first* served the temporary political and ideological purposes of the so-called struggle with revisionism and was not really intended for substantial discussion; it always returned whenever the next political vendetta had to be carried out.

The second was based at best on misunderstanding and at worst on demagogic exploitation of certain verbal associations. The reforms did not aim to liquidate central planning and thus did not mean a return to the situation in which the directions of economic development are formed as the resultant of uncontrolled actions, of independent micro-elements of the system. It was absolutely clear that it was a matter of changing the methods of constructing and implementing the plan, while maintaining the principle of calculation at the level of the 'system' as a whole (of the national economy) – both in relation to the objective function and to the function of outlay of resources. *In this sense* the 'decentralised model' of the socialist economy was to remain more centralised than any form of functioning of a modern capitalist economy, since the supremacy of the overall economic point of view was preserved (and indeed strengthened). The postulate of increased enterprise independence was in no case an expression of a tendency to deconcentration of production, but merely a concrete form of the general thesis of the need for relative autonomy of individual 'sub-systems' within the framework of the 'system' as a whole; this thesis did not in the least prejudge the scale of this autonomous unit; it could be the single enterprise as understood hitherto, or it could equally well be a specific form of integration of enterprises (for example, the association) on condition that this was not an administrative creature but was endowed with the essential economic features of the enterprise. The point also was that the scale of integration, the system of linkages (vertical, horizontal, mixed), should include the possibility of individualised solutions adapted to needs and economic possibilities rather than to the monolithic organisational pattern corresponding to the distribution of targets and resources to 'addressees'. The provision in the 'decentralised model' of instruments for shaping the long-term processes of development, influencing the structure of income distribution and consumption, etc., was intended to make the *possibilities* of realising the social goals of socialism (to put it most cautiously) no less than in the 'centralistic model'; use of these possibilities would depend, of course, on policy at the central level. To sum up, the criticism 'from the left', while not unfounded where extreme decentralisation solutions and attempts to introduce a free market mechanism were concerned (see chapter 2, section 3), were misdirected if applied to the 'model of a planned economy using a (regulated) market mechanism', and thus also when applied to the programmes of economic reforms discussed, which did not go beyond the framework of this model.

In substance the most important group of arguments was *the third one*, which was appealing in that it referred to the development of modern methods of steering and information techniques. Closer analysis of the meaning of computerisation of management, particularly after the first dazzle of the prospects of 'mathematically-enlightened' centralism has passed, shows, however, that modern methods and techniques of steering not only do not foredoom evolution in the direction of centralisation but on the contrary create the preconditions, the necessity even, for including various levels in the process of decision-making in order to optimise the result for 'the system' (the national economy) as a whole.[49] It is true that purely theoretically one can imagine today a totally automated information system replacing the market but in reality not only would such a system scarcely be realistic either today or in the foreseeable future, but also – which is the most important thing – it would be inadequate for the task which economic planning has to solve. This follows, putting it most generally, from the fact that optimisation of economic plans affects relations between people, so that (1) a number of essential choices (at times the initial ones) lie in principle outside the framework of formalised decision-making theory,[50] and (2) the production and processing of information itself cannot be treated as independent of human behaviour, nor of motivation and the incentives connected with it. For this reason, too, one of the Soviet theoreticians of optimal planning, A. A. Volkonsky,[51] seems to me correct in his formulation which treats the functioning of the economy as 'a man-machine system' where the elements of informal decisions and the system of incentives must be linked with the formalised decision-making processes in a single whole. From this point of view the activation of mechanisms operating automatically within certain limits but at the same time generally steered from the central level has quite exceptional significance for a socialist system, since it allows the demands of 'socio-economic rationality' (Lange) to be combined with the essential scope for the initiative and creative invention of people. The principles on which the 'centralistic model' is based, on the other hand, actually ignore the necessity of taking this specific human element into account in the system of functioning of the planned economy and are based on a mechanistic formulation: man operates only when activated by the appropriate external directive and he operates in the way this directive bids him. The problem of choice of a system of functioning of the economy which is proper for a socialist system thus goes very deep and the opportunities provided by modern techniques must be subordinated to the nature of the task.

Bearing in mind on the one hand the problems touched on above – the technical possibilities, and what some authors call 'the paradox of planning'[52] – and on the other the universally accepted thesis that it is possible to create a price system which approximately meets the conditions of optimisation, it becomes clear that the construction of an optimal plan must proceed through iteration *of a specific type*. The accent on the *specific type* of iteration here is most essential since basically no plan ever was or ever could be constructed at one stroke, without successive steps towards precision. But in a system based on absolute subordination to the central authority and the absence of autonomy at lower levels, the iteration process could lead at best to internal consistency, to the balancing of the plan, but not to its optimisation. A lower link reacted to the information sent out (instructions) in a passive manner, formulating only the physical conditions for implementation of the target, which from this point of view could be corrected (or compulsorily kept) until a balance was achieved. On the other hand, iteration which is to bring the programme closer to an optimal solution must consist in a *game* between the higher level and autonomous 'sub-systems' which have defined rules of behaviour (autonomous objective functions) and interests connected with them. The point of departure of the process of plan construction is a highly aggregated 'indicative' programme and corresponding evaluations of the constraints for the 'system' as a whole; these evaluations are the parameters issued for the 'sub-systems', which communicate their optimal programme constructed on the basis of them to 'above', which in turn corrects the quantities or the evaluations, thus taking the next step in the iterative procedure. It is clear that this type of iteration must assume genuine multi-level planning.

There is no need to describe the process more closely here, still less to present it in mathematical form. From our point of view what is essential is that a precondition of it is the relative autonomy of 'sub-systems' endowed with their 'own' objective function and that this function must be based on maximisation of a synthetic type of indicator (one which reacts to the totality of effects and outlays calculated in parametric valuations). With a suitably constructed and sufficiently strong material interest individual steps in the iteration process cease to be successive stages of passive adaptation to information flowing from above and generate (at each level) new information streams running in different directions and inter-penetrating each other. This kind of game is obviously possible not only through the medium of the market mechanism; it can also take place by means of direct transmission of information (e.g. in the course of successive stages in the construction of an investment plan using such a parameter as 'the marginal recoupment period of additional investment outlays'). But (1) it is always necessary to give the 'sub-systems' autonomy and an interest in the results of the game, of which we have spoken above; and (2) for the vast mass of current decisions connected with the construction of a short-term plan the market mechanism is at present the only practically available solution for organising an iterative process of this type. The harnessing of the market mechanism *in this sense* to the procedure of planning should contribute to the objectivity of plans and thus to increasing the real degree of planning.

Thus, too, it was no accident that the most prominent representatives of the mathematical-cybernetic trend in economics (Lange in Poland; Kantorovich, Nemchinov and Novozhilov in the USSR; Kornai and Liptak in Hungary; Habr, Pelikan and Kyn in Czechoslovakia; and others) were decided advocates of abandoning the centralistic system, and some of them voiced far-reaching conceptions of decentralisation. Deeper acquaintance with the effects and opportunities offered by the development of cybernetics and computerisation of the flow of information for methods of steering large systems led many former opponents of the 'decentralised model' type of solution to withdraw later from the position they had taken. To this must also be added the reflection, which is irresistibly suggested by the experience of the socialist countries, that computerisation is precisely one of the fields whose development suffers most because of centralistic rigidity, and the prospects of eliminating the obstacles – technical, organisational and in personnel – are clearly connected with radical reform of the system of functioning of the economy. . . .

Thus it would be hard to accept that the failure of the 'first wave' of reform was decided by well-founded considerations of substance. It is true that many questions became much clearer later, but sufficient basis existed at the time too – at the end of the 1950s – for treating the arguments against reform with less confidence.

The influence of the political factor was evident. This is borne out, too, by the interesting correlation between the retardation and reversal of reform and certain features of the economic situation, especially in Poland and the USSR. We mentioned that an incentive to taking initiatives from above for improving the system of functioning of the economy was the urgent political need to get results in the sphere of consumption. Meanwhile in the years 1955–8 these results appeared, despite the fact that the system of functioning of the economy had not undergone any essential change. The sources of these relative successes were rather shallow; the peculiar kind of reserve stemming from past mistakes could not last long. But in political wishful thinking this temporary progress was magnified and treated as a weighty argument against embarking on a dangerous, or at least uncertain, wave of reform. When after a few years of relaxation of the burden of accumulation there followed, in 1958–9, renewed tightening of the screw and the opening of a new cycle of expansion of investment, this, too, was interpreted not so much against decentralisation as simply in favour of recentralisation of those decisions which had previously been transferred to lower levels; compulsory indicators and allocation of means of production were also restored to their former extent.

The fate of the 'first wave' of economic reforms confirms the interrelationship between the economic and political aspects. The postulate of reforming the mechanism of functioning of the economy, which grew solely out of criticism of the inadequate economic efficiency of the existing system, quickly acquired a dual significance: on the one hand it remained a purely pragmatic economic postulate, on the other it became an element in a broader programme of political transformation. The authorities strove to eliminate the second aspect at all cost, particularly after their recovery of freedom of manoeuvre, which was limited in certain situations (e.g. Poland in 1956) by strong social pressure. When it appeared possible, the striving to eliminate the political consequences was ultimately expressed in the abandonment of economic reforms. This, however, contained an internal contradiction, since the constraining influence of political fears was bound to make it more difficult to obtain the economic results which were necessary – in the specific conditions of the post-Stalin period – for maintaining the monopoly of power. This contradiction became especially evident in the 'second wave' of reforms.

Before we go on to discuss the 'second wave', let us draw attention again to the fact, which is characteristic of Poland, that – in spite of everything – the slogan of changes in the system of functioning of the economy never disappeared from the official political arsenal and at moments of increased demand for propaganda trumps was even brought to the fore. Economic reform figured in the resolutions of all successive congresses of the PUPW, including the III Congress (1959) which in reality was an important stage in the process of return to the old methods of management. This is yet another (minor perhaps, but symptomatic) indicator of the differences between the Stalin and the post-Stalin period, when reformist attire began to be desirable garb for the authorities.

The 'second wave' is the name we give to the renewed activisation of reformist tendencies in the middle of the 1960s. It is true that this did not have uniform practical effects in the different countries, but the coincidence in time and – to a certain degree – in conception was sufficiently large to enable us to find a number of common causes.

The basic causes of course stemmed from the economic sphere. The 'reserve of past mistakes' was quickly exhausted, just as were the extraordinary resources in Poland (American credit, the return of overpayments by the Soviet Union) or Hungary (stabilisation assistance after the 1956 uprising). On the other hand, the sources of irrationality connected with the essentially undisturbed system still operated, both in direct form (inadequate rate of decline or even increase in capital intensity, material intensity and labour intensity of manufactures) and in direct form (the so-called misdirected production, i.e. not suited to the needs of customers and therefore causing excessive growth of stocks). In the new conditions – of the higher general level of the economy and the growing role of international division of labour – the inefficiency of the system of functioning placed a greater and greater burden on the economy, particularly on the final reflection of its results in the level and growth of incomes of the population. It was also more and more difficult to make this area play the role of universal shock-absorber for economic disturbances, and if the authorities forgot this and went too far the threat of a social explosion appeared. The internal political and economic contradictions were supplemented by external ones: the necessity of keeping up with the scientific, technical and organisational revolution in Western countries.

It follows from the nature of the causes mentioned that they were bound to appear especially strongly in the most developed socialist countries – East Germany, Czechoslovakia and also Hungary – which were marked by non-existent or insignificant reserves of labour and relatively strong dependence on foreign trade. This meant that there was no, or only very limited, possibility of compensating for insufficient growth of labour productivity by additional employment. With their weak internal raw material base, particularly in relation to their developed processing industry, especial importance attached, on the one hand, to the ability to use raw materials efficiently and, on the other, to the steady growth of industrial exports. This last problem was closely connected with the preconditions for innovation, not only in methods of production but also in the use value of manufactures, their competitiveness on foreign markets. With inadequate productive efficiency, economic growth in countries of this type was bound to come up against a more and more serious barrier, and the standard of living of the population to remain disproportionately low in relation to the general level of development of productive capacity. True, not everywhere did this appear so strongly as in Czechoslovakia, which suffered a real collapse in the years 1962–4,[53] but the effects were keenly felt in East Germany, too (particularly in 1962 and 1965), and in Hungary (the slackening of the rate of growth in 1964 and

1965). In addition it so happened that in each of the countries mentioned a natural inclination appeared to compare their own results with the neighbouring capitalist countries with which they had had strong and close links in the past and which had formerly represented a more or less analogous level of economic development, incomes, and conditions of life (Czechoslovakia and Hungary with Austria, East Germany with West Germany). The negative results of these comparisons, particularly vivid probably in the case of the contrast between the Czech lands and Moravia *vis-à-vis* Austria, were bound to strengthen criticism of the existing system of functioning of the economy, and not only from the public but also from certain groups within the party leadership. It was thus no accident that the first harbinger of the 'second wave' was East Germany although it was one of the principal bastions of political and ideological dogmatism in the socialist camp. Somewhat later the slogan of reform was taken up in Czechoslovakia, but in a completely different manner, both as far as economic solutions and political implications were concerned.

In the Soviet Union and in Poland, and also in Bulgaria and Rumania, the objective situation allowed reform to be postponed to a greater extent since there still existed extensive factors of growth – in particular, reserves of labour. In addition to this there were specific features in the individual countries: in Poland the relatively favourable growth of agricultural production up to a certain time; in the Soviet Union, the growth of production and export capacity associated with the development of its raw material base; in Bulgaria, the rapid increase in revenue from tourism; in Rumania, partly tourism, but mainly the substantial investment credits from the West, etc. All this meant that, although the 1960s brought a slackening of the rate of growth in comparison with the previous decade, this was not so clear as it was in the first group of countries. Also, the slow growth of real wages was, as we saw, partially counteracted by the growth of average real incomes per inhabitant.

Nevertheless, in this group of countries, too, the economic failures of the 1960s showed that the centralistic system of functioning of the economy was more and more clearly contrary to the requirements of the development of productive forces. A fairly important element in the exacerbation of this contradiction was the very fact of the delay of reforms, while at the same time the slogan of changes was maintained and changes were simulated by minor practical moves: first the objective economic conditions deteriorated, which made it more difficult to undertake a reorganisation which, particularly in the initial period, would demand extra reserves to ensure a minimum freedom of manoeuvre; second, society's confidence in the programme of reforms was being shaken. The change in social climate was particularly evident in Poland: while in the October 1956 period and shortly after, an atmosphere of hope and even enthusiasm reigned, in the second half of the 1960s reform generally evoked a mood of scepticism and passivity. An attempt was made to assuage this mood with the help of the quasi-scientific propaganda argument that the conditions for the introduction of reform matured only at the conclusion of the phase of extensive growth and the transition to the intensive phase. This was intended to preserve the principle of infallibility of the party leadership, which by definition always used the correct methods for the given period. This in addition overlooked not only the party's own programme slogans of the past, but also the whole of the substantial criticism of the waste unnecessarily caused by the centralistic system even in conditions where extensive factors of development predominated.

A major role in the renewed growth of interest in economic reforms was played by external economic factors. The more developed countries were feeling the need for change more acutely and – in the 'second wave' – set about them more energetically; this thus gave rise to a situation where the weaker countries had no choice, since – assuming the economic effectiveness of reforms – to preserve the old system threatened to open the gap in economic levels wider. What was regarded as especially dangerous here was the achievement by others of predominance in the controversial area of exports – most of all to capitalist hard-currency markets, but within Comecon too, since the people's democracies are in competition, among other things, to ensure themselves the highest possible deliveries of raw materials from the USSR. With the course of time it became more and more difficult to obtain these supplies (from the purely economic aspect) without the possibility of making payment in relatively attractive commodities which diverged less from world standards. The centralistic system of functioning of the economy showed less and less ability to meet the growing import needs with industrial exports, and this restricted the possibilities of technical reconstruction of a number of branches, of increasing labour productivity and of modernisation of the structure of production. The weakness of market instruments for regulating economic relations within Comecon made the processes of integration more difficult which, in the face of the progress of the West European Common Market, intensified economic difficulties and political troubles. Hence, among others, such apparent paradoxes as the fact that the countries least advanced in internal reforms (Poland in the 1960s) put forward the most radical postulates for introducing the market mechanism within Comecon.

Thus, in the middle of the 1960s the pressure of economic needs once again raised the problem of reform of the system of functioning of the economy in all countries with the etatist model, but particularly sharply in Czechoslovakia, East Germany and Hungary. The political factors which operated against reforms appeared as before, and probably were uniformly strong everywhere. The distinctive resultant of the different intensity of needs and the similar degree of political fears was the fact that the three concrete attempts at a comprehensive reform were undertaken precisely in East Germany, Czechoslovakia and Hungary.

The economic reform *in East Germany* was initiated in 1963 – with the maximum caution so as not to permit any weakening of the monopoly of power. This aim was successfully achieved, which – combined with the relatively favourable economic results in the period following – would have made East Germany an attractive model for the ruling groups in the other countries, were it not for fears that untransferable national features and the conditions in which the country found itself were operating here (among other things the influence of its special type of economic relations with West Germany). As far as the reform solutions themselves were concerned, they of course moved towards greater autonomy of enterprises and associations (the latter play a considerable role in East Germany) and broader use of the market mechanism, but they remained closer to the centralistic point of departure than in the 'decentralised model' conception. The number of obligatory indicators transmitted from the top down to the enterprise level was substantially restricted, but they were not totally eliminated; in this area the principle of directive hierarchical plans at successive levels remained in force. Although a connection appeared between profit and the enterprise's development potential and its labour force's earnings, it was fenced round with a number of restrictions: in the investment field the possibilities of implementing projects not anticipated in the state plan were basically very small; in the field of earnings the link between profit and bonuses went through the filter of a series of detailed indicators (the so-called partial indicators) the fulfilment of which governed the relation between actual payments and the amount due on the basis of the financial results. In principle all prices were fixed by state organs, as were the other parameters of calculation. The central level of course took the basic decisions about development directly. Foreign trade, despite a higher degree of autonomy than previously, retained a number of directive elements in its management methods.

In Czechoslovakia the programme of reforms was undertaken by the Novotny team still, under pressure of the special economic difficulties, with the aim of relieving the tension through changes confined to the economic sphere. These calculations misfired, however; a mass movement of revival developed in all fields of social life, headed by democratisation of the political system. The changes in the system of functioning of the economy became in the 'Prague Spring' period part of a complex programme which was to acquire a concrete form at the XIV Congress of the Communist Party of Czechoslovakia in September 1968; as far as one can judge on the basis of the steps already taken in practice and the numerous statements in the literature, these changes were to be far-reaching, in some elements even going beyond the conception of the 'decentralised model' which the author of these words has become accustomed to treat as a point of reference. The intervention of the USSR and four other Warsaw Pact countries and the process of 'normalisation' initiated thereafter arrested the development of 'socialism with a human face' and thus also the implementation of the economic reform; some of the elements of the new system which had already been introduced were withdrawn. It is true that this does not foredoom the future of reform (economic requirements are operating as before and thus tending towards rationalisation of the functioning of the economy within the existing system of political relations too), but it remains a fact that the end of the decade 1961–70 found Czechoslovakia with a system of planning and management not greatly different from the previous one.

In Hungary the complex reform prepared over a period of a few years was put into operation on 1 January 1968. The system as it finally developed is the one which in our opinion most fully implements the conception of 'the model of a planned economy with a regulated market mechanism'.This is expressed above all in the break with the principle of hierarchical construction of the plan based on obligatory indicators addressed to economic bodies at successive levels, including the lowest. The central plan and the plans of lower levels (branches, enterprises) are organisationally independent of each other: apart from exceptional cases there are no obligatory indicators nor a system of rationing of factors of production. The growth of resources at the disposition of enterprises and the growth of their workforces' earnings are linked in a defined manner with the financial results achieved by the enterprises, subject of course to taxation for the budget. The independence of enterprises applies mainly to current operation but also extends partially to the sphere of investment, a certain portion of which is self-financed from current or future revenues (in the latter case through bank credit). Efforts are made to ensure the supremacy of the central plan, in accordance with the foundations of the 'decentralised model', through: (1) retention at central level of the basic long-term decisions on the pace and directions of economic development (the investment rate, allocation of the basic part of investment resources), on the general proportions of the distribution of income for consumption (in particular between private and public consumption), and on priority social and political aims and the resources for implementing them, etc.; (2) the setting at central level of a concrete objective function ('rules of the game') for enterprises; and (3) the concentration at central level of a set of instruments of economic policy which permit direct determination or effective control of the basic magnitudes entering the economic calculations of enterprises: prices, interest rates, tax rates, exchange rates, etc. As far as prices are concerned the principle that they should be parametric in relation to enterprises is realised not only by the method of setting prices by appropriate state organs, but also by means of prescribing limits of fluctuation or even permitting free movement of prices for those groups of commodities where market competition is a sufficient check against oligopolistic manipulation (in 1968–70 the group of free prices did not exceed one fifth to one quarter of the total value of retail turnover). In accordance with the importance attributed to foreign trade, the degree of independence of enterprise has grown considerably in this area, as has their direct interest in the financial results of transactions and the connection between exporting and importing and activity on the internal market; it is considered – correctly – here, that the new system, which radically increases the flexibility of the economy, does not undermine the validity of the 'state monopoly of foreign-trade', of which the essential content for a planned economy consists in the assurance of effective control over external economic relations rather than in convulsive clinging to forms introduced in the past.

The Hungarian solution, which in general is economically cohesive, was also accompanied by certain elements of political evolution. True, the institution of worker self-management was not introduced (it is hard to say whether owing to lack of confidence in it as an organisational form or because of its political implications), but some liberalisation was to be observed there – cautious and slow, but clear enough in relation to the other countries. This liberalisation, although intently observed from outside, i.e. by other socialist countries, did not encounter open criticism, which can be regarded as a sign that it did not undermine the principle of 'the leading role of the party', i.e. the effective control of the entire political life of the country by the party leadership. In any case this is a doubly interesting phenomenon: first – it is yet another link in the rather specific development of the situation in Hungary where from 1956 there had actually been no zigzags but a continuous – albeit initially, exceedingly slow – ascent from a very low starting point; second – the example of a complex economic reform and accompanying relative liberalisation which nevertheless does not violate the foundations of the political system, and does not evoke intervention from outside, can exert an influence on the course of further evolution in other countries (the tendency sometimes described by the term 'kadarisation' has won popularity in some of the peoples' democracies, including Poland after the convulsion of December 1970).

In other countries no deeper changes in the system of functioning of the economy had followed up to the end of the decade. In the USSR an economic reform was proclaimed in 1965, but neither its basic assumptions nor a time scale for its introduction were spelt out in detail. The general direction was towards increasing the role of the market mechanism (economic calculation, in Soviet terminology) by reducing the number of directive indicators and increasing the independence of enterprises – implemented gradually in selected branches and regions, but not reaching a degree which would permit us to state that a new, internally logical system had arisen. Also characteristic of Soviet relations was the extraordinary sensitivity to fluctuations in the political climate surrounding reform (e.g. the omission of the description 'economic reform' at the XXIV Congress of the CPSU), which produced corresponding jumps in the intensity of practical activity.

In Poland in the second half of the 1960s official 'declarations of intent' to introduce a reform of the system of functioning of the economy rained down almost continuously. Even after the events of March 1968, when the ideological campaigns against revisionism denounced 'market socialism' with reinforced vigour, there was an announcement of an increase in the decision-making powers of enterprises, growth in the role of profitability and the basing of economic incentives on financial results, etc. But in fact the changes were not carried out, and in 1970 on the other hand there was an attempt to make use of the idea of reform in order to camouflage the drastic deflationary policy. From 1 January 1971 the so-called new system of economic incentives was to come into force, laying down a two-year wage freeze and relatively narrow limits on growth thereafter. Together with the increase in the prices of necessities, this unfortunate system of incentives was among the direct economic causes of the workers' demonstrations in December 1970.

In Bulgaria in the middle of the 1960s a fairly broad economic reform was announced, but later the situation developed in a basic-ally analogous way to the Soviet Union. Rumania was for a long time the only country which did not bring out any general pro-gramme of reform of the system at all, although certain changes (in the same direction as in the other countries) were in fact introduced.

To sum up – despite the fact that in the second half of the 1960s the economic need to abandon the centralistic system of functioning of the economy was almost universally recognised and included in official programme documents, reform was introduced only in two cases, and in a consistent manner in only one: the Hungarian reform, however, passed over the problem of workers' self-management. This means that in general no basic changes in the system of functioning ensued in the post-Stalin period, which would contribute to the democratisation of the system, either directly at enterprise level or indirectly through a reduction in the degree of concentration of power at the centre. Thus, on this plane, too, the evolution of the etatist model in the post-Stalin period brought no new features from the point of view of the criterion of socialisation we have adopted.

In sum, then, an analysis of the processes taking place in the USSR and the people's democracies in the post-Stalin period leads to a conclusion which seems unequivocal: on all the planes considered – the socio-economic, the methods by which power is exercised, the system of functioning of the economy – changes were carried out, which it would be mistaken to underestimate but which did not transform public ownership into social ownership *sensu stricto*, according to the definition we have adopted. True, the extreme forms of totalitarian dictatorship receded – gradually and not without relapse – and the flexibility of the system, its capacity to adapt to changed conditions, increased to a certain extent, but the fundamental features of the production relations making up the etatist model of socialism remained undisturbed, in particular in the sector which we recognised as crucial, namely, in the political system, the real structure of power. Neither the whole of society nor the working class, whose dictatorship is supposed to be the essence of the socialist state, held power in the post-Stalin period, and thus neither did they become the owners of the nationalised means of production.

Notes

1 With the exception of the military sectors, in which progress was assured but with incommensurably high outlays. A significant contribution to the thesis of the contrast between military industry and all the rest is provided by the story of the hero in the Soviet writer Dudintsov's book *Not by Bread Alone* (English edn, New York, 1956). In the absence of objective scientific analysis this type of literature had a value as evidence.

2 See, for example, Maurice Dobb, *Soviet Economic Development since 1917*, London, 1966, ch. 15.

3 See Janet Chapman, *Real Wages in Soviet Russia*, Cambridge, Mass., 1963, ch. 9, table 22.

4 According to the Soviet statistical yearbook *Narodnoe Khozyaistvo SSSR v 1969 godu* (*The National Economy of the USSR in 1969*), Moscow, 1970, real income per employee (on the above definition) was 2·7 times above the 1913 level in 1940 and exceeded the pre-revolutionary level 7·6 times in 1969; using indices of the growth of real incomes over 1960–9, from table 25 of *Statisticheskii ezhegodnik SEV, 1970* (*Comecon Statistical Annual, 1970*), and indices of wages and prices over 1953–60, from tables 173 and 175 of *UN Statistical*

M

Yearbook 1969, we obtain for 1953 a level four times higher than 1913. M. Kalecki's calculations for Poland in 1960 (in comparison with 1937) show an index of 173 for the broadest aggregate (the index declines as the coverage is narrowed – see M. Kalecki, *Z zagadnień gospodarczo-społecznych Polski Ludowej* (*On the Economic and Social Problems of People's Poland*), Warsaw, 1964, p. 91 ff.); if we deflate this result by the index of growth of real wages in Poland over 1953–60 we reach an index of 110 for 1953 in relation to 1937. As for total consumption of goods and services per inhabitant, Simon Kuznets's calculations for the USSR showed an index of 131 for 1950 (taking 1928 = 100) and 175 for 1955 (see *Economic Trends in the Soviet Union*, ed. A. Bergson and S. Kuznets, Cambridge, Mass., 1963).

5 See M. Kalecki, op. cit., and Ivan Strup, 'A comparison of the standard of living and the general efficiency of production in Czechoslovakia and France', *Politićka Ekonomie*, (*Political Economy*), no. 2, 1968.

6 At least in the Soviet Union and Poland (see W. Brus, 'Środki publiczne i środki ludnošci w gospodarce mieszkaniowej' ('Public and private resources in housing construction'), ch. 1, in *Materiały i Studia Instytutu Gospodarki Mieszkaniowej* (*Documents and Studies of the Institute of Housing Construction*), no. 2, Warsaw, 1970).

7 By a government decree of 1940, which simultaneously restricted student grants to those students who achieved very good results. The justification of this move by the increase in the standard of living of the population to a level which allowed them to bear these payments was a kind of sour joke. Free tuition in secondary and higher education was only restored after the XX Congress of the CPSU in 1956.

8 An accurate although strongly emotionally coloured description of 'the ladder of cults of personality' is contained in Władysław Gomułka's speech at the VIII Plenum of the CC of the Polish Communist Party in October 1956, published in *Nowe Drogi*, no. 10, 1956. This document is particularly valuable in the light of the later evolution of Gomułka's own regime.

9 According to persistent rumours circulating in the USSR at the time, the conviction of the accused at a show trial was to be the green light for a plan for mass deportation of Jews from the western and central regions of the country.

10 This case is particularly well known to the author, who—in accordance with the basic task of the 'courtly economics' of the time – was also employed in pseudo-scientific justification of successive moves in economic policy, most frequently with inadequate acquaintance with their real basis and practical consequences – which were kept secret by the authorities. On the case of the price increases in January 1953 see 'O działaniu prawa wartości w gospodarce Polski Ludowej (w związku z uchwała Rządu z dn. 3.1.1953 c.)' ('On the operation of the law of value in the economy of people's Poland (in connection with the government decree of 3.1.1953))', paper by Comrade Włodzimierz Brus, 4.1.1953, *Materiały dla lektorów* (*Documents for*

Lecturers), ed. Wydział Propagandy KC PZPR, Warsaw, January 1953. The paper served as the basis of the article 'O niektórych zagadnieniach działania prawa wartości w okresie przejściowym od kapitalizmu do socjalizmu', published in the theoretical organ of the Central Committee of the Polish Communist Party *Nowe Drogi*, no. 1, 1953 and subsequently reprinted in the Italian journal *Critica Economica*, no. 6, 1953 ('Su alcuni aspetti dell'azione della legge del valore nel periodo di transizione dal capitalismo al socialismo').

11   See J. Stalin, *Economic Problems of Socialism in the USSR*, Moscow, 1952.

12   The fates of books, as the proverb says, are surprising – in a sense the consequences of Stalin's last work were unexpected too. After his death and the change in political conditions the thesis of the objective character of economic laws was transformed from an instrument for presenting everything actual as rational into an instrument of criticism: if economic laws have an objective character, then there is a basis for contrasting policy with something which can serve as an external, independent standard.

13   See Janet Chapman, op. cit., p. 145.

14   *Wskaźniki rozwoju gospodarki narodowej Polskiej Rzeczypospolitej Ludowej 1950–1955* (*Indicators of the Development of the National Economy of the Polish People's Republic 1950–1955*), GUS, Warsaw, 1956. Similar relative increases can be derived from the estimates of the Economic Commission for Europe, which otherwise estimates the index for 1953 (1949 = 100) as considerably lower in absolute terms (88 instead of 105·8) (see *Economic Bulletin for Europe*, vol. 9, no. 3, table 11, p. 35).

15   This tendency – in the years which interest us directly, here, for Hungary, i.e. immediately after 1952, and for Poland and USSR for a slightly later period (in the absence of earlier data) – can be seen in table 8.20 in the Economic Commission for Europe volume *Incomes in Post-war Europe: a Study of Policies, Growth and Distribution*, Geneva, 1967 (E –ECE – 613–Add. 1).

16   Two such attempts – both concerning agriculture – used to be mentioned in rather repeatedly circulated rumours: the first was the idea, launched in 1947 by the then member of the Politburo responsible for agriculture, Andreev, of returning to the so-called links (small workteams) in the use of kolkhoz land; the second was the proposals for revisions in agricultural policy allegedly submitted in 1949 by the chairman of Gosplan, N. Voznesensky. The fate of Voznosensky was tragic – he was executed on the orders of Stalin; Andreev fell into disgrace and ceased to play any political role.

17   Władysław Bieńkowski, *Problemy teorii rozwoju społecznego* (*Problems of the Theory of Social Development*), Warsaw, 1966, p. 131ff, draws attention to the phenomenon of 'dynamic processes of petrification', warning against understanding petrification as a stationary state.

18   According to the papers presented to the Joint Economic Committee of the United States Congress up to 1961 (the building of the Berlin

wall) the disparity between the level of consumption per inhabitant in East Germany and West Germany was even diminishing constantly (the index for 1960 for East Germany is 72·1, taking West Germany as 100), whilst in subsequent years it began to grow again (*Economic Developments in the Countries of Eastern Europe*, compendium of papers submitted to the Sub-committee on Foreign Economic Policy of the Joint Economic Committee, Washington DC, 1970, No. 38–2210).

19 As far as the Soviet Union is concerned, according to the Economic Commission for Europe in *Incomes in Post-war Europe*, op. cit., table 7.12, the years 1956–8 showed a considerably lower rate of growth of incomes than subsequent years, which is to some extent the opposite of the peoples' democracies.

20 *Incomes in Post-war Europe*, op. cit., table 7.12.

21 Data from the same source for 1965 (1960 = 100) are: Bulgaria, 110; Czechoslovakia, 104; E. Germany, 113; Hungary, 109; Poland, 107; Rumania, 122.

22 This must surely be the source of Khrushchev's supposition of rapidly achieving the West European and even the American level of consumption of basic consumer goods per inhabitant, and also of the reticence in reforming the system of functioning of the economy, since its initial dynamism seemed to gainsay the need for institutional changes which would be politically risky from the point of view of the rulers.

23 *Rocznik Statystiki Międzynarodowej* (*International Statistical Annual*), GUS, Warsaw, 1970, p. 338. The index for the USSR differs from that given in the 1970 Comecon handbook (for 1968 (1960 = 100) it gives 123). *Gospodarka Polski na tle wybranych krajów* (*The Polish Economy Compared with Selected Countries*), GUS, Warsaw, 1971, table 6, p. 233, gives figures for average annual rate of growth (per cent) of real wages, excluding agriculture, over the period 1960–9. These are reproduced in Table A.

TABLE A

Austria	5·2	Poland	1·8
France	4·0	Czechoslovakia	2·8
W. Germany	4·9	E. Germany	3·0
Great Britain	2·2	Hungary	2·4
Italy	4·4		

24 *Incomes in Post-war Europe*, op. cit., ch. 11, p. 5.

25 See Egon Vielrose, *Rozkład dochodów według wielkości* (*The Distribution of Incomes*), Warsaw, 1960, pp. 34–7; Lidia Beskid, 'Płace realne w Polsce w latach 1956–1967' ('Real wages in Poland in 1956–1967'), *Ekonomista*, no. 6, 1968; Wiesław Krencik, 'Czy słuszne różnice płac?' (Are pay differentials correct?), *Polityka*, no. 45, 1971. The last author concludes:

the specific features of the structure of wages of manual and white-collar workers which we have presented are not only characteristic of 1970. The structure of wage differentials was analogous in 1965, 1960 and even, for manual workers, in 1949, when completely different conditions existed.

26 Evidence on the influence of territorial concentration of lower-paid branches of the economy on the earnings situation in the region concerned is provided by the characteristic example of the Polish textile centre, Łódź. When, at the beginning of 1971, compensatory supplements were awarded for wages which amounted to less than 2,000 zlotys monthly, they had to be given to over 60 per cent of all workers there, or double the average proportion in industry.

27 See W. Brus, *Środki publiczne i środki ludności w gospodarce mieszkaniowej* (*Public and Private Resources in Housing Construction*), IGM, Warsaw, 1970, tables 3, 4, 5.

28 See *Studia i prace statystyczne GUS* (*Works and Studies of the Chief Statistical Administration*), Warsaw, 1970, no. 19, annex, table 1.

29 See Michał Kalecki, 'Próba wyjaśnienia zjawiska przestępczości gospodarczej' ('An attempt to elucidate the phenomenom of economic crime'), in *Z zagadnień gospodarczo-społecznych Polski Ludowej* (*On The Social and Economic Problems of People's Poland*), Warsaw, 1964.

30 With other forms of repression, particularly economic, the position is different, especially in periods of political tension such as 1968 in Poland or in Czechoslovakia after the armed intervention by the Warsaw Pact countries.

31 '... the English Established Church will more readily pardon an attack on 38 of its 39 articles than on 1/39 of its income', *Capital*, vol. 1, author's preface to the first edition, trans. Samuel Moore and Edward Aveling, ed. Frederick Engels, London, 1889 (reprinted 1946), p. xix.

32 The controlled 'opening up to abroad' gave the authorities a new and unexpectedly effective instrument of pressure on the citizen – in the form of an appropriate policy on permission for foreign travel and contacts.

33 The principal note of this campaign in Poland was the alleged direct and immediate threat of invasion of Czechoslovakia by West Germany.

34 We shall call this process 'normalisation', employing the term which the Warsaw Pact countries used of the invasion of Czechoslovakia. This is substantially justified since in both cases the aim is the same – elimination of all violations of the political system proper to the etatist model.

35 This process is the subject of the book by Władysław Bieńkowski, *Socjologia klęski, dramat gomułkowskiego czternastolecia* (*The Sociology of Disaster; Gomułka's Fourteen Years*), Paris, 1971.

36 In this connection a public terminology even appeared, distinguishing between 'mandated' and 'non-mandated' places on the lists. Candidates placed in the latter are deprived in advance of all chance and usually receive a few per cent of the votes compared with the ninety-

odd per cent which the 'mandated' candidates get from simply untouched ballot papers (exceptions occur in elections to rural councils at the lowest level). In order to avoid completely discrediting 'non-mandated' candidates they began, from a certain point, to be given 'mandated' places for representative bodies at a lower level (a 'non-mandated' candidate for the Sejm would thus be a 'mandated' candidate for a provincial council).

37   At the VIII Plenum of the Central Committee of the PUPW in February 1971, that is, after the December 1970 events, Józef Cyrankiewicz, who had held the office of premier for a quarter of a century, described another similar case, when, fearing Gomułka's anger, he had first concealed the name of the author of a critical economic memorandum, and subsequently decided that he would not make the mistake of presenting expert reports any more. See *Nowe Drogi*, special number, May 1971.

38   See the next section of this chapter.

39   In particular the VIII Plenum of the Central Committee of the PUPW, February 1971; see *Nowe Drogi*, special number, May 1971.

40   We shall frequently use the shorter term 'economic reform'; this term is very widespread, although not fully precise, since economic reform can touch matters which extend beyond the problems of functioning.

41   This kind of attitude is evident in the series of resolutions of the Central Committee of the CPSU and the Council of Ministers of the USSR from 1953 and the beginning of 1954, in the resolutions of the II Congress of the PUPW in February 1954 and in analogous documents from the other countries; only in agriculture were certain changes initiated almost from the beginning which could be described as affecting the system.

42   The accepted terminology at the time for distinguishing between administrative and economic methods was not perhaps completely precise and would require additional interpretation, but nevertheless it reflected the general sense of the postulated changes.

43   *Dyskusja o polskim modelu gospodarczym* (*Discussion of the Polish Economic Model*), Warsaw, 1957, pp. 261–2.

44   *Ekonomika i matematicheskie metody* (*Economics and Mathematical Methods*), vol. 1, no. 5, Moscow, 1965.

45   See chapter 2, section 3.

46   Just as in the general political field, Gomułka's accession to power in October 1956 did not so much open up as terminate the maturing processes of change in the system of functioning of the economy. These processes grew up under the influence of the criticism of the existing state of affairs at all levels, particularly the lowest. A strong impulse to the drawing of conclusions from this criticism was given by the general congress of Polish economists in June 1956. The growth of social pressure, of which the most vivid illustration was the workers' demonstration in Poznan, made economic reforms an element in the broader programme of renewal of socialism. After the VII Plenum of the Central Committee of the PUPW in July 1956,

which properly sanctioned the general direction of reform, initiatives – at first individual, later more and more broad – began to appear in implementation of new methods of management in particular enterprises ('economic experiments') and spontaneous appointment of worker self-management organs (workers' councils). In order to avoid disorganisation, and also loss of political control over the whole process, a Party-Government Commission was appointed to reorganise the system of management. As a result of the work of the Commission in the space of a very short time three legal acts were prepared: resolution of the Council of Ministers No. 704 on the extension of the powers of state industrial enterprises; the law on workers' councils; and the law on the factory fund. It is true that all these legal acts were adopted in the course of the couple of weeks after the October VIII Plenum of the Central Committee of the PUPW, but they were in fact the result and the expression of the social and political situation of the pre-October period. Besides, these were the most far-reaching (compared with both earlier and later) acts in the direction of real change in the system (radical restriction of the number of centrally fixed targets (commands), a strong link, in the factory fund, between a part of remuneration and the financial results of enterprises, and what is most characteristic – use in the law on workers' councils of the formulation that the general management of the enterprise is confided precisely to bodies freely elected by the workforce and not formally subject to any hierarchical apparatus; appointment of the director required the sanction of the workers' council, which could also propose his dismissal).

After Gomułka had come to power the process of adaptation of other sectors to the situation created by the acts mentioned lasted for some time (e.g. the so-called small reform of trade), and individual enterprises were allowed to try particular experimental solutions for a limited time, but generally the process of reform outside agriculture was frozen, and soon the freeze changed in many sectors into retreat.

47 Some economists attached greater weight to this element of reform than to decentralisation and new forms of material incentives: see M. Kalecki 'Rady robotnicze i centralne planowanie' ('Workers' councils and central planning'), *Nowe Drogi*, no. 12, 1956, reprinted in *Zagadnienia gospodarcze i społeczne Polski Ludowej* (*Economic and Social Problems of People's Poland*), op. cit.

48 We should always keep in mind the reservation (see chapter 2, section 2) that 'the political monopoly of the party' has nothing to do with the discharge of authority by members of the party. It concerns the party as an institution, not as a set of people.

49 To avoid misunderstanding it must be pointed out that the term 'optimisation' is used here (and in other places) in a very general sense – as the attempt to obtain the best possible solutions with the given state of knowledge of the decision-makers, a given degree of uncertainty, and taking account of social, political and institutional constraints (most frequently non-quantified), etc. In practice, then, it

becomes choice among a group of *relatively* favourable eligible solutions rather than of an optimum in the language of mathematical programming models; these models can be extremely useful in the course of the logical preparation of the plan, but should not be treated as direct instruments for decision-making.

50   I have discussed this type of problem by way of an example in my article 'Economic calculus and political decisions' (see the collection of essays *Economics and Politics of Socialism*, London and Boston 1973). However, the problem does not just boil down to the questions touched on there of discounting the benefits of consumption in the shorter and longer run over time; it also involves many problems in the field of the social distribution of income.

51   A. A. Volkonsky, *Model' optimal'nogo planirovaniya i vzaimosvyazi ekonomicheskikh pokazatelei* (*A Model of Optimal Planning and the Interrelationship of Economic Indicators*), Moscow, 1967. See also Radmila Stojanović, *Veliki ekonomski sistemi* (*Large Economic Systems*), Belgrade, 1970.

52   'The paradox of planning' (in this context) consists in the necessity of simultaneously defining the structure of final product and prices, while there exists, obviously, an interrelationship between prices and quantities (quantities are needed for setting prices and prices for setting quantities). If planning applies to *the whole system* no magnitudes should be taken as externally given; a single national economy, or even a superstate integration in so far as it draws data from outside (world market prices), is a 'sub-system' of the 'system' the world economy. The consequences of the 'paradox of planning' for the problems of the functioning of the economy are discussed, among others, by Charles E. Lindblom, 'The rediscovery of the market', *The Public Interest*, no. 4, 1966 (New York).

53   The official index of national income for 1963 in relation to the previous year was 98, which, not counting such periods of convulsion as 1956 in Hungary, was a phenomenon unknown in Eastern Europe.

4

The prospects for socialisation
in the future

Both our analytical chapters have led to a negative conclusion;
socialisation of the means of production, defined precisely, has not
become a reality in the European socialist countries. This statement, as we have emphasised already and shall not hesitate to
repeat again, does not in the least mean that we underestimate the
depth of the change which has taken place in the economic system
and in social relations, and consequently in the degree of industrialisation and the general living conditions of the population. A central
point in our discussion is the recognition of the economically and
socially progressive role of the *nationalisation* carried out as a result
of the October Revolution and the analogous types of change of
system in the peoples' democracies. The problem turns on the extent
of the progressiveness, on whether there exists an objective necessity
for progress *forward* (the emphasis on the last word is essential!)
towards *socialisation*. The Marxist conception of socialism says
without doubt yes. Our comparison with the reality of the socialist
countries (confined basically to the etatist model) negates this
hypothesis. Is this sufficient evidence against the Marxist conception
of socialism?

No. As we stressed when summing up chapter 2, this type of
contrast of the Marxist hypothesis with the course of reality hitherto
in the socialist countries still does not entitle us to deny theoretically
the objective necessity of socialisation of the means of production as
a historical law. The conclusion that socialism meets the demands

of the development of productive forces through the establishment of relations of production based on public ownership without further definition, that is, what we regard as the 'Schumpeter version', would be substantiated if we could accept that the etatist model not only exists but is also rational, i.e. creates favourable preconditions for the further development of productive forces, is a driving force of rather than a brake on development. In other words, the question remains to be answered, whether we can say of the 'normal form' of the etatist model what we said of the Stalinist deformations, the elimination of which proved to be economically determined, in the categories of the dialectics of productive forces and relations of production. The answer will be more difficult this time, in that it cannot be furnished *ex post*, on the basis of more or less precise empirical material, but has to be an *ex ante* answer deduced by way of abstract reasoning (some will say intellectual speculation) from comparison of certain characteristics of modern technology and a modern economy and the features of the political system.

The risk in such a venture is evident, but it must be undertaken in order to bring the matter to a conclusion – with the obvious reservation that it is not a question of predicting whether, how, and when, the etatist model of today will give way to a democratic socialism based on socialised means of production, but of examining the general interrelationships between the economic and political factors of development and defining on this basis the long-term tendencies at present perceptible.

To defend the hypothesis of the necessity of socialisation it has to be shown that considerations of economic efficiency are creating a need for democratisation of the political system of the socialist countries, a need which is long-term and has no substitute. This means that we want to formulate the problem of freedom praxiologically; using Bieńkowski's terms,[1] we pose the problem of freedom as a 'factor of production' rather than as a 'consumption' good in itself. It is true that this contrast is handicapped in advance by a lack of precision, since the degree of satisfaction of consumer requirements always (including the case of feeling a need for freedom) in its turn exerts an influence on production – yet the fundamental sense of this formulation should be clear: it is a question of the connection between the democratism of a social organisation and its economic efficiency.

The methodological aspects of this problem have been formulated in an interesting way by the eminent Polish sociologist, Stanisław Ossowski. Analysing three types of collective behaviour and the 'three simple conceptions of social order' corresponding to them,[2] Ossowski deduces a fourth type of social order ('based on a system of understandings') from their intersection, of which he writes:[3]

> This fourth conception of social order, which – despite the protestations of old-fashioned liberals – is to reconcile the polycentric character of social life with a rational system of planning, imposes a problem of the first rank on men today and opens up a broad field for sociological research and 'sociological imagination'. It is a question here of the methods of planned cooperation on the broadest scale in a polycentric society. It is a matter of solving the conflict between the effectiveness of monolithic direction and the humanistic values of polycentrism.

The last sentence was read initially by the author of the present work as a suggestion for a peculiar kind of compromise, relinquishment of the 'effectiveness' of monocentrism *in favour of* the values of another type ('humanistic') represented by polycentrism. But this seems to be a superficial interpretation. Conflict – understood usually as a clash of alternatives which are mutually exclusive or at least weaken each other – appears, according to Ossowski, 'if we only take the three simple forms of social order into account'; then 'central planning can basically only be compatible with the third type'. On the other hand, when we go beyond the three simple types of social order the possibility is opened up of a solution which is supposed to reconcile 'the polycentric character of social life with a rational system of planning' and thus create a plane on which effectiveness and humanistic values are not substitutes but complementary to each other. Let us note that even assuming that the level of effectiveness remains unchanged the situation, in Pareto's categories, is better, since the realisation of the 'humanistic values of polycentrism' is attained; it is all the more so if – as the Marxist conception of socialisation would have it – greater freedom increases effectiveness, and in a cumulative manner ('positive feedback').

Ossowski's reasoning was directed expressly against those who – as he put it – cherish the traditions of nineteenth-century liberalism and 'are frequently inclined to link the system of central planning with a monocentric system of a military type';[4] he mentioned here Hayek (*The Road to Serfdom*) and could have added many others, in particular, among economists, Milton Friedman (*Capitalism and Freedom*). From the point of view of our own discussion this is fundamental in that right from the beginning (see chapter 1) we have recognised the objective character of the tendency for growth of the economic role of the state and planning. Exposure of the methodological error on which is based the thesis that planning and freedom are antonyms frees us from the need to engage again in a general polemic with the traditional liberal position.

But the view that there is an inseparable link between planning and 'the monocentric type of social order' (which could include the general outline of the 'etatist model of socialism', in our terminology) is professed basically by extreme opponents of liberalism, too – if not in words, then in their actual position. The conclusions they draw are the opposite: whilst the former reject central planning since it is incompatible with freedom, the latter reject freedom because it is incompatible with central planning; but for both liberals and the adherents of the existing forms of 'dictatorship of the proletariat' alike the postulate of central planning is a 'postulate of the rationality of the monocentric order', and, on the other hand, 'the monocentric order creates the simplest, easiest conditions for central planning and its implementation'.[5] Ossowski's methodological criticism thus indirectly hits at the opposite pole too.

Of course, even the most apt methodological plane does not by itself solve the substantial question of the economic determination of the evolution of the etatist model towards this 'fourth type of social order'. Let us then attempt a substantial analysis.

The development of productive forces in the contemporary era is marked not only by its rapid and constantly growing pace, but also by the complex nature of the changes, which extend beyond the simple continuation of mechanisation of the processes of production which is characteristic of the industrial period. Individual theoreticians rank the elements in the 'scientific-technical revolution' differently, but in general they always emphasise 'the victory of the principle of automation in a broad sense'; changes in the 'subjective aspect' of production, i.e. the gradual elimination of man from 'the area of merely executive, service, operative and finally even regulating functions in direct production'; and the wide penetration into production by science and its technological adaptations.[6] As far as this last element – which is of fundamental importance – is concerned, it seems that, in distinction from the period of the industrial revolution, when the progress of science impinged on production from the outside, as it were, as an exogenous factor developing 'behind the back of the old form of capital' (Marx) – modern scientific and technical progress, embracing both basic and applied scientific research and the whole problem of innovation, is more and more rarely the result of discoveries made by isolated individuals and more and more often the result of collective organised effort supported by the requisite outlays, which are borne by the prospective user or – particularly with the growth of the scale and time horizon involved – by the state. These changes in the mechanism of innovation are reflected in economic theory in, among other things, attempts to construct models of economic growth in which technical progress would be treated as an endogenous factor functionally related to outlays on science, education, etc.[7]

What is the connection between these features of the development of productive forces in the present era, in particular the rapid pace and the specific mechanism for generating innovations, and the postulate of evolution of production relations by way of democratisation of the political system in the socialist countries?

The general answer sounds simple but is not very illuminating: there are interrelations in different directions. On the one hand, correlations appear which – at least at first glance – could be described as negative, i.e. contrary to the hypothesis of economically determined democratisation of political relations; on the other hand, positive correlations appear which conform to this hypothesis. Our task therefore must consist in examining both types of correlation and evaluating the relative importance of each.

In general the elements of *negative correlation* are primarily connected with the high degree of concentration and the complexity of the economic problems which have to be solved by the decision centre, particularly at the level of the national economy as a whole, but also at the level of a branch of production or a large enterprise. Not only technical questions but evaluation of the economic profitability and the social effects of allocation decisions, too, are complicated and more and more removed from daily experience, from ordinary 'common sense'. The anticipation of the future which is required for the design and technical, production and personnel preparation of large-scale investment raises the importance of highly specialised knowledge and of coordination of the enormous number of parameters of decisions today, and above all of the ability for coordinated prediction of future changes in them, both their general trend and their specific course in particular phases. Since modern economics more and more widely rejects the initial premise of 'consumer sovereignty', which is supposed to form the structure of production through allegedly autonomous acts of choice on the market, it is alleged that the conception of the sovereignty of citizens as producers who would have to decide what, how and when to produce, would seem to be all the more unrealistic; and this after all is what in the last resort the use *by* society of the means of production or, in our definition, their socialisation, boils down to. It would follow from this that the character of modern productive forces demands not the democratisation of decisions but handing them over to a greater and greater extent to experts – scientists, technical specialists, organisers, economists, etc. The rise to prominence of these and similar factors is supposed to be the source of the most general premises for connecting the scientific and technical revolution with the 'managerial revolution', with the role of a technocratic oligarchy, which satisfies the material needs of the masses better or worse (with the course of time rather better) but always remains a distinctive élite with *de facto* disposition over the means of production.

The arguments cited apply both to state economic organisations and to large private share corporations. The latter, which formerly served some scholars and ideologues as a stepping-stone to the thesis of democratisation of the disposition over capital, are today more often an example of the atrophy of all signs of real influence by rank-and-file shareholders on the decisions monopolised by the management. The growth of the economic role of the state and the phenomenon which Galbraith calls – for contemporary American conditions – the superimposition of political over industrial authority[8] not only do not weaken the technocratic tendencies in economic management but, on the contrary, transfer them in a peculiar way to the sphere of politics, even where well-developed and operating democratic institutions exist. This would lead not so much to democratisation of the economy as autocratisation of politics, expressed among other things in decline in the significance of parliamentary control and appeal to the will of the electorate, with at the same time an increase in the role of every kind of private understanding between technocrats and politicians. This is also in essence the implication of Galbraith's conception of the technostructure, despite the author's effort to save society from its negative effects by appealing to the still latent power of intellectuals who could make beneficial use of their monopolistic position in the sphere of creation of the values indispensable to the existence and development of the modern world. For the prospects of evolution of the socialist political system the conclusion would be that the postulate of democratisation – particularly referring to the institution of parliamentary democracy – borders on anachronism 'even' for the developed capitalist countries. The transition of the economy from the sphere of private activity to that of public activity would then create the natural precondition for extension to the whole economy of bureaucratism in the Weberian sense:[9] hierarchical structure and a clear principle of subordination to higher levels, division of competence (and in particular separation of direction from execution), operation according to formalised rules, etc. There is no need to emphasise that according to Weber bureaucracy is not a harmful tumour on the body of an organisation but a condition for it to meet modern demands efficiently.

Another factor which is regarded as conflicting with the democratisation of the political system is the very fact of the use of the criteria 'superior social interest', 'social preferences', etc, that is, of categories which are inseparably linked with the nature of a socialist economy implementing the objective function of 'the system as a whole'. This thesis is advanced by, among others, adherents of extreme economic liberalism, who see the principle of superiority of the social interest as a violation of individual preferences: the social interest can be either the sum of individual interests – when it has no separate existence and cannot fulfil the role of a criterion – or it is regarded as an independent interest of the collective as such, which does not tally with the sum of individual interests – when it must be imposed on the members of society by compulsion. One can of course disagree with the conclusions which those who criticise socialism from liberal positions derive from this reasoning, but to a certain extent at least there is a real problem here, which we partially touched on in the introduction to chapter 2 when discussing the difficulty of defining the social interest unequivocally. In the first place there is the question of the different time horizons of individuals and society in the case of investments with delayed effects, and the consequent differing evaluations of the relation between cost and benefit from the point of view of the individual interest and of the collective interest. On this basis conflicts can arise which either cannot be successfully solved at all by means of democratic procedure, or can only be solved with great difficulty, at the cost of delay in taking decisions, and thus of losses. The most frequently cited example is that of a high rate of investment which threatens current consumption – essential for economic development in certain conditions, but liable not to be accepted voluntarily. There are a number of other problems of this type, and not only at the level of differences in time preferences (conflict between the level of wages and the level of employment where a reserve of labour exists, or between overall shortening of hours of work and lowering of the retirement age; some authors also include conflicts concerning policy for protection of the environment in this category). Because the direct *current* interest of the majority is in many cases obvious (lower accumulation, higher wages, shorter working week) it may be feared that choice by means of a democratic political mechanism will not take sufficient account of broader and long-term considerations. This provides the grounds for justifying the leading function of the political élite, the '*avant-garde*' which is conscious of 'the historical interests' of the working class and the people. This function falls, according to the doctrine, to the communist party. The Leninist conception of the *avant-garde* party is thus transposed from the conspiracy situation of revolutionary struggle to economic processes and the system of economic decision-making, and because conditions also undergo a fundamental change in the respect that the pre-revolutionary party of selected individuals is transformed in all socialist countries into a mass party, in which the way of thought of the rank-and-file members does not basically differ from the attitude of the majority of society, the thesis of 'the leading role of the communist party' and the claim that it represents the general social point of view lead logically to the conclusion that the capacity to take correct decisions lies in narrower and narrower circles of the party leadership.

We are not concerned with an exhaustive enumeration of all the factors which could be regarded – or at least interpreted – as conflicting with the hypothesis of economic justification for democratisation. It is sufficient to outline in general what type of factors can be included in this category and what kind of conclusions they can prompt.

Analysis of these factors seems to confirm that modern conditions of development of productive forces also contain objective elements which may not favour the democratic evolution of the political system. These elements are in a certain sense side effects of the tendency towards planning and transition from private economic to social economic criteria of rationality; they must not therefore be ignored. Taking account of the appearance of elements of negative correlation is a necessary antidote to the over-optimistic expectation of easy and immediate progress in all sectors as a result of taking the path of democratic evolution. The consequences, particularly in the initial phases, can also be to some degree or other negative, not only in respect of the political difficulties of the process of transformation itself (we are not in principle concerned with these problems) but simply in respect of the non-homogeneous character of the relationship between democratisation of the political system and the needs of the development of productive forces.

But if it would be wrong to abstract from the negative correlation, it would be still more wrong to make a fetish of it. One of the fundamental sources of such fetishisation, it seems to me, is the conviction that an objective precondition of democratisation is a progressive process of simplification of problems and methods of solving them. This conviction is connected to some extent with the view of socialism, which is widespread in the Marxist tradition, as an 'easy' system which solves all conflicts by the act of 'expropriation of the expropriators'. Such utopian simplifications include, among other things, the view of the extraordinary ease of democratic government of a socialist state. It may be that this view, repeated so many times, for example, by Lenin in *State and Revolution*, fulfilled a revolutionary mission in its time, since it emboldened the masses to take actions at which they could have baulked had they known the true scale of its complexity. However, this does not mean that it thus became correct, especially as today, unrevised in official doctrine, it plays a retrograde role since it helps to cultivate the fiction of the power of the people, which governs nothing easily while a narrow directing group solves only the difficult, that is, all the important problems,

N

Social reality, on the other hand, bids us seek the relationships between the development of productive forces and the evolution of the political system of socialism on the plane of *the growing complexity of the object and methods of decision-making.* It is on this plane, or – speaking cautiously – mainly on this plane, that we must find the elements of negative and positive correlation between modern development needs and political democratisation; on this plane, in my opinion, we can use the proper measure to evaluate the relative weight of each side and extract the predominant tendency. Our thesis runs: the growing complexity of the object and methods of decision-making is not only a source of elements of negative correlation (from which we began) but also a source of elements of positive correlation with the latter predominating and defining ultimately the direction of the long-run process.

We shall begin with problems which appear to be somewhat removed from the main stream of our discussion, namely those which are the concern of modern industrial and organisational sociology in relation to methods of management in the enterprise, broadly understood.[10]

The results of the studies by Western industrial sociologists and management and organisation theorists are especially interesting from our point of view because – despite, as usual, the great burden of hardly testable theoretical hypotheses based on arbitrary assumptions – these studies have a connection with the practical functioning of economic organisations both as far as their initial inspiration and criteria and the chance of implementation of their results are concerned. Industrial sociologists and organisers address their postulates and conclusions not to philanthropists but to businessmen, and thus base themselves on praxiological criteria – efficiency of operation, economic effectiveness. Of course many of these conclusions and postulates encounter scepticism at every stage – some exceed the capacity of practical men to adapt, some may simply be wrong – but nevertheless longer observation of the changes in the methods of management provides evidence that the general direction of the conclusions advanced by the consensus of representatives of the various social sciences studying the efficiency of organisations is confirmed in practice. This applies in particular to the universal abandonment of Taylorism which, unlike any organisational conception, was based on the assumption that the worker is in the nature of things a passive and recalcitrant creature, requiring ruthless external direction, limitation of his own field of invention (hence the tendency to the most far-reaching division of activity and the reduction of work to mechanical performance), stimulation to activity by means of a highly developed system of rewards and penalties (among others in the form of complete adoption of piece-work), detailed control, etc.

Modern management sociology and psychology not only come out against Taylorism but also take a sceptical attitude to the conception of so-called humanisation of relations in the enterprise, which they treat as a 'soft', paternalistic version of the same principle which underlay Taylorism (the 'hard', autocratic version), namely the external direction of the labour of man who is regarded virtually exclusively as a passive executor, an object of manipulation.[11] In opposition to this principle, and both versions of its application, the assumption is now advanced that people are by nature active and ambitious, capable of integrating their aims with those of organisations, inclined to accept responsibility and display initiative – while indications of the contrary should be ascribed principally to the long refusal to give them an active role. Hence the basic task of management is to create conditions favouring the manifestation of the features of man as the true subject of the process of work, above all by enabling him to organise his activity himself. Self-organisation in the broad sense assumes participation in decisions affecting, directly or indirectly, the given field of activity; McGregor emphasises strongly that this is a matter of real participation, because nothing is less effective and more demoralising than apparent participation, intended merely to 'impress upon people that they are fulfilling an important role'.[12]

It is worth noting the attempts to make the justification of the expediency of a democratic system of organisation dynamic. Autocratic and paternalistic methods lose their effectiveness not only with the growth in the complexity of organisations' tasks and in the cultural and professional level of the workers, but also with the higher degree of satisfaction of their material needs (including the need for security for the future) since this is accompanied by growth in the importance of another category of needs – for the affirmation of human personality, the use of potential for activity and creative possibilities. This hypothesis betrays a clear similarity to the Marxist theory of socialisation and disalienation of labour, or at any rate shows one of the possible sources of the veritable explosion of

interest in this latter in the broad circles of students of social problems in the West. If it is correct, it opens up new and fascinating
aspects of a number of important practical problems, including that
of the limits of effectiveness of economic incentives and the conditions for use of a higher order of motivation. We shall return to
some of the questions connected with this.

A consequence of this trend in the evolution of views on the
effectiveness of organisations has also been a changed understanding of the Weberian thesis of rational bureaucratisation of organisational structures. Instead of treating this conception as conflicting
with the postulate of democratisation, it is more and more
frequently considered to lie on a different plane, and that the
typology of systems of organisation is simply not exhausted by the
contrast of autocratism and democratism.[13] A formalised hierarchical organisational structure operating according to defined
rules can be a component both of an autocratic and of a democratic
system of organisation – in the latter case on the condition that both
the aims of the organisation and the system of relationships and the
principles of selection of people at particular levels, the rules of
behaviour, etc., will be democratically decided and controlled.
What is more, bureaucratisation in this sense, and in particular,
observance by every organisational level of the established rules of
behaviour, can in certain circumstances be an essential component
of democratism, since it counteracts arbitrariness.[14]

The tendency, briefly discussed here, to link the efficiency of an
organisation with the democratism of its structure resulted from
theoretical and empirical analysis of the functioning of private
enterprises, mainly large corporations. The area of practical applic-
ability of the results of this analysis under the capitalist system is a
problem with which we are not concerned here; if it is limited, then
we have in turn before us an indication of the contradiction between
the requirements of the development of productive forces and capitalist production relations.

From our point of view, however, the important question is the
justification for extending these conclusions to the socialist
countries at their present phase of development. There seems to me
to be no reason to question this. On the contrary rather, the connection between efficiency and democratism should be even greater
in respect of relations *within* socialist enterprises since for understandable reasons the expectation of partnership is greater here than

in capitalist enterprises and thus failure to fulfil it antagonises the workforce more strongly and is a greater barrier to integration. The most important premise, however, for the general significance of the thesis of *positive correlation* between democratism and efficiency stems from *outside* enterprises, from the sphere of basic economic decisions taken at central level according to general economic criteria. The postulate, put forward by the sociological trends discussed above, of integration of the workforce with the aims of the organisation acquires even greater weight at the macro-economic level because it not only determines the proper motivation but also has a substantial influence on the flow of information. Of course the information aspect plays a big part within enterprises too, but there can be no doubt that its role increases enormously at the macroeconomic level. It is from this problem, which is so specific to the planned economy, that we shall begin. In the nature of things, we shall have to go beyond the area of the problems which are the subject of interest of the sociologists and theorists of organisation.

The transition from the single enterprise – even the largest in terms of absolute size – to the national economy as a whole radically, one could say qualitatively, modifies *the problem of information flows* in the process of decision-making.

On the one hand – we are concerned in general with decisions which are not only on a larger scale (at least relatively, i.e. in relation to the size of the national economy) but which, at least by assumption, are coordinated and which must therefore take into account directly the consequences for other 'sub-systems' and for the 'system' as a whole. Since at the present stage of development of the socialist countries obvious solutions and obvious connections between them either no longer appear at all or are becoming rarer and rarer, choice must be based on comprehensive multi-stage and multi-level analysis of variants. The game element in the iteration process, the significance of which we emphasised when justifying the rationality of the 'decentralised model' (see chapters 2 and 3), plays not a lesser but a greater role in the weighing-up of different variants at the central level itself. The cardinal condition for elimination of inefficient solutions and taking the path of optimisation (in the sense of approximation to optimal solutions) is the availability of a number of variants which 'enter the lists' on equal terms and are defended in good faith in the process of choice. It is clear, too, that the optimisation procedure, understood as a gradual approach to a point which is at least *satisfactory* according to the criterion adopted, does not consist in seeking out a prepared solution which is merely hidden at the bottom of a bag, but must generate new information and thus have some influence on the final result. It is all the more indispensable, therefore, that decision-making should take the form of real analysis of variants.

On the other hand – central allocation of resources on the scale of the national economy as a whole, based on public ownership of the means of production, which belong to one and the same owner – the state, diminishes the relentlessness and directness of the *economic* pressure for the fullest and most scrupulous possible use of the optimisation procedure. The external pressure of competition which makes an enterprise which either is private or operates on analogous principles use all available sources of information does not exist; wrong decisions taken on the basis of incomplete, one-sided information do not and cannot bring responsibility with one's own money; the internalisation of many costs and benefits which are external to the individual enterprise does indeed express operation according to higher, socio-economic criteria of rationality, but at the same time it complicates the calculations. This does not mean, of course, that the central decision-making body is free of all pressure, including economic (among other things, in connection with international economic relations) but this pressure operates on it in a roundabout way over a longer time period, and there is the possibility of shedding responsibility or even directing it on to another party.

In a socialist economy, then, there appears both a necessity for a particularly well-developed and free flow of information to and from the central decision-making body and a particular possibility of restriction and manipulation of the information system. This conflict – if it is lasting – gradually becomes a more and more powerful brake on the development of productive forces, especially in the conditions of the scientific and technical revolution. The basic condition for eliminating it is democratisation of the political system, the creation of *political* pressure and control of a kind such that the decision centre must base its choice on full sources of information and really comprehensively use the method of variant analysis not just in respect of marginal matters but of the key problems of the plan.

In the socialist countries, particularly the USSR, a lot of attention is being devoted to improving the information system in a broad sense with application to economic problems. But the dominant aspect is the technical one, which clearly must not be ignored (the dependence of the quality of decisions simply on knowledge is obvious) but which, in spite of everything, plays a subordinate role under conditions of totalitarian dictatorship. Experience shows that backwardness in the field of information techniques can be made up in a relatively short time (if only by means of imitation) but this will not eliminate the 'information gap' without the creation of the appropriate political preconditions. It is difficult, for example, to accuse the Polish statistical service in 1970 of being professionally incompetent and technically badly equipped, yet it supplied both the decision centre and public opinion with false information, not by means of inventing figures but through one-sided material which, in the existing political conditions, could not be countered. The well-known decision to raise food prices in December 1970 was thus to a great extent an effect of the negative feedback between the political system and the information system. It was the same with the cata-strophic decision to end imports of grain and feed to Poland during the period from 1965 to 1970/1971: it was taken not in the absence of any other variant (which existed, but was not admitted for con-sideration) but on the basis of arbitrary assumptions and one-sided arguments; it was a classical example of the lack of a political mechanism which would have forced the authorities to make use of available information. A mass of such examples can be cited from every socialist country with the etatist model, and these are not chance phenomena but logically interrelated.

Democratism in the political system is the essential condition for a change in this state of affairs, among other things because it opens up the possibility of, if not full at least sufficiently broad introduc-tion of the principle that the members of organisations which supply information are not judged according to the success of the activities on which they are reporting. The implementation of this principle requires relative independence both of the appropriate local ('lower') links in the administrative and economic apparatus and of external generators of information. Objective precise situation reports, i.e. describing the effects of decisions taken earlier, must of necessity also contain a political evaluation of the actions of the central level; one cannot of course exclude the possibility of an 'enlightened absolutist' permitting a greater degree of objectivity in this type of reports in some area, but only the replacement of monopoly by political pluralism gives a *guarantee* of the creation of an objective information reporting system. The same applies to *ex ante* information, i.e. evaluation of draft decisions by the central level and the corresponding decisions of its subordinate links.

The institutional factors which guarantee information flows against distortions (and one-sided distortions at that, as we have pointed out) embrace not only freedom of expression of opinion but also the possibility of organisation in defence of one's own conception and of critical evaluations of official conceptions. Experience shows that denial of the right to defend a position – before and after a decision is taken – and all the more so exclusion of all forms of appeal to public opinion and manifestation of social pressure – has far-reaching negative effects on the effectiveness of the actions taken. Real control over the decision centres requires in addition the possibility of drawing personal-political conclusions from evaluations, and thus of the selection and changing of leading teams on the basis of the programme presented and the results achieved.

Against the background of the interrelationships analysed here the question of the rationality or arbitrariness of the decisions taken by political centres becomes clearer. The classical liberal argument disqualified socialism as being an irrational system precisely because under it economic decisions must be taken according to political criteria and not to what are allegedly the only rational criteria, namely those of the market. The polemicists (including Lange in 1936) initially accepted this plane, while showing that socialism does not exclude the use of objective information stemming from the market or from simulations of it. Today this plane – with a few exceptions – has been abandoned, since it is clear that the premises for rational economic decisions extend far beyond market criteria and must include broadly conceived social criteria. Economic decisions involving social criteria – mainly macro-decisions – are political in nature and should also be described as such. They must not, on the other hand, be identified *ipso facto* with arbitrary decisions – if they are taken on the basis of sufficiently broad information, not in the least limited to market-type information. Arbitrariness is a feature of *autocratic* political decisions, since they exclude the mechanism compelling use of all the available information and continual extension of its compass in the future. We can say, then, that under socialism – and in general under conditions where the state plays a prominent economic role – political democratism is an indispensable factor in the objectivity (which is always relative, according to the system of aims and the given state of knowledge) of the process of decision-making; it is thus also an indispensable factor in economic rationality and the full use of the development potential of society.

When discussing the elements of 'negative correlation' between the contemporary development of productive forces and democratisation we emphasised among other things the growing role of experts in the preparation of decisions. This statement is indisputable, but that does not mean that this indisputability also extends to the technocratic conclusions about the redundance of the democratic form of acts of choice. Specialised expert competence based on scientific knowledge is today to a greater and greater extent a necessary condition, and that all the more so the more complex and coordinated the character of the decisions or – putting it differently – the more they are planned, the more fully they take account of the connections between parts and the whole. Decisions of this type always have clear social implications, or are bound to exert a perceptible influence on the interests of the whole population or at least of large groups. This applies not only to such matters as setting the rate of accumulation, which is a measure of the sacrifice of the present in favour of the future, or to the allocation of accumulation between productive and non-productive purposes (including protection of the environment), or the social structure of the distribution of income, etc., but also to solutions which are apparently purely technically economic. For example, the long theoretical debate about the problem of optimisation of the choice of production techniques – the degree of mechanisation or automation of production – showed conclusively that evaluation of economic rationality in this field becomes senseless if it does not start from a given social situation (the magnitude of the reserve of labour), is not subordinated to a given objective function (maximisation of the surplus or of the net output from the given investment outlays), is not based on established time preferences (the fastest possible, or more protracted liquidation of unemployment), etc.[15] If it is, then the large and ever-growing role of experts does not conflict with the possibility of or the need for the democratic form of choice. The experts eliminate inefficient variants and thus delineate the set of solutions which can be taken into consideration; they do this better, with fewer errors, the higher the level of knowledge at their disposal and the more closely the political conditions of full use of available information and free presentation of the results of it are met. Choice among a correctly defined range of possibilities, on the other hand, ceases to be the domain of narrowly specialised competence and enters the sphere of interests, volition and value systems. As Gilles Martinet correctly states:[16]

> the basic alternatives of choice in a planned economy can be formulated sufficiently clearly and must be solved on the basis of political, not technical criteria. Precisely for that reason it is absurd to think that we shall eventually come to purely technocratic government.

This reasoning has substantial importance for our evaluation of the need and the possibility of the collective form of decision-making. Not only does the objection of the incompetence of collective bodies selecting one of the variants put forward disappear, but so does the objection that such bodies are not sufficiently operational, that a longer time is essential for thorough discussion and expression of opinions on a problem in comparison with the autocratic type of bodies. The nature of the problems faced by the modern planned economy is continually increasing the relative importance of long-term strategic decisions which create the framework for the more operational decisions. In relation to decisions of a strategic type economy of time is undoubtedly of less significance than the correctness of the choice and its social acceptance. In this connection new perspectives are opened up for the development and enrichment of the functions of parliament, and even of forms of direct democracy (referendum). To appeal to the crisis of Western parliamentarism as an argument against democratisation of the political system of socialism, in which the basic means of production are nationalised is – consciously or unconsciously – to transfer the conclusions drawn from superficial observation of the phenomena to completely different conditions and is therefore wrong. The crisis of Western parliamentarism – where it appears – consists not in incompetence and technical incapacity to make real decisions on crucial problems but in the absence of the social and economic conditions for the taking of such decisions through parliament; the centres of real economic and social power are frequently beyond the scope of parliament's authority, which not only leads to a lack of effective steering instruments but also weakens (and sometimes even destroys) the sovereignty of the peoples' representatives, who include advocates of powerful private interests. From this point of view the situation in the socialist countries is totally different: if the purely political reasons cease and if (which is beyond the subject of this work) the systems are formally properly constructed – in particular if parliamentarism is correctly linked with worker, terrtorial and cooperative self-management, with independent trade unions, etc. – a positive correlation between democratism and economic efficiency should clearly appear.

There exists, then, *a rational basis for democratism* in the way in which central decisions are taken. And if this is so, then there arises *an indispensable need for democratism* in view of the motivation factors, whose importance for relations within the enterprise is so strongly stressed by the sociology of organisations; the potential for activity, initiative, inclination to 'good work' and innovation can only be exploited on the basis of participation and mutual responsibility. Two additional features, the first a general one, the second specific to socialism, increase the importance of this conclusion further.

The first is the growing level of education coupled with the changing character of work in the modern phase of development of production technology (the reduction in the importance of simple manual actions and purely executive duties in relation to the brainwork or conceptual element); the aspirations of the educated worker of whom thought, independence and inventivenesss are demanded are bound to come into sharper and sharper conflict with his lack of the opportunity of effectively influencing the choices which decide his situation as an individual and as a member of society. This conflict is particularly harmful in normal situations, demanding *continuity of effort, and commitment,* as distinct from extraordinary situations, when a short-term burst can be achieved with the help of various extra means of encouragement.

The second feature is the official ideology of socialist social integration, which proclaims the principles of power to the people, equality, the broadest participation in economic decision-making, etc., through all educational channels. This ideology cannot be abandoned – it is after all the basis of the regime's legitimacy, just as the ideology of direction of enterprises by their shareholders is the basis of the legitimacy of capitalist managers; at the same time, particularly in the longer run, the contrast between this ideology and reality becomes the ultimate source of the breakdown of social morality and the formulation of attitudes which are a negation of the socialist relation to work and lead to negative economic effects – the more serious, the higher the consciousness that the disparity between ideology and reality has no justification in objective conditions. The attempts to mask this disparity with make-believe, ritual democratic forms (so-called elections, discussions which are either purely fictitious or concern secondary problems, etc.) have the reverse effect, precisely as described by McGregor in the passage cited above.

The negative effects of the contrast between ideology and reality are all the sharper, the more deeply society is conscious of the mistakes committed by the autocratic leadership, even from the point of view of its own scale of preferences. After a certain time it transpires that the costly solutions which were imposed and which demanded sacrifices from the population were not necessary at all, that alternatives existed. The feeling of the existence of choice between different variants of strategic conceptions and at the same time the consciousness, acquired through experience, that the solutions which best satisfy both the general and the individual interest are undertaken precisely at those times when the voice of society is most audible (both Polish turning points – 1956 and 1970 – are a classic illustration of this thesis) deepen the demoralising consequences of the lack of democratism. One of these consequences is the attraction and the admiration aroused by bourgeois patterns of success and aspirations to the capitalist 'consumer society' in the socialist countries. We do not of course identify the ideology of socialist joint management with asceticism, still less do we deny the role of economic incentives (we shall return to this question below), but we do want to emphasise that disillusionment about the possibility of real influence on general questions finds a natural outlet in a striving to make amends in private forms. In this way a mass of social energy is wasted.

All this is not the same as saying, as we have already discussed, that there is no possibility of taking wrong decisions by a democratic means, preferring the short-sighted interest of the majority or temporary advantages to the detriment of the long term. But it seems to me that in the final reckoning the advantages of the democratic mechanism outweigh the negative aspects which cannot be eliminated. Again, we would agree with Martinet who, to the question 'Will the verdict of the people be optimal?', answers:[17]

> Not necessarily. Political leaders commit mistakes – the people commit them too. But the latter have an educational value which the mistakes of political leaders have never had, since in the case of mistakes by the people the solution must be sought in the choice of a new policy, not simply in a change of leadership. A certain time must elapse before this type of democracy will be capable of functioning really satisfactorily. Furthermore, it will be necessary to create the proper preconditions in the shape of a reform of the education system in which an important place will be occupied by preparation for and stimulation of growing participation by the citizen in the direction of society. Without this there can be no thought of democracy.

Both the diminution in the threat and the scale of wrong decisions and the inculcation of the spirit of joint management of the public means of production are only possible in the process of real development of political democracy. The argument for waiting 'until the masses are mature', particularly in the present internal and international conditions, must be treated either as evidence of ignorance or as a disguise for the desire to maintain the existing monopoly of power. What was one of the principal theses of the Marxist theory of revolution – the necessity for the masses to learn by their own experiences – is fully applicable here, and besides – at least in relation to socio-economic choices – the costs of learning would certainly be much less than what has been and is being paid by the socialist countries of Eastern Europe for the arbitrary decisions of autocrats. Experience shows, among other things, that the pressure for better satisfaction of current material and cultural needs (those suppressed 'inclinations to consumption' which have always been alleged to threaten the development and security of socialism), which is associated with democratisation of the method of macro-economic decision making can, apart from in exceptional situations, have a positive influence on economic rationality, for it brings the decision centre up against constraints which compel it to seek more efficient solutions, instead of patching up all the holes at the expense of consumption (and social services) which are treated as a residual magnitude. It is probably not even necessary to add how important it is for the fate of socialism that the centre should be conscious that its freedom of decision is subject to constraints of a social nature, and how slight is the probability of this consciousness existing permanently rather than being something short-lived, produced by an explosion, without a democratic mechanism of joint decision-making and control. Thus not only the masses but the leaders, too, must learn democracy by practice.

An important aspect of the economic determination of the democratic evolution of the socialist political system is the problem of *the selection of leading personnel* at all levels. This problem has persistently run through both fragments of our analysis of the etatist model, in its Stalinist and its post-Stalinist versions. The conclusions were totally unambiguous and rather truistic: the negative selection of personnel is an inseparable feature of the totalitarian political dictatorship which, in the interests of self-preservation, maintains the closest possible control over personal appointments, using as its criteria of preference servility and conformity, that is, qualities which are simply lethal from the point of view of the requirements of the dynamic development of society, particularly in the period of the scientific and technical revolution. The differences between the Stalin and the post-Stalin period in this field are fairly substantial: in the former, servile conformist attitudes took especially drastic forms, since they developed to a great extent under the influence of physical threat; in the latter, the main factor was a conscious policy of discrimination and privileges in the way of a political or professional career and the possibility of satisfying creative ambitions or stability of living standards, although the threat of physical coercion and 'civil death' is never totally excluded for the openly resistant. However, we should not overestimate the direct effects of these differences: they can be seen in the growth of the number of 'dissidents' and their increased chance of staying on the surface, but not in any fundamental improvement in the appointment of personnel to 'line' and 'staff' positions in the economy, science, or culture, not to mention the political and administrative apparatus. Furthermore, the elimination of the extreme forms of totalitarian dictatorship in the post-Stalin period, the abandonment of dogmatic differentiation on the basis of social origin, political past and ideological positions, with the increased appeal to general national and state motivations, makes it easier for some people, particularly among the intelligentsia, to justify opportunism to themselves. Thus the mitigation of the methods is not at all bound to mean a reduction in their effectiveness, all the more so since reality – that most effective of educators – invariably bids one to ignore the liturgical calls to boldness and criticism and, on the other hand, teaches one to base one's actual attitudes on the facts, which stubbornly show that obedience pays while every 'deviation' is punished.[18]

The dependence of the quality of personnel on the degree of political pluralism seems to be particularly large in the socialist system, greater than in capitalism. The socialist state concentrates in its hands control over the whole course of man's life: education, employment, professional advance, assurance for old age; because of this, only democratic political control over the controllers can create the preconditions for the functioning of a personnel selection mechanism which meets the requirements of modern society and can ensure at least a minimum guarantee against exploitation of the concentration of power which socialism creates in the interests of maintenance and strengthening of the regime's monopoly. It must also be taken into account that *positive selection of personnel* consists not only in making the road to advance dependent on favourable assessment of a man's present ability and prospects, with a particular preference for an inclination to 'revisionism', i.e. to breaking down conservative opposition and inertia, but to at least the same extent in concern to ensure the institutional conditions for the display of all these features in practice. The sources of the weakness of the leading personnel at different levels in the socialist countries today frequently stem not from lack of training and individual potential for development, but from the organisational situation which makes it impossible for people to spread their wings, stifles initiative and gives rise to continual conflicts between actions which conform to the imposed 'rules of the game' and rational and socially useful actions.

The problems, failure to solve which brings severe negative consequences from the point of view of the dynamism of economic personnel, include that of the director's right to take risks and responsibility. No other element in what is now after all several decades of experience provides so much cause for satisfaction to the critics of socialism as this one – the importance of which does not require underlining. Let us recall once again Hayek's[19] prediction that the socialist enterprise director would constantly be driven to one of two extreme positions; either that of an insurer trembling at every risk, if the system of sanctions is sufficiently effective, or at least is believed to be such, or alternatively that of an irresponsible risk-taker, conscious that he is immune from penalty. It is easy to confirm the relatively high degree of accuracy of this prediction, but the sources of the phenomenon stem not from an 'organic' impossibility of solving the problem, but again from the political system, which, first, does not create a feeling of joint ownership and, second, excludes any democratic mechanism for evaluating the justification for the decisions taken and the degree of risk involved in them.

In our discussion of the factors claimed to support the thesis of positive correlation between the requirements of the development of productive forces and the democratisation of the political system we have concentrated up till now on questions of a more general nature, trying to extract the features which seem particularly essential in the era of the scientific and technical revolution. But at the beginning of the 1970s in the USSR and the peoples' democracies a particular factor is also operating, namely *economic reform*.

It can be accepted that – despite all the obstacles, which we examined in detail in chapter 3 – decentralisation of the system of functioning of the economy and the associated extension of the area of the market mechanism will eventually be implemented in all socialist countries of Eastern Europe. The pressure of economic needs – the need to make production more flexible, reduce material content, stimulate the growth of labour productivity, etc. – especially in the face of the necessity of solving the problems of further growth and technical progress with *at the same time* greater concern for consumption than hitherto, are forcing the exploitation of the reserves which flow from improvement of the system of functioning. But because economic reform contains elements which influence the political system – through the delegation of some categories of decision to lower levels, the strengthening of the material preconditions for reality of worker self-management, and a certain possibility of rationalising personnel policy in enterprises – it must by itself be treated as one of the components of the economic determination of political democratisation.

Our analysis of the self-management model, however, brought us to the conclusion that decentralisation in socialism has definite limits, that it cannot apply to basic macro-economic decisions, the objective function of 'sub-systems' and their external parameters of operation; in view of this – while acknowledging the importance of decentralisation, particularly as the real basis for workers' self-management – we took a critical position towards the conception of socialisation of the means of production by way of complete or almost complete elimination of central allocation of resources. It followed from this that the *direct* political significance of economic reform – although substantial – cannot be decisive, that the question of socialisation is decided not on the plane of 'depoliticisation of the economy' but of 'democratisation of politics'. And it is precisely on the plane of 'democratisation of politics' that economic reform seems to have an *indirect* positive significance; this stems not from the area of problems which it solves but on the contrary from the problems and contradictions which it only reveals or exacerbates.

The reconstruction of the system of functioning of the economy according to the principles of the decentralised model or similar ones, making the incomes of employees to some extent dependent on overall economic results, should contribute to the better coordination of individual interests with the interests of the collective and the enterprise as such. If its basic assumptions are fulfilled, in particular including the development of self-management, there should follow not only an increase in the economic efficiency of enterprises but also growth of the degree of integration of the collective, of group solidarity and of the feeling of separateness from other groups. It is easy to see that in one breath we have mentioned results which are unconditionally positive and some which require to be qualified by additional examination. This second category includes the influence of economic reform on the relations between groups of employees (the workforces of enterprises), and above all on the relations between these groups and society as a whole. Our thesis is as follows: in a situation where decentralisation and the development of worker self-management at enterprise level[20] are not followed by democratisation of the centre the contradictions between 'sub-systems' and 'the system', and the tendencies towards disintegration, increase. The theoretical argument seems simple: on the one hand, the area of decentralisation must, as we have seen, be restricted – on the other, failure to democratise the centre means that enterprises' workforces are deprived of any influence on the general decisions which limit their independence and the possibility of achieving their own interests; undoubtedly grounds for conflict arise, and the very fact of the considerably greater strength of a

o

group, in comparison with the individual, makes the conflict sharper. The movement to which this contradiction is ultimately bound to give rise can lead in two directions. The first is further decentralisation, either intentionally or only incidentally in conformity with the conception of the self-management model but with the political autocratism of the centre maintained; this direction, however, does not augur success, in view of both the more and more harmful effects of exceeding the economic limits to the rationality of decentralisation and the fact that being weighed down under the pressure of a particularism alienated from the totality will lead not to saturation but rather to strengthening of the tendencies towards disintegration.[21] The reaction to this failure can be an attempt to return to extreme centralism, i.e. resort to a medicine of which it is hard to say whether it is not worse than the illness itself. The second direction is democratisation of the centre, mutual integration of the 'system' as a whole with the 'sub-systems', through participation by the latter in general decisions; in our opinion this is the only direction which offers a proper solution, since it permits rational proportions of centralisation and decentralisation to be maintained, and favours the coordination of group interests (and through them individual interests) with general social interests, the definition and implementation of which is the task of the community. It is precisely in this sense that economic reform is indirectly one of the factors in the economic determination of the democratic evolution of the political system.

Against this background a more general problem emerges – *the role of material incentives* from the point of view of social integration under socialism.

It is well known that the use in the socialist countries of material incentives – both individual and, above all, collective ones linked to market criteria – is the principal object of the criticism from the 'New Left'. The objections are that incentives appealing to an egoistic motivation prolong and strengthen it and are thus a source of a consumption-oriented social consciousness analogous to the bourgeois one and of a psychology of self enrichment which is contrary to the ideals of equality and social solidarity. If this criticism is taken literally – as the basis of a postulate of equalisation of remuneration without regard to quantity or quality of work – it is hard to describe it other than as utopian and failing to reckon with social realities. It is obvious that to ignore the undoubted need for

differentiation of remuneration according to the principles of 'distribution according to work' would not only have negative economic
effects but would also tend to destroy the social bond.

A correctly constructed system of material incentives – individual
and collective, based on enterprises' results – will long remain an
essential element in the stimulation of productive activity, and at
the same time a factor in socialist education, since it teaches the
interrelationship between personal interests and the social interest
on the scale of the collective and on a global scale by direct experience, in a palpable and comprehensive way. Yet the criticism 'from
the left' deserves thorough examination since – apart from its literal
interpretation – it draws attention to the danger, which in the light
of practice is far from abstract, of relying *exclusively* on material
incentives without simultaneously creating the real preconditions
for the formation and development of the feeling of being joint
owners of the public means of production. We would like to underline the last point strongly, as it is of fundamental significance in
distinguishing our position from the views of those who would
diminish the role of economic incentives and try to replace them
with verbal 'moral incentives' – particularly in situations where economic incentives operate badly and conflict with the assumption of
coordination of personal and social interest.[22] The solution should
thus consist not in neglect of the role of economic incentives but in
proper construction of the system of incentives and consistent coordination of direct material interest with all those elements which
make up the process of socialisation of the means of production
sensu stricto, and hence in the first place with democratisation of
the political system. Only if this condition is met can efficient operation of the economy be expected, since even the best system of
material incentives is not in a position to cope with many problems,
particularly long-term ones, the scale and importance of which are
growing; it is not chance that hitherto attempts to use material
incentives have proved relatively least successful in the field of key
investments. Only if this condition is met can we expect material
incentives to operate not in favour of but against the tendency to
maximisation of personal advantage at the cost of the advantage of
others and of society as a whole, and to lead not to the limitation
but to the gradual extension of that part of national income which
must be allocated according to criteria of social solidarity, of the
needs of 'investing in man' and his environment.

O*

And one further question. We mentioned above, referring to the
findings of modern sociology and industrial psychology, that with
the growth in the complexity of production problems and the rise in
the level of the labour force the effectiveness not only of the 'hard'
but also of the 'soft' version of direction of people from outside,
from above, was declining. 'People take advantage of the "soft"
approach. They continually expect more, but they give less and
less.'[23] Similar phenomena – mainly associated with the elimination of the simplest capitalist forms of economic compulsion to
work – are well known in the socialist countries. Everyone who
has encountered the problem of labour discipline or labour turnover
knows perfectly well how often managerial personnel complain of
the demoralising influence of the state of full employment and yearn
for 'at least a little' unemployment as a medicine for ignoring work
duties; these complaints and longings extend to higher levels, too,
and also to certain pitiable economists, who do not yet declare
aloud, but deeply believe in, the expediency of creating a small
percentage margin of surplus labour. The same thing applies to
some social payments (particularly payment for justified absence),
the negative effects of which it is attempted to counteract by means
of an extended system of bureaucratic control, a complicated network of conditions, and sometimes even mechanical limitation of
payments. It must be admitted that the problem is by no means
imaginary but really exists and causes a mass of troubles and can
even – quite apart from other factors – retard the extension of the
system of social payments. Only it is not in the least a product of
age-old features of human nature, but of conditions in which on the
one hand there was an increase in the bargaining power of labour
and, on the other, there was no changeover from the external direction of people to real integration of their individual aims with the
aims of their organisation. Only the creation of the preconditions
for such integration and the assurance of its gradual implementation can cut this miserable knot of contradictions and thus, among
other things, ensure the necessary harmony between economic
rationality and a programme of social rights fitting to socialism.
From this aspect too, then, let us note the positive correlation
between the requirements of the development of productive forces
and the democratic direction of evolution of the political system
under socialism.

The basic question which we had to answer in this book was: do there exist economic laws determining the necessity of real socialisation of the means of production and thus setting the direction for the further evolution of socialism in relation to the form which it has taken in the USSR and the peoples' democracies? In particular, is the evolution of the political system ruling today in these countries economically determined? Our answer is positive. We consider that nationalisation of the means of production does not sufficiently fulfil the conditions for the development of productive forces in the present era, and that it is essential for them to be socialised, and thus for public ownership to be transformed into social ownership *sensu stricto,* which consequently means the necessity of political democratisation.

We have attempted to examine the various aspects of the relationship between the conditions of progress of productive forces in the modern era and the political system under socialism. It is not a one-way relationship: alongside elements of what we have called positive correlation, i.e. those supporting the necessity of democratisation of the political system, there appear elements of negative correlation. Despite this, in our opinion it seems quite possible to assess the relative weight of the factors operating in the different directions. It is true that not every element of negative correlation has a direct counterpart in a corresponding element of positive correlation which neutralises its effect, yet – taking into account, too, the introductory arguments presented in chapter 1 – the intensification of the economic need for political democratism is undeniably the dominant tendency. In this sense – taking counter tendencies into consideration – we consider the thesis of the economic determination of the democratic evolution of the political system under socialism to be established. To this must be added the humanistic merit of freedom as a value in itself, which is of immense significance for the social factors in the development of socialism.

The consequence of this conclusion – in accordance with the assumptions and definitions we have accepted and with the whole course of our argument – is recognition of the justification of the Marxist hypothesis of socialisation of the means of production as an historical law. This law is not fulfilled by the etatist model of socialism in the post-Stalin period either (in what we have described as its 'normal' form) mainly because it retains an undemocratic political system which excludes disposition over the means of production by society. Critical analysis of this system also leads to the conclusion that the requirement of creation of the political preconditions for real socialisation of the means of production is not satisfied by an ordinary correction within the framework of its present foundations. A fundamental change is necessary – from totalitarian dictatorship, unrestricted monopoly and uncontrolled power in the hands of a narrow leading élite, to effective dependence of government on society, i.e. the creation of a mechanism which permits legal questioning, modification and ultimately rejection of government policy and its replacement by a different policy enjoying the support of the majority.[24] Effective dependence of government on society or – to formulate the same point in a different way – effective social control over government assumes real freedom of speech, freedom of association, the rule of law and, above all, the necessity of periodically seeking a social mandate for power by way of elections in which there are both personal and political alternatives. This is equivalent to allowing, on the basis of socialism, centres of political initiative which are independent of the government, and thus, to call things by their proper names, legal forms of organised opposition too.

The absence of the political preconditions for socialisation of the means of production makes the etatist model at present a brake on the development of productive forces; with the passage of time its negative influence, particularly on scientific and technical progress, will become more and more strongly visible. Of course this does not mean that maintaining the etatist model is bound always to cause absolute stagnation or even retrogression, leading ultimately to the explosion of the whole social and economic structure.[25] It does mean, on the other hand – even if a certain development occurs – waste of part of the productive potential of society and continual increase in the disparity between possibilities and reality.

The conclusion of economic determination of the evolution of the political system permits us to define more precisely the dialectics of the interrelationship between the basic categories of historical materialism – productive forces, relations of production and political superstructure – under socialism. In connection with our analysis of developed state interventionism in chapter 1 we have already drawn attention to the modification of the relationship between economics and politics; our definition of social ownership

(chapter 2) in a certain sense reversed the base-superstructure relationship, as it derived the character of ownership from the character
of power and thus defined socialist production relations on the basis
of the essence of political relations. Now we can add the last link,
namely economic determination of the evolution of the political
system. The general laws of historical materialism are thus subject
to modification in socialism but their most fundamental feature
remains – that in the last instance the development of productive
forces plays the decisive role. The category of production relations
is inseparable under socialism from the way in which power is
exercised, contradiction between productive forces and the relations
of production appears primarily as contradiction between productive
forces and the political system, and the law of necessary conformity
of productive forces and production relations operates in the direction of adapting the political system to the demands of the
development of productive forces at the given stage.

The answer to the question posed has been given. But is it possible
to base on it any prognosis of the process of socialisation of ownership of the means of production in the socialist countries – of the
paths, phases and forms of this process? Can we at least acknowledge the democratic perspective for the evolution of the political
system as unequivocally determined and thus predictable within an
observable time horizon for all the socialist countries? These are
after all the problems in which, as we mentioned in the Introduction, many readers are most interested, and who is to say whether or
not they are right.

Let us state clearly and without qualification: no – our answer
still does not create sufficient basis for this kind of prognosis. We
have tried to establish the objective need for socialisation, and
therefore political democratism – we have not on the other hand
been concerned with the question whether and how this need can be
satisfied in concrete conditions. From this point of view the result of
our analysis does not close but only *opens up* the problems of the
evolution of socialist production relations in Eastern Europe as *the
problems of the interaction of living social forces* in all their concrete complexity, with their changes over time and their connections
with all the economic and non-economic aspects of the development
process. The author finds it hard to assess how far in general this
type of analysis can be carried out on the basis of today's state of

knowledge of the socialist societies, their true political stratification and the sources and potential for resistance and pressure in relation to changes. The only thing that is certain is that changes in the political system cannot be detached from contradictions, and therefore from struggle between social forces – despite the official doctrine which declares that incidental flaws in the fundamentally democratic system of the socialist countries are eliminated by the leadership itself, without opposition or the necessity of pressure, simply as a result of consciousness of a 'mature need'; the thesis of the absence of conflict in the relations between leadership and masses leads in practice to driving conflicts below the surface, whence they force their way out every now and then at different points in the socialist camp in the form of violent outbursts, compelling the authorities to make partial concessions.

The list of problems which would have to be discussed if we were to attempt to go on from our general conclusions to construct a scientific prognosis of real processes is long and imposing. It covers both the question of the forms of the political system and the, in the author's opinion considerably more important, question of the conditions, paths and methods of the transformation.

As regards the forms of a political system which would satisfy the need for both democratism and the efficient functioning of the centrally planned economy, the leading problem here is the one, discussed above, of the possibility of making use of parliamentarism and the principle of division of power (including judicial supervision over the legality of the administration's actions) as instruments of control over economic decision centres. In deciding the concrete forms of such a system (and particularly the means for linking parliament with worker, territorial and cooperative self-management) it is essential to place the accent on the effective improvement and enrichment of parliamentarism, on adapting it to contemporary social and economic requirements, and not on erasing it; it seems to me that considerable weight should be given here to the negative experience of the effects of the fallacious theory which in principle rejects parliamentarism, the division of power and the principle of 'limitation and retardation' in the institutional structure of the state for socialism.

In the light of the historical experience which we have also analysed in the pages of this book there is presumably no need to prove that even the most refined democratic forms can be devoid of essential content; what is more – there are grounds for stating that the *differentia specifica* of the form of totalitarian dictatorship which has developed in the socialist countries of Eastern Europe consists, among other things, in the broad use of legal-state camouflage. Precisely for this reason the most important question is the ways and methods of ensuring the reality of changes.

From the point of view of this last question the disposition of social forces and the way they change during the evolution of socialism are of decisive significance. Among the many problems opened up in this field there is also the question of the class character of the state in a situation where the means of production are in public ownership but have not passed into social ownership *sensu stricto*. We have consciously passed over this question, although it obviously called for consideration on our declared Marxist methodological plane. But the author recognised that he lacked adequate grounds to take up a position, both as a result of the weakness of the attempts made hitherto at empirical analysis of political stratification and as a result of the failure to elucidate fundamental theoretical problems of the sociology of socialist society; in particular the reversal (in comparison with capitalism) of the direction of causality of the connection between ownership and power seems to make it totally useless to formulate the relations of rule and subordination on the basis of public ownership in the categories of the dichotomy of classes, unless we give the concept of class a completely different sense from the traditional one. Is this not a purely abstract problem, a kind of tribute laid on the altar of fossilised doctrinal scholasticism? It is hard to say, but one certainly encounters the view that the way this question is decided is important for assessment of the strength and character of the resistance which the ruling groups pose to any attempt at democratisation of the political system; if a new exploiting class is exercising power the eventual democratism can only be implemented ultimately by the overthrow of the 'new class' (which incidentally does not exclude partial concessions 'on the way', if the ruling class is sufficiently flexible and succeeds in activating the mechanism of 'dynamic petrification'); if on the other hand the political hierarchy in the socialist countries is not a class hierarchy, then the chances of reform and the possibility of permanently attracting a large part of the party and state apparatus, including high levels, on to the side of democratic changes are increased (which in turn does not mean that the role of social pressure diminishes).

Assessment of the strength, directions and effectiveness of social pressure demands deeper and sharper analysis of the political aspects of the various forms of stratification. It is a question of the political consequences of the changes which economic development has brought about and will bring about in the numerical proportions of the traditional classes and social layers (the working class, the peasantry, the petit bourgeoisie and the intelligentsia) and in the internal structure of each of them, and also in the system of values and associated aspirations; of particular importance here is assessment of the political aspirations of the working class, which has the greatest possibilities of exerting mass pressure (its effectiveness is multiplied, among other things, by the ideology of the proletarian legitimacy of the authorities), but about which the conventional opinion frequently persists, that its demands are limited to the economic field. It is also a question of analysis of the new social stratification patterns, and especially of the political potential of the so-called 'new middle class' – a rather heterogeneous social layer, but in which the greatest part is played by the technical and economic intelligentsia in managerial positions at various levels; the undoubted growth in the importance of this layer is often linked with technocratic tendencies, which do indeed undermine the monopolistic political position of the power apparatus but can at the same time come into conflict with general democratic aspirations.

The next group of problems which cannot be passed over in formulating a prognosis is the question of the external conditions – both in relation to individual countries and to the socialist camp as a whole. It could be said that the first aspect of the external conditions is of no significance here as general discussions apply similarly both to Poland or Czechoslovakia and to the Soviet Union. This is correct, but it does not mean we can assume equal degrees of development in the individual countries, so in this sense it does not eliminate the problem of external conditions within the compass of the socialist camp. The experience of Czechoslovakia in 1968 is historical evidence of the possibility of overcoming internal resistance and turning the communist party on to the road of democratic evolution (as distinct from Poland in 1956 when this process was halted to a considerable extent by internal forces); but at the same time – and precisely because of the complete internal success of the democratic forces – Czechoslovakia was brutally reminded of the weight of the external factor. Despite this, a one-sided – fatalistically negative – formulation of the role of external conditions seems to me unjustified. We have mentioned some external impulses stimulating abandonment of obsolete, retrograde structural forms at various places in this book. Even considerations of global power strategy cannot operate in one direction only in this respect. At any rate, a full picture of the preconditions of the motive forces and the brakes on the evolution of socialism would demand a proper discussion of this circle of problems too.

Finally there is the very important set of problems, which are sometimes linked with the previous ones, but which, despite their diversity, can be subsumed under the common roof of 'the influence of the past on the future'. We have in mind here not so much the historical constitutional traditions in individual socialist countries (excessive weight is sometimes attached to these traditions) as the specific difficulties which the process of socialisation (and therefore political democratisation) is bound to encounter during and as a result of the prolonged maintenance of totalitarian dictatorship. It is worth recalling that modern history has no real precedent for the democratic transformation of totalitarian dictatorship due to the influence of internal factors. The monopoly of power and information, based on deep police penetration aimed at suppressing all attempts at organisation in the embryo stage, has not only material effects after a time but also brings about permanent changes in mentality; as a result of many years' experience belief in the success of authentic social political initiative disappears. And in addition, after all, we are concerned here – as we have tried to bring out in the whole of this book – not with a process answering the reactionary position of the opponents of 'all' dictatorship and 'every' socialism, but with a progressive process of socialisation of public ownership, even if starting out from the original sin of compulsion. Yet conviction of progressiveness, together with the most sincere desire to purge this original sin (and subsequent ones) by themselves do not eliminate the consequences – among them the psychological ones – of the etatist model. These consequences endure, quite independently of one's assessment of whether and to what extent this model was a necessity of the period of revolutionary change and forced industrialisation (acceptance of this necessity leads to interesting theoretical problems of contradiction between the conditions of nationalisation and the conditions of socialisation). One of the most poisonous of these consequences is the identification of the ruling political system with the essence of socialism – an identification which incidentally the official propaganda basically strives to consolidate. This is the source of the scepticism of some and the fear of others – fear of an uncontrolled reactionary outburst as an allegedly inevitable consequence of radical violation of the principles of the ruling system. Because the extreme forms of totalitarianism are generally going out of use and the standard of living, in the nature of things, is bound to rise, stabilising tendencies are developing, tinged at times with a feeling of conscious resignation, but often supported by an active ideological foundation, in particular with a nationalistic character. This opens up to the power apparatus – which is conservative in view of its interest in preserving its political monopoly – the possibility of finding support in certain situations in the (of different origin, but that is not important . . .) conservatism of part of society. It is precisely here that the authorities can find a basis for the mechanism of 'dynamic petrification'; if they succeed in making use of it skilfully it is hard to exclude the possibility of maintenance for some time of a relative social and economic balance, despite the unfulfilled postulate of real socialisation of the means of production.

Against the background of this long, although probably still incomplete, list of open questions, which are of undoubted importance for a more concrete prognosis of the future course of development of the socialist countries, there arises the natural question: in relation to this what is the value of the analysis attempted in this book and of the conclusions drawn on the basis of it? Can a general statement that the postulate of socialisation of the means of production is in conformity with contemporary tendencies in the development of productive forces, and thus that the democratic evolution of the political system is economically determined, be regarded as useful from the point of view of the many dilemmas facing socialism and its future in the modern era?

The author is convinced that it can. In spite of the conscious limitation of the area and degree to which the problems were dealt with concretely, the answers which we have attempted to give here have a fundamental significance for the understanding of real phenomena, and consequently for participation in their shaping.

Accepting that they are correct answers, they indicate the objective basis on which the complex, many-sided and contradictory processes of the further evolution of socialism are proceeding and will proceed. This basis does not prejudge the shape of the future; it writes nothing in the book of fate, but it reveals the historical sense of human activities, both institutionalised and spontaneous, and allows us to apply the criteria of progressiveness and reaction to them. Social and economic progress is not a simple function of time, but as long as in general we acknowledge the justification of the category of progress in this field, to establish the objective progressiveness of one of the possible directions of development is of enormous importance for assessment of the relative chances of its realisation, and thus also for the corresponding stimulation of the activity of people.

Furthermore, in our opinion the usefulness of the conclusions resulting from looking at the problems of the evolution of socialism through the prism of the Marxist theory of historical materialism extends beyond the framework of the USSR and the peoples' democracies, which were the direct object of these discussions. These conclusions are important for countries in which transition to socialism 'in a state of immaturity' and the 'rapid industrialisation approach' can, under certain conditions, though by no means always, justify revolutionary force: consciousness of the price which will have to be paid for it should cause them to weigh up meticulously the real scale and the time period of the necessity for restrictions on freedom, and above all to remember that these are restrictions and not permanent, normal, fully socialist forms of democracy. To an even greater extent these conclusions are important for highly developed countries in which attempts to implement socialism on the principle of the allegedly universal experience of the Soviet Union would be bound to cause in an enhanced form the negative results with which we are familiar. On the other hand, successful adoption of a course of real socialisation would have crucial significance on a world scale, among other things through its feedback effect on the fate of East European socialism.

In 1956 in Poland the workers' description of democratic socialism as 'socialism which can be liked' became popular. The year 1968 will pass into history as the time of the Czechoslovak attempt at 'socialism with a human face'. It is not, and cannot be, without importance for us to be conscious that socialism which can be liked, socialism with a human face, is not only an expression of natural yearnings but also a condition for meeting the demands of the epoch.

Notes

1 *Motory i hamulce socjalizmu* (*The Motors and Brakes of Socialism*), Paris, 1970.

2 a) The order of 'collective perceptions'; social life based on social conformism regulated by traditional patterns.

b) Polycentric order: social equilibrium achieved automatically thanks to 'natural laws' of interaction, as a result of individual uncoordinated decisions, with observance of certain rules of the game (norms of social life).

c) Monocentric order: social life regulated by central decisions by an organisation which keeps watch on their observance (*O osobliwościach nauk społecznych* (*On the Peculiarities of the Social Sciences*), Warsaw, 1962, ch. 2, 'Koncepje ładu społecznego i typy przewidywań ('Conceptions of social order and types of forecasting'), p. 86).

3 Ibid., p. 115.
4 Ibid., p. 106.
5 Ibid.
6 See Radovan Richta et al., *Cywilizacja na rozdrożu. Konsekwencje rewolucji naukowo-techniczej dla społeczenstwa i człowieka* (*Civilisation at the Crossroads. The Consequences of the Scientific-Technical Revolution for Society and Man*). Polish translation, Warsaw 1971, from Czech original (Prague, 1969), ch. 1 'O istocie rewolucji naukowo-techniczej' ('On the essence of the scientific-technical revolution').

7 See E. Denison, *Why Growth-Rates Differ. Postwar Experience in Nine Western Countries*, Washington DC, 1967; E. S. Phelps, 'Models of technical progress and the golden rule of research', *Review of Economic Studies*, April 1966; S. Gomułka, *Inventive Activity, Diffusion and the Stages of Economic Growth*, Aarhus, 1971.

8 J. Galbraith, *The New Industrial State*, Harmondsworth, 1968.
9 Max Weber, *Wirtschaft und Gesellschaft. Grundriss der verstehenden Soziologie* (many editions).
10 These questions were mentioned in our analysis of the self-management model (see chapter 2, section 3).
11 See Douglas McGregor, *Leadership and Motivation*, Cambridge, Mass., 1966.
12 'Participation as a device for kidding people into thinking they are important', in ibid., p. 18.
13 See Maria Hirszowicz, *Wstęp do socjolgii organizacji* (*Introduction to the Sociology of Organisation*), Warsaw, 1967, ch. XI 'Ustroj organizacji' ('The system of organisation').

14 See Michael Crozier, *The Bureaucratic Phenomenon* (Tavistock, London, 1964). Maria Hirszowicz, citing the view of Crozier on this matter, refers to the accepted thesis in political rights in modern states (op. cit., p. 354). The same applies, of course, to the functioning of the economy, particularly in conditions where the state occupies a strong economic position, and therefore certainly under socialism. Oskar Lange drew attention to this many times (in *The Economic Theory of Socialism* (Minneapolis 1938) and also in the lecture, of which only a summary has been preserved, 'Is democratic socialism possible?' delivered at Iowa State College on 14 February 1939, in the Oskar Lange archives). The replacement of arbitrary decisions by established rules of behaviour is among the most important postulates of the economic reforms in the socialist countries of Eastern Europe (see ch. 3).

15 See, among others, M. Dobb, *An Essay on Economic Growth and Planning*, London, 1960, chs 3 and 4, and the polemic with this position in M. Kalecki, *Zarys teorii wzrostu gospodarki socjalistycznej* (*An Outline of the Theory of Growth of a Socialist Economy*), ch. 10 in *Selected Essays on the Economic Growth of the Socialist and the Mixed Economy*, Cambridge, 1972. See also Zofia Dobrska, *Wybór technik produkcji w krajach gospodarczo zacofanych* (*The Choice of Production Techniques in Economically Backward Countries*), Warsaw, 1963.

16 Gilles Martinet, *Le Marxisme de notre temps*, English edition, Monthly Review Press, 1964, p. 79.

17 Ibid., pp. 80–1.

18 It is particularly instructive in this respect to look at the personal consequences of radical changes at the very top of the party-government hierarchy, changes which, in the nature of things in the totalitarian dictatorship system, take place violently and astonish public opinion – like, for example, the fall of Khrushchev in 1964 or of Gomułka in 1970. Such changes are accompanied over a certain area by purges in high positions and the introduction (at least of a 'guaranteed minimum') of people trusted by the new leadership. But because the basic criterion – loyalty and obedience to the regime – retains to the full its importance for the new team, loyalty and obedience to the old one at any rate does not prejudice, and in general helps in the maintenance of one's position 'after the flood'. In March 1968 in Poland the circles which had criticised the whole of Gomułka's policy and warned against its consequences were given short shrift; in December 1970, when these consequences appeared in the open, the critics of course remained 'out', and their oppressors remained 'in', often still in even better places, even though up to the last minute they knew precisely that the current incarnation of Marxism-Leninism was the Gomułka line, just as from the first moment after the change they knew equally precisely that the Gomułka line was a negation of Marxism-Leninism, a departure from 'the Leninist norms of party life', etc. (The abruptness of the events caused the leading roles in

this truly Orwellian grotesque to be played not only by the official journalists and publicists but also by the members of a high party body, the Central Committee, which in the space of six days twice unanimously accepted two different policies and two different leading teams). The paradox is of course only apparent; in essence we have here the impeccable internal logic of the political system. Society is perfectly well aware of this logic, so that one can hardly be surprised at the long-term psychological effects of this kind of lesson, particularly for young people.

19 See chapter 1 of this book, p. 22.

20 It should be remembered that we include in the concept of the enterprise bodies of different sizes, including also large organisations of whole branches if they have the appropriate economic basis.

21 These tendencies are especially strong if the economic antagonisms are combined with antagonisms of a different type, with their roots in the traditions of the past, such as racial, national or religious antagonisms. While trying to avoid drawing hasty conclusions, it does seem that this is the direction in which we should seek the essential – although certainly not the only – sources of the many negative phenomena which appeared at the turn of the 1960s and 1970s in Yugoslavia, and particularly of the growth of nationalistic moods on an economic basis in individual republics, principally Croatia.

22 See W. Brus, *The Market in a Socialist Economy*, London and Boston, 1972, 'Conclusions', pp. 192–5.

23 Douglas McGregor, op. cit., p. 7.

24 The term 'government' and its derivatives are clearly used in a broad sense here – to describe the centre of power, independently of the internal institutional structure (political bureau of the communist party, council of ministers, presidium of the supreme soviet, etc.).

25 See the general theoretical discussion by Michał Kalecki in the article 'Econometric model and historical materialism' in the collection *On Political Economy and Econometrics. Essays in Honour of Oskar Lange*, Warsaw, 1964, pp. 237–8.

Index

LIBRARY OF DAVIDSON COLLEGE

Books on regular loan may be checked out for **two weeks.** Books must be presented at the Circulation Desk in order to be renewed.

A fine is charged after date due.

Special books are subject to special regulations at the discretion of library staff.